THE  BOOKS OF

# GALATIANS &
# EPHESIANS

## BY GRACE
## THROUGH FAITH

Advancing the Ministries of the Gospel
**AMG** *Publishers*

*God's Word to you is our highest calling.*

TWENTY-FIRST CENTURY
BIBLICAL COMMENTARY SERIES®

THE  BOOKS OF

# GALATIANS &
# EPHESIANS

## BY GRACE
## THROUGH FAITH

JOHN
WITMER
MAL
COUCH
GENERAL EDITOR
ED HINDSON

The Books of Galatians and Ephesians: By Grace through Faith
Copyright © 2009 by Scofield Ministries
Published by AMG Publishers
6815 Shallowford Road
Chattanooga, TN 37421

Unless otherwise noted, Scripture quotes are taken from the NEW AMERICAN STANDARD BIBLE, Copyright © 1960, 1962, 1963, 1968, 1971, 1972, 1973, 1975, 1977, by the Lockman Foundation. Used by permission. (www.Lockman.org)

Scriptures marked ASV are from the American Standard Version of the Bible.

Scriptures marked KJV are from the King James Version of the Bible.

Scriptures marked NIV are from the HOLY BIBLE, NEW INTERNATIONAL VERSION®, NIV®. Copyright © 1973, 1978, 1984 by International Bible Society. Used by permission of Zondervan. All rights reserved.

Scriptures marked NKJV are from the New King James Version. Copyright © 1982 by Thomas Nelson, Inc. Used by permission. All rights reserved.

TWENTY-FIRST CENTURY BIBLICAL COMMENTARY SERIES is a registered trademark of AMG Publishers.

ISBN–13: 978–0–89957–817–0

ISBN–10: 0–89957–817–9

First Published: August 2009

Cover Design by ImageWright, Inc.
Editing and Text Design by Warren Baker
Editorial assistance provided by Patrick Belvill and Weller Editorial Services, Chippewa Lake, MI

Printed in Canada
14 13 12 11 10 09 –T– 8 7 6 5 4 3 2 1

# Twenty-First Century Biblical Commentary Series®

## Mal Couch, Th.D., and Ed Hindson, D.Phil.

The New Testament has guided the Christian church for over two thousand years. This one testament is made up of twenty-seven books, penned by godly men through the inspiration of the Holy Spirit. It tells us of the life of Jesus Christ, His atoning death for our sins, His miraculous resurrection, His ascension back to heaven, and the promise of His second coming. It also tells the story of the birth and growth of the church and the people and principles that shaped it in its earliest days. The New Testament concludes with the book of Revelation pointing ahead to the glorious return of Jesus Christ.

Without the New Testament, the message of the Bible would be incomplete. The Old Testament emphasizes the promise of a coming Messiah. It constantly points us ahead to the One who is coming to be the King of Israel and the Savior of the world. But the Old Testament ends with this event still unfulfilled. All of its ceremonies, pictures, types, and prophecies are left awaiting the arrival of the "Lamb of God who takes away the sin of the world" (John 1:29).

The message of the New Testament represents the timeless truth of God. As each generation seeks to apply that truth to its specific context, an up-to-date commentary needs to be created just for them. The editors and authors of the Twenty-First Century Biblical Commentary Series have endeavored to do just that. This team of scholars represents conservative, evangelical, and dispensational scholarship at its best. The individual authors may differ on minor points of interpretation, but all are convinced that the Old and New

Testaments teach a dispensational framework for biblical history. They also hold to a pretribulational and premillennial understanding of biblical prophecy.

The French scholar René Pache reminded each succeeding generation, "If the power of the Holy Spirit is to be made manifest anew among us, it is of primary importance that His message should regain its due place. Then we shall be able to put the enemy to flight by the sword of the Spirit which is the Word of God."

It has long been observed that few books have had a profounder influence on the history of humankind than Paul's letter to the Galatians. The late Merrill Tenney went so far as to suggest, "Christianity might have been just one more Jewish sect, and the thought of the Western world might have been entirely pagan had it never been written." Martin Luther credited his study of Galatians as the launching pad of the Protestant Reformation and the very basis of the rejection of Roman Catholicism. Timothy George observed, "From first to last Galatians is a book about God—God's grace, God's sovereignty, God's purpose, and God's gospel."

Paul's letter to the Ephesians is also both doctrinal and personal. William Hendrickson said: "Here is Paul in person, pouring out his heart and praise in Thanksgiving. . . . It is both a spontaneous utterance of his heart and a careful composition of his mind. The gold that pours forth from his heart has been molded into definite and artistic shape by his mind (so that) his words and ideas are the words and ideas of the Holy Spirit." F. F. Bruce called Ephesians "quintessence of Paulism," and E. J. Goodspeed added that it is the "great rhapsody of Christian salvation."

In these two letters to the Galatians and Ephesians, we discover both the heart of the apostle and the heart of the New Testament gospel. In both epistles we learn that salvation is by grace alone through faith alone and Christ alone.

# Contents

# THE BOOK OF EPHESIANS

# Foreword

The apostle Paul, originally named Saul (see Acts 7:58; 22:20), presumably after the first king of Israel (1 Sam. 10:19–24; 11:12–15), was a Jew born and raised in Tarsus, the chief city of Cilicia, located on the river Cydnus near the coast of the Mediterranean Sea in the southeastern corner of Asia Minor, now modern Turkey. Tarsus was both important and strategic. Just to its north ranged the Tarsus Mountains, penetrated by a deep pass called the Cicilian Gates, through which all commerce, military forces, and visitors had to pass. Although Tarsus was roughly ten miles from the Mediterranean coast, it was a port city, because the Cydnus was navigable to that point. In addition, the citizens had developed a lake on the river between the city and the sea to keep the river from flooding the city.

Tarsus therefore absorbed the culture of both the East and the West for several centuries before Saul was born. Sometime in the last century before Christ, perhaps by Pompey, Roman citizenship was conferred on the residents of Tarsus to reward them for cooperation in achieving stability in the area. It was designated a Roman city. This citizenship was passed from generation to generation, and Paul proudly announced and claimed the benefits of his Roman citizenship (Acts 16:36–39; 22:25–29; 25:10, 16). Tarsus became a cosmopolitan city, the home of Athenodorus, teacher of Augustus, and the locale for a group of Stoic philosophers. Borrowing the phrase of Euripides, Paul described Tarsus as "no insignificant city" (Acts 21:39).

Although born in Tarsus, Saul was "brought up in this city" (Jerusalem), and "educated under Gamaliel, strictly according to the law of our fathers" (22:3). A Pharisee (5:34) and member of the Sanhedrin (vv. 21, 27, 34, 41), Gamaliel was "a teacher of the Law, respected by all the people" (v. 34), and is still highly regarded by Jews today. A properly raised Jewish boy, Saul was "circumcised the eighth day, of the nation of Israel, of the tribe of Benjamin" (as was King Saul, 1 Sam. 10:20–24), "a Hebrew of Hebrews" (Phil. 3:5). As a result of this training, Saul also was "as to the Law, a Pharisee" (v. 5). "Under Gamaliel" he was "educated . . . strictly according to the law of our fathers, being zealous for God, just as you all are today" (Acts 22:3). He claimed to be "as to the righteousness which is in the Law, found blameless" (Phil. 3:6), in all likelihood a true claim. Saul was like the rich young ruler who came to the Lord Jesus asking what to do to inherit eternal life (Luke 18:18–23). Only such a person as Saul of Tarsus—a zealous Jew with Roman citizenship and yet familiar with Grecian culture—could be God's instrument to carry the gospel of His grace and love through the finished redemptive work of the Lord Jesus Christ, God's Messiah, to all the people, Jews and Gentiles, of the Roman Empire.

This was the Lord's statement about him to Ananias of Damascus when he demurred from visiting Saul, citing his persecution of the believers in Jerusalem and his coming to Damascus for the same purpose (Acts 9:10–14). The Lord repeated his instructions, revealing Saul's spiritual condition and explaining, "He is a chosen instrument of Mine, to bear My name before the Gentiles and kings and the sons of Israel" (v. 15). Saul (Paul) also realized that God had set him apart, even from his mother's womb, that he "might preach [Christ] among the Gentiles" (Gal. 1:15–16).

Although the apostle Peter was the first to take the gospel to the Gentiles in his God-directed ministry to the household of Cornelius the centurion (Acts 10:19–11:18), it was Barnabas and Saul (later Paul) who later were commissioned by the assembly at Antioch at the direction of the Holy Spirit to take the gospel to the synagogues beyond Palestine, and they "sent them away" (13:2–3). After ministering in Seleucia, Cyprus, and Perga (vv. 4–5, 13), they came to Antioch in Pisidia and preached the gospel in the synagogue on the Sabbath at the invitation of the elders, a common courtesy with visiting teachers (vv. 14–15). The first Sabbath the message was well received, especially by the Gentiles (vv. 42–43), but on the second Sabbath it was rejected by the Jews. Then Paul told the Jews, "It was necessary that the word of God should be spoken to you first; since you repudiate it, and judge yourselves unworthy of eternal life, behold, we are turning to the Gentiles" (Acts 13:46). This became the pattern of Paul's ministry. Wherever he went, when possible, he preached the gospel to the Jews first, and when they rejected it, he turned to the Gentiles (cf. Acts 28:17–29).

After fruitful ministry in and around Antioch (13:49), Jewish opposition forced them to leave and go to Iconium, approximately fifty miles to the southeast (v. 51). Almost immediate opposition there (14:1–5) led them to go to Lystra about twenty miles almost directly south, where they ministered and Paul performed a miracle (vv. 7–18), until opposition came from Antioch and Iconium. After Paul was stoned to death and restored to life by God, the apostles (first called that in v. 4) moved on to Derbe, farther to the southeast (v. 20). They then retraced their path through the cities in which they had ministered, creating churches (literally, "assemblies") and appointing elders (vv. 21–23). They finally reached their home base in Syrian Antioch. Their report to the church there indicated "how [God] had opened a door of faith to the Gentiles" (v. 27).

After some time strict Jewish believers came from Judea and insisted that gentile believers had to follow the Mosaic system with the men circumcised in order to be saved, a view that Barnabas and Paul rejected. Dispute over this issue led the church at Antioch to send Paul and Barnabas with others to Jerusalem to take the question to "the apostles and elders" (v. 2). Some of the strict Pharisaic believers insisted that gentile believers must be circumcised and required to obey the Law of Moses (v. 5).

Peter ended the dispute by repeating his experience at Caesarea in Cornelius's house, when God sovereignly gave the Gentiles the Holy Spirit, "just as He also did to us" (v. 8). This is undoubtedly a reference to the experience of the believers worshipping in the temple area on the Day of Pentecost (Acts 2:1–4). Then the group listened as Barnabas and Paul described what they had experienced, after which James concluded that no burden should be placed on gentile believers to follow the Mosaic Law and Jewish practices except that they should take proper care to avoid offending their Jewish brethren in Christ. The council asked only that gentile believers should "abstain from things sacrificed to idols and from blood and from things strangled and from fornication" (v. 29), actions deemed necessary to avoid offending Jewish believers.

# GALATIANS

# Background of Galatians

## Canonicity

The Pauline authorship of this letter has been questioned by only the most radical of New Testament scholars. Even the liberal Tubingen school of the nineteenth century accepted Paul as its author. This is true not only because the author identifies himself as Paul (1:1; 5:2), something he does in all his letters except Hebrews (a possible argument against his authorship of it), but also because of the abundance of autobiographical information contained in it. With the possible exception of Philippians, Galatians is probably the most autobiographical of Paul's letters, although he includes some personal information in all his letters. However, in Galatians not only the abundance but also the nature of the personal information confirms its Pauline authorship. Wilson and Stapley add, "Paul is stated in 1:1 to be the author, and 5:2 mentions his name again. No case of any real merit has been brought forward to the contrary, and *few* books of Paul have been so unquestionably accepted as genuine. Many of the Early Fathers make mention of it and quote it. Furthermore the historical data and personal history of chapters 1 and 2 authenticate its Pauline authorship."[1]

## The Area of Galatia

The letter is addressed "To the churches of Galatia" (1:2). The name Galatia originally referred to an area in the central plateau of Asia Minor where nomadic Gauls settled and established a kingdom close to three hundred years before Christ. The emperor Augustus expanded the Roman province of Galatia to include areas of Phrygia, Lycaonia, Pisidia, and Pamphylia to the south and west of the original, ethnic Galatia. This area, in which Barnabas and Paul established the churches named, was often and properly called Galatia because it was a legal part of the province. Long and protracted arguments have been put forward as to their identity, and we probably shall never know with certainty. Two suggestions have been made as to these people, one based on the geographical/racial use of the word *Galatia*, the other on its political usage to describe the Roman province including Southern Galatia.[2]

# Theories of When Galatians Was Written

### The Northern Galatian Theory

Those who propound the northern Galatian theory believe that Paul was writing to the Gauls who inhabited the northern plateau known as Galatia and that reference to Paul's work among them is mentioned in Acts 16:6 and 18:23. This was the view of the early church. As explained in tradition, it allowed for the two visits to Galatia recorded in the Acts and implied in the epistle (see 4:13). The apparent fickleness of the Gauls seemed to be seen in their change of attitude to Paul (see 4:16). The towns where the churches were established were reckoned to be *Pessinus, Ancyra,* and *Tavium,* leading cities in northern Galatia, or Galatia proper.[3]

### The Southern Galatian Theory

The southern Galatian theory was first propounded in Europe toward the close of the eighteenth century but has been particularly popular among English theologians. It has been demonstrated that the province of Galatia extended southward to include the towns of Antioch (in Pisidia), Iconium, Lystra, and Derbe. The argument is that we have no record of churches in the north but that we do have a record of churches in the south. Certainly it would seem strange that Luke should say so much about the churches in the south (Acts 13 and 14) and that Paul should never mention them.

However, the identity of the Galatians does not affect the teaching of the epistle. Whoever these people were, they were in grave danger through the presence and influence of false teachers preaching another gospel. Upon their return and report to the church in Syrian Antioch, Barnabas and Paul "spent a long time with the disciples" (Acts 14:28). During that period of time, apparently toward its close, the council at Jerusalem, as stated above, met to decide the issue of the relationship of gentile believers to Jewish customs and the Mosaic Law. This was to avoid having gentile believers offend Jewish believers living among them.

Some time later Paul left on his second missionary journey, this time accompanied by Silas (Acts 15:40–41). During this trip he revisited the churches he had established on his first visit. At Lystra, Timothy was added to the party. "While they were passing through the cities, they were delivering the decrees, which had been decided upon by the apostles and elders who were in Jerusalem, for them to observe" (Acts 16:4). This statement makes it evident that Paul's letter to the Galatians preceded his second visit, or else he would have supported his rebuke of the Galatian gentile believers by reference to those decisions. This would place the writing of Galatians sometime prior to the Jerusalem Council, following a report of those believers' defection from the truth of salvation by grace through faith. This would make Galatians Paul's earliest epistle, written sometime before AD 49. This date is accepted by Donald Campbell, which he calls "the best of the available options."[4]

## *Which View Is Correct?*

The date of the Galatian epistle has been the subject of much controversy, and no doubt many saints will feel that the time of writing is unimportant, and what really matters is the teaching. However, the following viewpoints may be noted:

1. Those who accept the north Galatian theory must place the date *after* the events recorded in Acts 18:23, and so Lightfoot suggests it was written around AD 57 or 58.

2. Those who hold to the south Galatian theory obviously see it as written much earlier. Here again there are differences of opinion depending on the identification of Paul's visit to Jerusalem mentioned in Galatians 2:1–10 (as will be discussed later). Those who connect the visit of Galatians 2 with the famine relief visit of Acts 11:29–30 maintain it was written *before* the Jerusalem Council of Acts 15 and suggest AD 48 or 49.

3. Those who see the visit to Jerusalem in Galatians 2 to be the same as that of Acts 15 place the date *after* the council. Again opinions differ, some holding it was written during the second missionary journey around AD 52; others maintain it was probably during the third missionary journey, thus making the date around AD 55 or 56.

Consideration must be given to the other visits made by Paul to Jerusalem. The problem is as follows. Luke in Acts reports three visits by *Paul:* (1) Acts 9:26–29; (2) 11:30–12:25; (3) 15:1–29. However, in Galatians Paul mentioned only two visits (see 1:18–2:1). There is little doubt that Acts 9:26–29 and Gal 1:18 refer to the same occasion. The question now arises: does Paul's *second* visit in Galatians equate with the one in Acts 11 or 15? Is it the same as the famine relief visit of Acts 11 or the meeting with the council in Acts 15? As so many scholars and commentators have differed radically, it does not become one to be dogmatic.

*Thesis 1:* Galatians 2 is same as Acts 11. Those who maintain the above connection maintain it is the most straightforward and natural way to look at the incidents, removing any suggestion of Paul omitting to mention his going to Jerusalem on the famine visit when he outlines his movements in Galatians. It is pointed out that if the council took place before Galatians was written, all Paul needed to do was to refer them to the decrees that had been publicized. It is also noted that Galatians indicates a *private* meeting, whereas Acts points to a *public* meeting. Likewise, attention is drawn to the fact that Titus is mentioned in Galatians but not in the Acts account, emphasizing that the word "again" in Galatians 2:1 means "the second time" and must refer to the famine visit. The omission could have played into the hands of his enemies, who could have charged him with misrepresenting the facts. If he had been more often in Jerusalem than he had stated, then his contact with Jerusalem was more than he was willing to admit.

*Thesis 2:* Galatians 2 is same as Acts 15. As indicated earlier, the difference of judgment among eminent scholars points to the fact that one cannot be dogmatic, but the weight of evidence lies with this identification. It is important to go back to the points raised in the previous thesis (to the identification of Galatians 2 and Acts 11).

Paul does not mention the famine visit, because it had nothing to do with the point at issue. It was a mission of mercy, there being nothing in the references (11:30; 12:25) to indicate that it had in view anything other than handing over the collection to the elders. Note, too, there is no mention of the apostles. Being a time of persecution, with James having been murdered and Peter having been imprisoned, maybe the rest of the Twelve were keeping a low profile.

Paul had given the Galatians the decrees issued at Jerusalem (see Acts 16:4, 6), but obviously the false teachers had so undermined Paul's authority that they had lost confidence in him. These teachers, claiming to have come from headquarters (Jerusalem) and obviously representing an element in the church that rebelled against the decree, were able to sway the Galatian converts. Galatians 2:2 would seem to allow for both a public meeting (v. 2a) and a private meeting (v. 2b).

It is true that Titus is not mentioned by name in Acts 15, but it would seem the expression in verse 2, "and certain others of them" would make room for him as well as others.

Scholars observe that the word "again" (*palin*) is the usual word so translated and is more indefinite than the word translated "second" in the New

Testament. It should be noted that Galatians 2:2 indicates that Paul made known to the apostles the gospel he preached to the Gentiles, and his work was confirmed by them (see vv. 7–10). This he could not have done during the famine visit of Acts 11 before his first missionary journey.

A number of other matters should now be noted that identify Galatians 2 and Acts 15:

1. *Circumcision:* see Acts 15:1 and Galatians 2:3.

2. *Speakers:* Paul, Barnabas, Peter, and James being mentioned in each account.

3. *Declaration:* how God had worked among the Gentiles (Acts 15:12; Gal. 2:2, 8, 9).

4. *Agreement:* see Acts 15:22; Galatians 2:9, noting too the agreement of Peter (Acts 15:10) and James (v. 19).

5. *Special pleading:* Judaizers in each case contending for circumcision: see Acts 15:5; Galatians 2:4–5.

Finally, as to chronology, if the famine visit of Acts 11 is the same as recorded in Galatians 2, it must have taken place around the time of the death of Herod Agrippa I (AD 44). If this was fourteen years after Paul's conversion (Gal. 2:1), that places his conversion in AD 30, during the life of the Lord. Obviously, this cannot be. It should be noted that many believe the fourteen years should be added to the three years of (1:18), making seventeen years in all. Some, however, say Herod's death was not until AD 46 and, using the old inclusive reckoning, would make Paul's conversion in AD 33. This very neat reckoning is based on the assumption that the fourteen years are dated from Paul's conversion but is ruled out entirely if the fourteen years are additional to the three years of 1:18.

As the gospel began to be preached in gentile territory and Gentiles began to profess faith in the Lord Jesus, so the problems began to increase. These problems were raised by Jews. What was the relationship of the Gentiles to the Law of Moses? Were they to be allowed to ignore it completely? Had it not a place seeing it was of divine origin? And what about the rite of circumcision? If the Gentiles were to be among the people of the covenant (as they would say) should they not carry in their bodies the mark and seal of the covenant?

Wider issues arose from such questions: was the church only to be an extension of Judaism? If salvation was for all, was faith in Christ sufficient? Were Law works needed to complete justification? And what about table and meal fellowship?

Could Jews and Gentiles eat together and eat the same food? Clearly, Paul had preached a pure gospel. Law keeping did not enter into it: salvation was in Christ alone. The Law condemned, but on the cross Christ had borne its curse.

Then word came through that the Galatians were turning back to the Law. False teachers had come from Jerusalem claiming to be from James and having his support. They proclaimed that faith in Christ was insufficient, that the converts must be circumcised and keep the Law, and that Paul's doctrine of the gospel was wrong.

Paul was deeply moved. The teaching destroyed the foundations of the gospel. Christianity would finish as a sect of Judaism, an extension of the Jews' religion.

The attack on Paul was threefold:

1. They attacked Paul's claim to be an apostle. If they could undermine his authority, they could destroy his teaching. He was not one of the original Twelve called and sent forth by Christ: he was apart from them. Well meaning in his preaching, nevertheless, he was on his own. All must look to Jerusalem and the Twelve for the true gospel. Paul answers this challenge in chapters 1 and 2.

2. The gospel preached by Paul was good but insufficient. It did not go far enough, for it left out the Law, and no one ever knew God among His people without observing it. Christ had honored it, and the apostles too. Who was Paul to set all this aside? Paul answers such teaching in chapters 3 and 4.

3. Not only so, but the Law was necessary for good living. Its precepts were to help all to live a good life. Life for God without Law must inevitably lead to lawlessness and immorality and every kind of excess. Paul answers these arguments in chapters 5 and 6 as he sets before them a Spirit-filled life.

It is important to note that although the Galatian problem was a first-century problem, the emphasis of modern charismatic teaching on Christ plus experience has the same root.[5]

## The Territory of Galatia

The epistle to the churches of Galatia is so called because it is addressed *to the churches of Galatia* (1:2); moreover, the addressees are mentioned throughout the book as, *O foolish Galatians* (3:1). The question then comes up: Where were these churches and who were these Galatians? Can they be found in the territory of the former kingdom of Galatia or somewhat else in the more extensive Roman province of Galatia, which also included the former kingdom with a lot more area added? Were the recipients of this epistle Galatians in the ethnic sense, or only in the political sense, as citizens of the Roman province that was identified with that name?

## The Word *Galatia*

The Greek word *Galatia* is a variant form of *kevltai* or *kevltoi*, "the Celts" (Lat., *Galli*). When the Celts are first seen, they live in Central Europe, in the Danube basin. Some place names in that area retain Celtic thought forms even today. For example, Vienna (Lat., *Vindobona*) is a good example. All the way, then, they came from the Danube basin as they migrated in a westerly direction into Switzerland, southern Germany, and even as far as northern Italy, and then on into Gaul and Britain: they also migrated toward the south and settled in north-central Asia Minor, giving their name to their new homeland, just as they also did to Gaul (Lat., *Gallia*, Gk., *galativa*).

The Celts who moved toward the southeast ravaged Thrace, Macedonia, and Thessaly, and then went on and invaded Greece; however, they got no farther than Delphi. They were driven out from there in 279 BC. The following year a large body of these people crossed the Hellespont into Asia Minor. They came at the invitation of Nicomedes, king of Bithynia, who thought he could use their military power against his enemies. For about a generation they menaced their neighbors in Asia Minor, until a series of defeats at the hands of Attalus I, king of Pergamum (c. 230 BC), confined them within fixed limits, in territory that had formerly belonged to Phrygia.

## The Romans and Galatia

The Romans were influential in Asia Minor, apart from the period (88–65 BC) during which Mithridates VI of Pontus held sway over the area. The Galatians quickly appreciated the wisdom of keeping on good terms with Rome. With Roman permission or connivance, they augmented their territory during the second century BC. They suffered severely under Mithridates because of their friendship with Rome, but when he was finally defeated by Pompey in 64 BC, their loyalty was rewarded by Galatia's receiving the status of a client kingdom. Augustus reorganized the kingdom as an imperial province (25 BC).

## The Area of Galatia

In 6 BC inland Paphlagonia on the north was added to the province of Galatia, as three or four years later were some areas to the northeast that had formerly belonged to Pontus. These latter areas were henceforth known as Pontus Galaticus. By analogy with this, it has been inferred that, for example, those parts of Phrygia and Lycaonia that were included in the province were known respectively as Phrygia Galatica and Lycaonia Galatica, to distinguish them from that part of Phrygia that lay within proconsular Asia (Phrygia

Asiana) and from Eastern Lycaonia (Lycaonia Antiochiana), which from AD 37 to 40 and again from AD 41 onward, belonged to Rome's ally Antiochus IV, king of Commagene. These terms are convenient enough, but without proper attestation we cannot assume confidently that they were part of the official Roman nomenclature.[6]

# Section One

# THE APOSTLE OF GRACE
# BY FAITH

## GALATIANS 1:1-2:21

**CHAPTER 1**

# A True Apostle Defends the True Gospel
# Galatians 1:1–24

**Preview:**
*Paul had received reports of problems in the Galatian churches and begins to address them immediately. Apparently some were listening to false teachers who were preaching a perversion of the true gospel and sowing seeds of doubt as to Paul's true apostleship.*

## Paul's Salutation (1:1–5)

After stating his name, Paul identifies himself as "an apostle" (v. 1). In a very limited sense, this title is used only of the twelve disciples chosen by our Lord and Matthias, chosen to replace Judas Iscariot. Their qualification was to "have accompanied us all the time . . . beginning with the baptism of John, until the day that [Jesus] was taken up from us," their responsibility to "become a witness with us of His resurrection" (Acts 1:21–22). In a very broad, literal sense, it means "a person sent out" and can be applied to every missionary. Paul used the title in a technical sense, but differently from the Twelve. He had seen our Lord in his resurrection and could be a witness of it (Acts 9:3–4, 17; 1 Cor. 15:8–9).

Paul had been formally commissioned by Jesus "to bear My name before the Gentiles" (Acts 9:15; cf. 13:2–3) and had been sent off by the church at

*11*

Syrian Antioch. Thus he was also "an apostle" in the literal sense. Paul imme-diately makes it clear, however, that his sending was not "from men, nor through the agency of man" (v. 1). Instead, it was "by Jesus Christ" and, even then, not Jesus alone, but also "God the Father" working in harmony as always, "who raised Him from the dead." Ronald Fung adds, "The emphatic contrast with which Paul describes his apostleship is intended to underline its divine origin: he asserts that his apostolic commission, with regard to both its source and its mediation, was from God and Christ, just as a little later on he will categorically declare that his gospel, with regard to both its source and the manner in which it was communicated to him, was a direct revelation from God" (1:12, 16).[1]

The supreme evidence of God's almighty power is the resurrection of our Lord Jesus from the dead, which is also the assurance of the believer's resur-rection by faith to eternal life. There is no life after death apart from the work of Christ on the cross and His coming forth from the grave. Because He is the Holy One, the grave could not hold Him—that is, the Second Person of the Trinity could not undergo decay (Ps. 16:8–11; Acts 2:25–31). The resurrection is what makes Christianity unique among religions of the world. The great fear of humanity is conquered by Christ's resurrection (1 Cor. 15). It is this Christ, and His heavenly Father, who has commissioned Paul. Paul does not speak, witness, nor minister through his own authority. He stands tall as an apostle because of the person of the Lord Jesus.

In his greetings Paul includes "all the brethren who are with me" (v. 2). This is also a clue that Paul was writing from Syrian Antioch. He sometimes mentions his companions by name in his greetings but never more than two (1 Thess. 1:1; 2 Thess. 1:1), because he always traveled light. This reference implies a larger group, which would be true in Syrian Antioch, which was con-sidered Paul's home base because he resided there for some years and fellow-shipped with the believers. He and Barnabas had reported on their mission-ary journey, undoubtedly rejoicing the hearts of the believers (Acts 14:26–28). James Dunn adds:

> It is also relevant to note that in what are probably his two earliest letters, Paul does *not* introduce himself as an "apostle" (1 Thess. 1:1; 2 Thess. 2:1), whereas, as we have already seen, it became his almost unvarying practice thereafter to describe himself as "apostle of Christ Jesus." If Galatians is the third (or second) of his extant letters, the implication is obvious that a claim to authority as "apostle of Christ," which was unquestioned before (1 Thess. 2:6), became a matter of some sensitive-ness for Paul and something he felt it important to assert from the first in all dealings with his churches from then on. This shift in emphasis was

almost certainly occasioned by the crisis in Galatia, and by the fact that his message was being challenged there by means of a challenge to his apostolic status.[2]

It is interesting to note that in many of Paul's letters he mentions other brothers who are with him. He is not saying that they have equal apostolic authority but that they are confirming him, what he says and what he does. However, they do impart a greeting with Paul to the churches he is addressing. How many were represented in Galatia is not known. But without doubt, the gospel spread far and wide in this territory and must have had a profound effect on the population.

Paul uses his usual words of greeting (v. 3) to the Galatians that he uses in his other letters—"grace and peace"—except that to Timothy he adds "mercy," evidently feeling that this young disciple needed mercy as well (1 Tim. 1:2; 2 Tim. 1:2). Although often customary, this greeting in Paul's writings was not ordinary, nor simply routine. In the inspiration of Scripture, no words are wasted. They are not simply "filler" words. Paul truly desires that God's grace and peace impact the lives of those to whom he is writing. The word translated "grace" is related to a usual Greek greeting that means to rejoice and signifies a favor bestowed upon the individual addressed. The word translated "peace" is a translation of the Hebrew word *shalom*, still used by Jews today. It can have a variety of implications, such as "be healthy, be in community, in fellowship." R. C. H. Lenski adds: "'Grace' is fundamental; 'peace' is its result. This order is never reversed. The grammars supply the optative form *eimi* to indicate a wish: 'May grace and peace be with you.' We prefer to supply nothing and regard the statement as an exclamation: 'Grace to you and peace!'"[3]

Both of these qualities come "from God our Father, and the Lord Jesus Christ." This is the valid order of these two persons of the Godhead, because the Father is the ultimate sovereign of the universe and bestower of all blessings, and Jesus Christ is the Sinless One who provided the righteous way for the Father to bestow them. This is what Paul is explaining by saying that Christ "gave Himself for our sins, that He might deliver us out of this present evil age." This supreme deed, as all of Christ's work (John 8:29), is "according to the will of our God and Father." Paul then closes his greeting by invoking glory (praise, honor) on God "forevermore" (literally, "unto the age of the ages") and seals it with an "Amen."

As Donald Campbell observes, in this salutation "Paul had already drawn the lines of battle by touching on two vital concerns. He had affirmed his own apostleship and had declared that the basis of man's salvation lies solely in the work of Christ and not in any human works."[4] In addition, although only in a cursory way, he has touched on the doctrine of last things by speaking of believers being rescued "out of this present evil age" (v. 4). Paul does not fail to remind his readers of what Christ did on the cross. He voluntarily gave up His life "for our sins." Notice how Paul includes himself as a beneficiary of Christ's death. But there is more. Christ died that He might "deliver us out of this present evil." There is a past benefit with Christ's death. He took away the judgment that was placed on all humanity. He also died that believers might be presently liberated from the power and clutch of sin. But eternal salvation also awaits believers after death. The Greek word used here for "age" is *aiōn*. Regarding this, Frederic Rendall comments:

> In early Greek this word denoted the appointed lifetime of a man, and so combined the thought of an overruling destiny with the course of human life. From the conception of individual life was developed that of corporate life, whether of families, nations or societies, and the idea of divine appointment was more distinctly fastened on the word in Scripture, so that every successive dispensation of God was designated as an *aiōnē*. . . . This sweeping condemnation of the existing world corresponds to the language of [John] the Baptist and to Christ's own denunciations of the evil generation to which He came. In spite of all that revelation and conscience had done to leaven it, He found the faithful few in number, and evil predominant in the mass.[5]

This rescue into God's presence will take place ultimately for each believer either individually through death (cf. Luke 23:2–43) or corporately through the translation of the saints called the rapture (1 Thess. 4:15–17).

It is worth noting that Paul calls God "our Father" (Gal. 1:5), suggesting God's paternal concern for believers not only physically as his creatures (Gen. 1:26–27; Acts 17:28–29) but also spiritually as the result of our faith in the completed redemptive sacrifice of Jesus on the cross (John 19:30) and the regenerating work of God the Holy Spirit (John 3:5–8). As a result of that regenerating work, the Holy Spirit indwells the believer, who then from his heart calls God his Father (Rom. 8:15–16).

In verse 5 "the glory" (*doxa*) is speaking of the preeminent glory that belongs to God the Father, with whom no one can compare. The glory of the Lord Jesus Christ is also the glory of God the Father. This is the particular splendor that is ascribed to deity alone. The child of God acknowledges this radiance and majesty to the one and only Lord and Master. No mere human can receive such an accolade.

In this insertion of such a brief doxology, the mind of the apostle Paul is but following an inner impulse of worshipful praise. The apostle is not simply filling space when he writes these words—he is continually struck by the greatness of his God. And when he writes, "forevermore," he is using a Hebraic expression for time that is infinite and unending. The words here are actually in Greek multiplied indefinitely and could mean "for all possible ages." Actually, the words are "unto the ages of the ages," a phrase very specifically used by Paul, for example, in his doxologies to God (Phil. 4:20; 1 Tim. 1:17) and to Christ (2 Tim. 4:18).

The same words are used to define the duration of the punishment of the harlot of Babylon (Rev. 19:3) and of the devil, the Beast, and the False Prophet (20:10). The same words "unto the age of the age" can be found in Hebrews 1:8 as quoted from Psalm 45:6 (LXX).

The word *amen* is also a Hebrew word that is found in Deuteronomy 7:9, "the faithful God"; Isaiah 49:7, "the LORD who is faithful; and 65:16, "the God of truth," or "the God of Amen." The "amen" said by the Lord can mean "It is and shall be so," and by people, "So let it be." Christ usually used "amen" to mean "verily," by which He introduced new information or revelation concerning the mind and heart of the Father. In the Gospel of John the word is usually repeated as "Amen, Amen." In the New Testament, one time "Amen" becomes a title of Christ (Rev. 3:14), since He is the finality of God and His purposes and plans are established through the Son.

## Paul's Introductory Rebuke (1:6–9)

In most of his letters Paul followed his salutation with a statement of praise and thanksgiving for some aspect of the Christian witness of the recipients. This is true even of the Corinthians, whom he then rebuked for so many failures (1 Cor. 1:4–9). Here, however, without any commendation, he declared his amazement at their deserting God—"Him who called you by the grace of Christ" (v. 6). Paul was the human agent of their calling, but God obviously was the caller. These are strong words. The Greek word translated "amazed" could be translated "dumbfounded, flabbergasted" in the vernacular, and the Greek verb is in the continuing mode, indicating that Paul was in a state of astonishment. Paul, up to this point, has been pleasant in his words to the Galatians. But now he hits head-on the problem he has with these churches. While it would be too extreme to say that all believers in Galatia had departed from the basics of the gospel, this departure was prevalent enough to mark these churches as clearly moving away from the truth. In his wording it seems as if Paul did not expect this to happen. He had no warning of the change. He seems stunned that it took place at all.

The word translated "deserting" is a military term representing a serious action. They are turning to "a different [literally, 'another'] gospel." The participle "deserting" is also in the continuing mode, implying the situation was in a state of flux. John MacArthur says:

> The Galatian Christians not only were being confused and weakened in their confidence to live by grace but were actually **deserting**. The term behind **deserting** (*metatithēmi*) was used of military desertion, which was punishable by death during time of war, much as in modern times. The Greek verb is reflexive, indicating that the act is voluntary. The believers were not passively *being* removed, as the King James translation suggests, but were in the process of removing themselves from the sphere of grace. The false teachers were accountable for their corruption of God's truth, but the Galatian Christians were also accountable for being so easily misled by it to pursue legalism.[6]

Paul adds the clause "which is really not another" (v. 7). With this statement he is saying, "There is no relationship between what you now believe and what you apparently accepted when you trusted in Christ!" When it comes to doctrinal error, the apostle pulls no punches. He speaks out forthrightly and with righteous indignation. Doctrinal departure cannot be tolerated. Error is like a cancer that will destroy the body. Henry Alford explains that the literal translation, "another gospel" was "a paradoxical expression, there being in reality but one Gospel. Paul appeared by it to admit the existence of many Gospels, and he therefore explains himself more accurately, how he wishes to be understood."[7]

Paul uses a deliberate play on words with those translated "different"—literally, "another"—and "another." The Greek word translated "different" means literally "another of a different kind," as apples are one fruit and pears are another fruit, but another of a different kind. The word translated "another" in the clause literally translated "which is really not another," means "another of the same kind." The fact remains, however, that when circumcision and observance of the Mosaic Law are required in addition to faith in Jesus Christ for a person to be saved, it is another in the sense of a different gospel. By proclaiming that there were "some who are disturbing you" through their teaching, Paul wisely did not name them or say whether they came from Judea or whether they were led by one person, which is usually the case. However, these troublers, undoubtedly led by a ringleader, were "trying to pervert the gospel of Christ."

There have been many theories put forth as to who these troublers were. Although Paul never speaks to them directly, their impact was undoubtedly significant as they are mentioned in every chapter.[8]

Since there were Jews and Gentiles living in Galatia, along with the new believers in Christ, one view is that these instigators were local Jews attempting to convince these new Christians that Judaism was the correct path to God. This view, however, suffers from the evidence in the book of Acts that shows that false teachers were following Paul into the cities he visited, attempting to pervert his teaching (Acts 15:1, 24). Also, from 1:6–7, it appears that theses troublers were Christians, and not Jews, as they were presenting "a different gospel" and not pure Judaism.[9]

Another view has Paul fighting two different groups: one made up of local gentile Christians who had been swayed by local Jews to adopt the Judaizer's view, and a group of radical gentile Christians who wanted a complete break with Judaism. The problem here is no biblical evidence to show that Paul was fighting with two separate groups in Galatia.[10]

Perhaps, since Paul did not spend as much time with some churches as with others, this view arose: these false teachers were actually Gentiles whose conversion took place under the teaching of Paul, yet they had not been taught completely by Paul and now believed they had to follow the practices of the church in Jerusalem. This view is refuted by Paul's grammar in speaking to the disciples. When he speaks to his followers, he does so in the second person, but when he speaks of the troublers, it is in the third person. This sets a distinction similar to that in his letters to the Corinthians and reinforces the idea that these false teachers are coming into Galatia from the outside.[11]

One less specious view, held by Schmithal, is that these troublers were Jewish Christian Gnostics. To arrive at this view, Schmithal makes some rather doubtful assumptions, such as the interpretation "the heretic's demand for circumcision as a means of securing release symbolically from the dominion of the flesh."[12] There is no basis for this view in the letter; nor is there any other reference to elements of Gnosticism that Paul addressed in other letters, such as the *gnōsis* (or knowledge) in 1 Corinthians. In fact, the focus of the false teachers in Galatians is on adding Jewish legalism to Christianity, which would not agree with Gnostic thought.[13]

None of these views offer convincing evidence to overthrow the traditional view, that the false teachers were indeed Judaizers: Jewish Christians who believed that it was necessary for gentile believers to be circumcised and to follow the Law in order to be "truly" Christian.[14]

So emphatic is Paul about the uniqueness and singularity of the true gospel that he pronounces eternal condemnation (*anathema* in Greek) on the hypothetical cases of even himself or "an angel from heaven" (v. 8) preaching a gospel different from the true gospel he had already preached. To return to reality, the fact was that someone was preaching a false gospel, so Paul pronounces anathema on anyone preaching a gospel different from the one the Galatians had believed—salvation for eternity by the grace of God received by faith in Christ's redemptive sacrifice plus nothing. Christians today need the same zeal for the purity and simplicity of the gospel. Paul uses hyperbole and a certain amount of needed sarcasm to shake these churches back into reality. He stands firmly on what he is writing on the basis of his apostolic authority that was given him by Christ (v. 12).

In verse 8 the apostle must have in mind Barnabas when he uses "we." This would probably refer to their first visit (Acts 13:13) and on a later occasion with Silas and Timothy (15:40; 16:3–6). As mentioned, "An angel from heaven" is of course hyperbole and exaggeration, though it could refer to an incident in 14:11–13, when during the first visit to Lystra, a city in Galatia, the people thought the apostles were gods. "A gospel contrary" is really in the Greek text "other than," or "beside." The apostle Paul is adamant that the gospel he and his colleagues are proclaiming is complete, absolute, and final.

In the LXX the Greek word *cherem* means *something devoted to God*. Later in the development of the word there came about a wider use, a more negative meaning, a sense of disfavor from God (Isa. 34:5; Zech. 14:11; Mal. 4:6), thus *anathema* (*accursed*). This is how the word became most used later on in the New Testament. Paul uses it in Romans 9:3; 1 Corinthians 12:3; 16:22; and elsewhere only in Acts 23:14, where it is used as a verb, *anathematize*. Anyone communicating another presentation of the gospel could not be saved by that gospel. Therefore they are heretics and stand under the judgment of God. Again, Paul knows the force and power of error. He knows how easy it is to move away from truth. Satan the deceiver never tires or slumbers. Those laboring in the ministry cannot relax their vigil.

When Paul says "we have said before" (v. 9), he uses the Greek word *pro-legō* ("before said") with the sense of "we have before spoken plainly." Then to make sure they get it, he adds, "so I say again now." To make sure that they connect previous warnings he had given on an earlier visit, he repeats himself with all of the authority granted to him by the Lord.

Paul keeps up the unrelenting pressure of his authority and adds "if any man is preaching to you a gospel contrary to that which you received, let him be accursed." His repetition of this judgment illustrates he had given it not simply with passion but with deliberation, as a matter not just from emotional feeling but from the fact of how serious the matter is with God!

That gospel that the apostle was so jealous about was not simply that which was spoken from the outset, but which they had accepted, that had brought light from out of the darkness, and set them free as bound slaves just released from their bondage. In this case their enslavement was to sin (see 1 Cor. 15:1; 1 Thess. 2:13).

## Paul's Apostleship Questioned (1:10–11)

To support the false gospel they were selling the Galatian believers, the Judaizers questioned the validity of Paul's calling and apostleship. This was one of their primary objectives. They knew that it would be very difficult, if not impossible, to weaken his teaching of the gospel; therefore they questioned his legitimacy as an apostle, saying that he had appointed himself and only wanted to build up his own following.[15]

This strategy apparently worked; otherwise Paul would have had no need to make a defense. There is no evidence that the early church ever questioned the apostleship of the original Twelve—even Matthias, after he was added. But Paul was a different story. After all, hadn't he been a Pharisee and a well-known persecutor of the church? He had never followed Jesus during His first coming. Perhaps another sticking point was his reference to himself as an "apostle of Gentiles," (Rom. 11:13). This may have made Jewish believers suspicious, due to their inbred hatred toward Gentiles that they needed to overcome. Last, the fact that Paul had to defend and affirm his apostleship many times in his various letters gives the impression that it was frequently questioned.[16]

To introduce his defense of himself, Paul asks whether he is trying to please men or God. Dunn states:

> Having caught his audience's attention with the language of his introduction and indicated beyond doubt the gravity of the issues at stake, Paul can now begin his self-defence, or rather, the defence of his gospel. The atmosphere in the congregations in Galatia when the letter was first read out to them must have been electric. Their own astonishment and upset at the charges already leveled against them would ensure careful attention to and careful scrutiny of what he was about to say. The tactic was no doubt deliberate. Paul was a practised public speaker, and in thus gaining his audience's attention he was following the simple techniques which all successful orators have known how to use.[17]

And MacArthur offers this grammatical analysis:

*Gar* (**for**) has numerous meanings, which are largely determined by context. It can also be translated "because," "yes, indeed," "certainly," "what," and "why." It can also sometimes mean "there," which is a helpful rendering in this verse. **For** is not an incorrect translation, but "there" seems to follow better the flow of Paul's argument in this context. "There," he is saying, referring back to the strong anathemas of the previous two verses, "does that sound like I am a people pleaser? **Am I now seeking the favor of men, or of God? Or am I striving to please men?**" Obviously Paul's pronouncing a curse on men (v. 9) does not fit with the accusations of the Judaizers against him. Rather, it unquestionably seeks to honor God, whose truth was being perverted.[18]

Obviously he is not trying to please men, since he rebuked the Galatian believers and he denounced the false teachers. The only logical conclusion is that he is trying to please God. Paul then states plainly that his gospel message is not of human origin but came directly "through a revelation of Jesus Christ." In addition to stating the divine source of his gospel, Paul may be subtly alluding to the human origin of the message that demanded the observance of the Mosaic Law, including circumcision for men, to insure salvation proclaimed by the Judaizers.

In verses 10–11 Paul reinforces that what he is giving is not of human origin. And he receives no human reward for his message. He is driven only by his calling from God. When Paul in verse 11 says, "I would have you know," he uses the Greek word *gnōrizō*, a word often used to convey communicating something not previously known (2 Cor. 8:1), or sometimes used when recapitulating things already well known (1 Cor. 15:1). The apostle is not here intending to say that the Christians in Galatia had not before known the basis of his claim to apostleship, but is justly reminding them of this fact, lest they question his authority as the messenger of the truth about salvation only in Christ.

When the apostle says the gospel he is preaching "is not according to man," he goes from an imperfect (past tense) to a present tense as a reminder that the gospel had not changed in its form, in its scope, or in its character. "According" is *kata* and carries the thought of "not of man's devices," or not in accordance with human thinking or human ideas. This gospel was not conceived in the mind of man. It is from God and not from the religious thoughts of people. The Judaizers had interpreted the gospel as something created by Paul, something "after man," humanlike in its doctrine, origin, and object. Paul speaks of the gospel as "my gospel" in Romans 2:16, but he does not mean in the self-created sense. He simply is conveying there that the revelation about this great salvation was given to him for God to communicate and propagate to lost humanity. The facts of the gospel have to do with the death, burial, and resurrection of the Lord Jesus Christ (1 Cor. 15:1–3).

Paul is a walking miracle who encountered the Lord Jesus face-to-face on the Damascus road. Concerning Paul, the Lord said to the pious Jew Ananias, "Paul is a chosen instrument of Mine, to bear My name before the Gentiles and kings and sons of Israel" (Acts 9:15). Paul's life turned around immediately, and he was filled (controlled) by the Holy Spirit (v. 17) to begin "to proclaim Jesus in the synagogues, saying, 'He is the Son of God'" (v. 20).

| **Paul's Early Life** |
| --- |
| *Raised in Tarsus (Acts 21:39)* |
| *A Roman citizen (v. 39)* |
| *Studied under the famous rabbi Gamaliel (22:3)* |
| *Studied in Jerusalem (22:3)* |
| *Of the tribe of Benjamin (Phil. 3:5)* |
| *Of the sect of the Pharisees (Acts 23:6)* |
| *Originally named Saul, probably after King Saul (9:1)* |
| *His sister's son resided in Jerusalem (Acts 23:16–22)* |
| *Probably had a wealthy father* |
| *Was advancing as a leader in Judaism (Gal. 1:14)* |
| *Was zealous for his Jewish traditions (v. 14)* |
| *Set out to destroy the church of God (v. 13)* |
| *Was given authority by the chief priests to murder Christians (Acts 9:1, 14)* |

# Paul's Changed Life (1:13–17)

In these verses the apostle Paul wants to reestablish a connection with his readers and his much coveted past. He was a Jew of the Jews, the most pious of the pious! No one could outdo his religious devotion and fervor for tradition.

Having put forth the idea he is seeking to defend (1:1–12), the apostle turns to the first line of the defense itself—that is, his conduct just before his encounter with the risen Christ. He evidently thought it important that he should start there. His readers needed to be reminded that he knew Judaism from inside and indeed was a prime exponent of it. Paul realized what the attractions and appealing strengths were. Note how he focuses on praxis: his beliefs about Jesus were not what were paramount to the Galatian crisis; his conduct was. This emphasis reflected both the character of Judaism and presumably also the problems at issue in Galatia. Already there is a hint that what was at issue in Galatia was what was in practice in the lives of those who confessed their faith in such statements. It was a form of raw legalism.[19]

Paul says that the Galatians had heard of his "former manner of life in Judaism" (1:13), undoubtedly from his own lips as a part of his testimony when he and Barnabas brought the gospel to them (Acts 13:14—14:26). The use of the Greek aorist "you have heard" speaks of a past event related to the action of the present. Paul's story must have been familiar to the Galatians and served to show how divine his conversion had been. Only God could change the heart of one who had been such a terror to the church.[20]

When Paul mentions his "life in Judaism," he isn't speaking strictly of the religion. He is speaking about how he carried himself, his spiritual heritage, and his zeal for God even though it was misplaced. Rendall says that Judaism "denotes Jewish partisanship, and accurately describes the bitter party spirit which prompted Saul to take the lead in the martyrdom of Stephen and the persecution of the Church. Incidentally the partisanship was based on a false view of religion, for the narrow intolerance of the Scribes and Pharisees was a prevailing curse of Jewish society at the time; but *Judaism* expresses the party spirit, not the religion."[21]

Paul accurately confesses that he "used to persecute the church of God beyond measure, and tried to destroy it" (cf. Acts 8:3; 9:1-2). The Greek clearly describes the extent of Paul's hostile actions toward the church. "Used to persecute" is an imperfect, active, indicative verb meaning that Paul's persecution was persistent and continual. His sole focus in life was to destroy the Christian church, which, in his converted state, he now recognizes as the "church of God."[22] He knows now and freely admits that his actions as a zealous Pharisee were directed against the one true God and His Son, Jesus Christ. By saying, "beyond measure," is to imply that he went beyond normal boundaries. Trying to destroy the church indicates the fact that he probably would have loved to see the Christians killed. In Paul's mind they were destroying and distorting Judaism as he knew it. Being blind to the truth, he could not see that the message of Christ was bringing about a fulfillment of the Old Testament prophecies of the death, and then later, the reign of the Messiah!

Paul explained that he was "advancing in Judaism beyond many of my contemporaries among my countrymen being more extremely zealous for my ancestral traditions" (cf. Phil. 3:4–6). The Greek word for "advancing" literally means to cut a way forward, as in blazing a trail. Saul kept cutting his way forward through Judaism and would let nothing stand in his path, especially Jewish Christians.[23] As for Paul's "ancestral traditions" (v. 14), MacArthur says:

> **Ancestral traditions** refers to the body of oral teachings about the Old Testament law that came to have equal authority with the law. Commonly known as the Halakah, this collection of Torah interpretations became a fence around God's revealed law and all but hid it from view. Over a period of several hundred years it had expanded into a mammoth accumulation of religious, moral, legal, practical, and ceremonial regulations that defied comprehension, much less total compliance. It contained such vast amounts of minutiae that even the most learned rabbinical scholars could not master it either by interpretation or in behavior. Yet the more complex and burdensome it became, the more zealously Jewish legalists revered and propagated it.[24]

When Paul says he was "extremely zealous" (Gk., *zēlōtēs*), he is saying that he was *a zealot* in the fact that he was an uncompromising partisan for Judaism. By this name the most ardent group of the Pharisees, especially marked by their bitter antagonism to the Romans, practiced hatred and resistance. Such Pharisees were often called the *Cananaean*, which became an equivalent Hebrew term for those who were most zealous in their defiance of Roman rule (Matt. 10:4). Simon Peter also belonged to this group (Luke 6:15; Acts 1:13). Here in Galatians and in all other New Testament references, the word *zēlōtēs* is an adjective. Paul is not saying he belonged to the Zealot party any more than he meant that the Jews to whom he spoke in Jerusalem belonged to them (Acts 22:3, cf. 21:20). Paul is simply reminding his readers of his solid loyalty to Judaism in the days before he become a believer in Christ. The word *zēlōtēs* can be used in an admirable sense—that is, Christians can be "zealous for good deeds" (Titus 2:14) and "zealous of spiritual gifts" (1 Cor. 14:12).

Paul was on his way to becoming known throughout history as the persecutor, perhaps even the destroyer, of the followers of Christ. As a result, when Jesus arrested him on the road approaching Damascus, Paul deserved to be struck dead and his soul consigned to hell for eternity. God, however, had other plans. God had set Paul "apart, even from [his] mother's womb" (a strong argument against abortion) and had called him "through His grace" (1:15). There is a grace for salvation and a grace for living. Paul realized that he had been called by God's sovereign grace. His salvation was no accident.

The first part of this statement was especially poignant to Paul's Jewish readers. Fung explains:

> The idea of God consecrating Paul before his birth and subsequently calling him is strongly reminiscent of Isa. 49:1ff., where the Servant of Yahweh (addressed as Israel) is called to be a light to the Gentiles, and of Jer. 1:4f., where Jeremiah appears as one consecrated before his birth and appointed a prophet to the nations (i.e., the Gentiles). Paul's application of these biblical expressions to himself has the effect of aligning himself with those OT figures in the history of salvation: God's call to him was essentially the same as his call to them, a renewal of his will for the salvation of the Gentiles. More specifically, whereas the analogy with Jeremiah reflects Paul's "apostolic self-consciousness," the allusion to Isaiah (together with other similar references: cf. Rom. 15:21 with Isa. 52:15; Acts 13:47 with Isa. 49:6; Acts 18:9f. with Isa. 43:5) reveals Paul as "the Apostle specially selected to continue the work of the Servant of Yahweh."[25]

Paul supremely demonstrates what is true for each believer, that the grace of God is the free, abundant, and unconditional bestowal of his acceptance, blessing, and favor upon a person who deserves his righteous rejection and condemnation. God's design and desire were "to reveal His Son" in Paul, the same desire that He has for each believer in Jesus Christ. The eternal plan God had for Paul was that he "might preach [Jesus] among the Gentiles" (cf. Acts 9:15). Wherever Paul went to preach the gospel, he went first to a Jewish synagogue (see, e.g., Acts 13:14; 14:1; 17:2, 17; 18:4; 19:8) or place of Jewish worship (Acts 16:13); but upon the Jews' rejection of his message concerning Jesus Christ, he would turn in his ministry to the Gentiles (see, e.g., Acts 13:46; 18:6; 19:9; 28:17–28).

Paul makes the point that, when confronted by the ascended Christ on the road to Damascus, he "did not immediately consult with flesh and blood" (any other man). Paul's emphatic use of "immediately" may give some insight as to the charges brought against him by the Judaizers, as verses 16b and 17a appear to be refutations, possibly of lies being told about him.[26]

Perhaps the Judaizers had told the Galatians that Paul, at first, had listened to their sound teaching but then broke away and acted wrongly in discarding the legal requirements of Judaism. This could have influenced the Galatians by implying that legalistic Christianity was the original teaching, which Paul had adhered to after studying under other teachers. Paul refutes this possibility soundly in verse 16b.[27]

Acts also makes it plain. At God's directive, Ananias went to Saul in Damascus and ministered to him, explaining what had occurred (Acts 9:19), but Saul did not consult with any man as he had been trained by Gamaliel as a youth (Acts 22:3). Neither did he then go to Jerusalem to see and seek instruction or endorsement from "those who were apostles before me." Lenski writes:

> It would have been wrong for Paul to have consulted the Twelve or any number of them whom he might have found in Jerusalem. It will not do to say that they would undoubtedly have approved. They would have rebuked Paul for trying to consult them regarding God's own revelation. Not one of them would have ventured a word where God himself had spoken. Were they higher than God? By his revelation God had not only made Paul an apostle but had equipped him in every respect as he had equipped them, the Twelve, on Pentecost.[28]

Instead, he "went away to Arabia" (v. 17) where he was instructed by the Lord through study of his Hebrew Scriptures, meditation, and direct revelation. Then he returned to Damascus, when he evidently carried on the ministry described in Acts 9:20–22. Where is Arabia? It is first mentioned in the Old Testament in 2 Chronicles 9:14 and mentioned last in Ezekiel 27:21. It is mentioned in the New Testament only here and in Galatians 4:25. In the Old Testament Arabia would include the Asian peninsula between the Red Sea on the west and the Persian Gulf on the east, covering a territory of about 1.2 million square miles. It is a wide and broad area, and Paul is not distinct as to a specific place of geography. In the New Testament some scholars believe it covered the land of the Nabateans, including southern Jordan, the desert of Israel, and even possibly all the way up to Damascus.

There is no place in the New Testament where this testimony is given about why Paul went to Arabia. This journey could have been made soon after his baptism and before the "certain days" recorded in Acts 9:19. Or, possibly the narration in Acts may somehow be continuous with Paul remaining in the city of Jerusalem until after the "many days" of verse 23. These "many days" were possibly brought to a finish by the attempt to arrest him (v. 25; 2 Cor. 11:32–33). As to the duration of the apostles' stay in Arabia, there is no hint. The narration may suggest that it was short; on the other hand, it might have taken quite a bit of time and occupied the larger part of the three years mentioned in Galatians 1:18.

## Paul's Contact with Jerusalem (1:18–24)

Three years went by after the conversion of Paul (Saul) before he met with any of disciples. Dunn comments on why Paul goes into this part of his conversion history:

Paul was evidently concerned to give an orderly account of his *cursus vitae*. So having described the earliest phase of his adult life as a zealous Pharisee (1.15–14), and his commissioning, its independence from Jerusalem and its immediate sequel (i.15–17), he begins to describe his actual relationship with Jerusalem. **Then** in verse 18 is the first of three (i.18, 21; ii.1), which are obviously intended to mark out in chronological sequence the most relevant events which followed his encounter with the risen Christ and his time in Arabia and Damascus; though most think that Paul reckoned the three years from the Damascus-road encounter itself.[29]

---

### Paul's Conversion

*He was set aside for the gospel ministry from his mother's womb (Gal. 1:15).*

*He was struck to the ground from heaven on the Damascus road (Acts 9:3).*

*The Lord Jesus spoke to him out of heaven (vv. 4–5).*

*Saul was temporarily blinded from the revelation of Christ (v. 8).*

*He was called "a chosen instrument" to bear the Lord's name to others (v. 15).*

*He was baptized shortly after his conversion (v. 18).*

*He immediately began to teach that Jesus is the Son of God (v. 20).*

*The Jewish leaders set out to kill him for his conversion to Christ (v. 23).*

*The Christians in Jerusalem were afraid of Paul as he tried to associate with them (v. 26).*

*He remained out of the mainstream of service for fourteen years (Gal. 2:1).*

*Barnabas helps launch Paul's ministry with the disciples in Jerusalem (Acts 9:27).*

---

Peter was one of the first apostles Paul met up with (v. 18). Here Paul uses the Aramaic name Cephas instead of the Greek name Peter, which means "a stone." His original name was Simon, or Simeon (Acts 15:14), but he was renamed Cephas, or Peter, by Jesus. Some scholars have surmised that the change of name by the Lord would reflect in strength when the apostles began witnessing of the death, burial, and resurrection. Jesus originally said to him, "You shall be called . . ." (John 1:42), but this was changed to "You are . . ." in Matthew 16:18. Paul is the only writing disciple who uses the name Cephas. The Aramaic name may have been more understandable to the Jewish community Paul was addressing.

Paul's saying he became "acquainted" with Peter may imply that it took some time for the two to get to know each other. Paul was an outsider; nevertheless, Peter gave him hospitality for fifteen days.

Paul's visit to Jerusalem "three years later" could have been only one full year and probably occurred upon his escape from Damascus (Acts 9:23–26). The apparent contradictions between Paul's statement that he went "to become acquainted with Cephas [Peter]" and "did not see any other of the apostles except James, the Lord's brother" (v. 19) and Luke's account in Acts 9:26–29, are explainable in light of the differing purposes of the two statements. Paul, who affirmed "before God that I am not lying" (v. 20), is emphasizing his independence from the other apostles, while Luke is seeking to set forth the unity of the church in its history. A. R. Fausset writes: "Probably it was reported by Judaizers that he had received a course of instruction from the apostles in Jerusalem from the first; hence his earnestness in asserting the contrary, to vindicate his apostleship as derived directly from Christ."[30]

Paul's reference to James as "the Lord's brother" (v. 19), carries a twofold meaning. First, it serves to differentiate this James from James the son of Zebedee who was still alive during the first visit of Paul to Jerusalem. Second, it supports the scriptural evidence in Acts that this James was not considered an apostle but was (as ecclesiastical tradition holds) the bishop of Jerusalem. To be authenticated by James was an important step for the sake of the acceptance of the Christian community. Persecution was increasing, and of course, Paul played his part in this early on. All of the evidence concerning James's life shows that he stayed in Jerusalem as head of the church there and never undertook missionary duty as did the apostles.[31] That Paul could have lied about his acceptance by Peter and James must have crossed the minds of some of his detractors. Because he was so bold, and because the Lord led him to sharply define the gospel and bring the churches on line doctrinally, many wanted to defame him and find cause against his ministry.

Paul was forced to flee from Jerusalem (Acts 9:29–30) and "went into the regions of Syria and Cilicia" (v. 21). He was personally "unknown by sight to the churches of Judea," who only heard the report that the former persecutor of the believers was "now preaching the faith." This properly caused them to praise God.

Paul's saying, "I was still unknown by sight to the churches of Judea" (v. 22), likely indicates that these churches had been formed subsequent to his persecution. To identify the good people from the bad was important to the early church assemblies. They were in enough trouble as it was in their own communities. And they walked softly with the authorities wherever they lived. After the time of Paul, persecution would come upon the churches with a vengeance. Thousands would die over the coming decades. However the churches had heard of him, they seemed to have feared reprisals. The word had gotten out earlier about his great hatred of this new movement of Christianity. He adds that these congregations were "in Christ," a suggestive reminder to the Judaizers that these bodies of believers had been under the influence of the twelve apostles. They were not part of those who were strongly retaining certain Judaizing tendencies.

What took place in Ephesus also happened in Jerusalem and affected the entire region of Judea (v. 22). Sooner or later the disciples of Christ everywhere separated from the Jews who were mixing Judaism and Christianity (Acts 19:9).

It took some time for the assemblies in Judea to trust Paul. It is important to mention Judea. This was the largest tribal "state," in which Jerusalem was located, and the gospel had touched them early on. This problem had to be bridged! The Judeans kept saying, "He who once persecuted us is now preaching the faith which he once tried to destroy" (v. 23). While there is no exact count of the number of believers, the figure is probably small. Yet "the faith" was becoming so enshrined in the souls of a great many Jews that the Jewish leadership began its campaign to wipe the belief in Jesus from the map. In describing himself as the one who "persecuted" the Jews, Paul uses a participle showing that doing this had become a very part of his being. He was driven to stop the spread of the gospel.

Verse 24 cites the fact that the people in these churches were not simply praising God but were "glorifying" Him because Paul was converted and had become a missionary of the truth. The congregations were giving credit for Paul's transformation from a persecutor into a zealous and bold speaker of truth. They were not simply looking at the man in whom such great changes had been worked, but to the Lord God who carried out such miracles in his life. As the churches became comfortable with Paul, feeling he was genuine, they saw the hand of the Lord working in him. Because God had converted a man such as Paul, who had possessed power and authority, the new Christians could do nothing less but give the honor to Him.

## Study Questions

1.  Who was responsible for Paul's call to be an apostle?

2.  What supreme spiritual work did the Lord Jesus Christ accomplish?

3.  What situation in the Galatian church "astonished" the apostle Paul?

4. What were these people in Galatia doing with the gospel of Christ?

5. How exclusively did Paul declare the "gospel of Christ" he proclaimed?

6. What judgment did Paul pronounce on anyone who preached a different gospel?

7. From whom and where did Paul receive his gospel message?

# CHAPTER 2

# Paul Defends the Gospel in Jerusalem and Antioch Galatians 2:1–21

**Preview:**

*In the defense of his apostleship, Paul recounts his acceptance as an equal by Peter, James, and John in Jerusalem and his work among them to strengthen the gospel message, keeping it free of false Judaistic legal requirements. This work includes a confrontation with Peter in Antioch regarding his outward walk.*

## The Issue of Gentile Circumcision (2:1–10)

Verse 1 is most important in Paul's narration. When he says, "I went up again to Jerusalem," this may have taken place in Acts 11:30–12:25, or some believe it could be referring to chapter 15. The former may make more sense, because he is arguing that he never had an opportunity to learn from or receive authority from the twelve apostles. Interestingly, Luke does not mention such a meeting between Paul and the Twelve. Some think his going up to Jerusalem took place when Peter was in prison (12:4–5) or during his subsequent absence (17:19). R. C. Lenski explains:

> Root and branch Paul destroys the allegation of the Judaizers that his gospel is not the original gospel but that of the other apostles, and that he is not a genuine apostle, sent by the Lord like the Twelve, but has come from or through men only. He continues to let the facts speak their crushing language. In chapter 1 the facts reveal that Paul had his gospel by rev-

elation, that during a long period of time he had only fifteen days' contact with Peter and slight contact with James, but that Jerusalem and all the Judean churches glorified God because he preached the very faith he had once persecuted. So much for *the source.*

Now he presents *the contents* of his gospel regarding the very point assailed by the Judaizers, Christian liberty and circumcision in particular. Paul advances to the time of the great apostolic convention at Jerusalem when he came into fullest contact with the other apostles, yea, with all the leaders and with the church officially assembled. This was the decisive occasion when the first Judaizers were publicly and officially discredited and their Judaistic claims rejected. *They* were disowned; Paul was most fully acknowledged. Not that he needed such endorsement—he had never needed it. But if anything was wrong with either Paul's apostleship or his gospel of Christian liberty, this wrong would most certainly have been exposed at this convention in Jerusalem, regarding which Paul now presents the pertinent facts.[1]

Paul, accompanied by Barnabas, went to Jerusalem again after fourteen years. Donald Campbell observes:

While chapter 2 continues Paul's defense of his apostolic authority and the gospel he preached, he focused not on the source of his message but on its content. Further, whereas in chapter 1 he emphasized his independence from the other apostles, he now demonstrated that there was a basic unity between himself and them.[2]

Regarding this gap in time between visits to Jerusalem, James Dunn notes:

Paul could skate over the intervening years very quickly (i.21–4) because they had been spent far away from Jerusalem, with no contact, beyond the third-hand reports of his exploits which had circulated among the churches of Judea Even his earlier visit to Jerusalem could be passed over briefly (i.18–20) since it had been so inconsequential for the matter of present moment—he was prepared to swear to that. But now the pace slows. Paul begins to go into more detail. His second visit to Jerusalem was obviously of greater importance.[3]

The apostle mentions again (see 1:12) in verse 2 that he received a special revelation to go up to Jerusalem and preach the gospel. He went quietly and without fanfare. Though he is called of God to do what he is doing, he is careful as to the methods he employs. Paul is not afraid but simply moving with caution.

The fact that Paul was "taking Titus along also" is significant, because Titus was an uncircumcised Gentile (v. 3). Although Titus became a missionary companion of Paul (2 Cor. 2:13; 2 Tim. 4:10) and Paul wrote a letter to him (see 1:4), he is mentioned only a dozen times in the New Testament, most of them in Paul's second letter to the Corinthians. As a result little is known about his background except this reference that he is an uncircumcised Greek (v. 3). He apparently had been in the church at Syrian Antioch for an indefinite time without being circumcised until some Judaizers—whom Paul called "false brethren"—joined the assembly and insisted that Titus be circumcised.

Paul says they "had sneaked in to spy out our liberty which we have in Christ Jesus, in order to bring us into bondage." This Paul and Barnabas opposed, and Paul went to Jerusalem to see if he "might be running, or had run, in vain" (cf. Acts 15:1–2a). Paul says he went "because of a revelation," but Luke says Paul and Barnabas were sent by the church in Antioch (vv. 2b–3a). These statements are not contradictory, but complementary. James Boice explains:

> There is no real contradiction between this account [Acts 15:1–5] and Paul's statement. . . . Either the church at Antioch prayed about what should be done and then commissioned Paul and Barnabas in response to what they believed God told them to do, or else the revelation was a parallel and confirming one to Paul. Undoubtedly, Paul mentions the matter of revelation only to emphasize once again that at no time was he at the call of the other apostles. On the contrary, his movements as well as his Gospel are to be attributed directly to the revealed will of God.[4]

This visit was apparently what became known as the Jerusalem Council (Acts 15:4–30). Paul says he met with "those who were of high reputation," and he did so, "in private." Lenski observes:

> Paul adds information that is perhaps new to the Galatians, that he laid this gospel of his "in private (*de*, also) before those in repute," the leaders in Jerusalem. This was not in any way a secret conclave; it furnished direct personal opportunity for the leaders to learn from Paul all they might desire to know; we take it that Paul had Barnabas with him. Paul was very glad to tell everything, and, no doubt, James, Peter, and John were equally glad to hear all they could from Paul and Barnabas. It was a rare opportunity of which all concerned made the most. Whether any others of the elders of Jerusalem were present at this private meeting we cannot determine; it is possible.[5]

"Those who were of high reputation . . . contributed nothing to me" (v. 6), Paul writes. Instead, they recognized that Paul was called to preach "the gospel to the uncircumcised" just as Peter had been to the circumcised. God was working through both Peter "as an apostle to the circumcised" and Paul "as an apostle to the Gentiles." As a result, the "reputed . . . pillars"—James, Peter, and John—recognizing the grace given to Paul, gave Paul and Barnabas "the right hand of fellowship." Rendall remarks: "They saw in the marvelous success of Paul and Barnabas a visible token of their divine commission and of the grace bestowed upon them. These were doubtless the real authors of the final resolution adopted by the Council; and its hearty appreciation of their *beloved Barnabas and Paul, men that have hazarded their lives for the name of the Lord Jesus Christ,* coincides with the language of the Epistle."[6]

All that the leaders of the church asked of Paul and Barnabas was to "remember the poor," something Paul said, "I also was eager to do" (see 1 Cor. 16:1–3; 2 Cor. 8–9). The nature of this request was not so much doctrinal as it was practical. The church at Jerusalem had been hard-pressed economically for some time, even prior to the famine spoken of in Acts 11:28. This was due to the great increase in its numbers. In 2:41 there were about three thousand members added, and over the years many hundreds or thousands more may have come to Jerusalem, been saved, and decided to stay. Most probably had little money, and being a Christian in those days could be a hindrance in getting work. They did share what they had with each other (v. 45), but those resources wouldn't last long.[7] John MacArthur adds:

> To take care of the poor is not only a practical but a spiritual responsibility, because to forsake that responsibility is to disobey God's Word. "Whoever has this world's goods," John declares, "and beholds his brother in need and closes his heart against him, how does the love of God abide in him?" (1 John 3:17). James says that it is a sham believer who says to "a brother or sister . . . without clothing and in need of daily food . . . 'Go in peace, be warmed and filled,' and yet [does] not give them what is necessary for their body."[8]

Boice calls attention to the order of the names as significant.[9] When Paul spoke of missionary work among Jews, Peter is mentioned; but when the leaders of the church in Jerusalem are listed, James, the apparent official head (cf. Acts 15:13–21) is mentioned first. A similar change of position is seen in the relation between Paul and Barnabas. When God directed the church in Syrian Antioch to send them as missionaries, Barnabas was listed first, the apparent leader (Acts 13:2). Paul soon became the spokesman (vv. 9, 16; 14:8, 12b), but Barnabas continued as the leader (v. 12a; 15:25). Paul, however, took the initiative to go on a second missionary journey (15:36).

## Paul's Rebuke of Peter (2:11-17)

Regarding the incident at Antioch: the apostle has now made his chief point in the exposition of the thematic statement in 1:11-12. The gospel he preached (in Galatia as elsewhere) was not derived from the Jerusalem leadership of apostles, nor did it get its authority to them. Just the opposite. They had formally recognized in the Jerusalem Council that God had commissioned Paul and had distinctly given approval of his preaching of the gospel. That point having been made, Paul turns at once to the sequel: despite this agreement on the gospel, it had not been honored in the incident. The Antioch dispute was not just an example of the independence of Paul's gospel but instead derives its significance directly from the Jerusalem agreement as safeguarding *the truth of the gospel.*[10] Paul takes no time to set up the scene. He wanted to set the issue in 2:9 and that at Antioch as sharply as possible: the Cephas who had shaken his hand in 2:9 was the very same person he had to face down in verse 11.

Peter's visit to Antioch mentioned here apparently occurred after the council in Jerusalem. In many respects Peter was the leading apostle, having been the speaker on the Day of Pentecost (Acts 2:14) and the beginning of the church (v. 41). He also introduced the message of salvation in Jesus Christ to gentile believers (10:44-48). He truly had been given "the keys of the kingdom of heaven" (Matt. 16:19), because he became the human instrument to introduce both Jews and Gentiles into the church.

However, Peter could and did make mistakes (Matt. 16:22-23; 26:33-35, 69-75). Paul had to have courage to rebuke Peter. He says, "I opposed him to his face, because he stood condemned." While Peter was not a heretic, nor preaching raw heresy, he still was not at this point preaching the pure gospel of the grace of God. He even withdrew from eating with the gentile believers who were uncircumcised because he was pressured or forced to do so by some of the Jewish Christians. A. R. Fausset astutely observes, "The apostles were not always inspired; but were so always in writing the Scriptures. The inspired men who wrote the Bible books were not at other times infallible, much less were the uninspired men who kept them." He then points out, "The Christian fathers (in the sense of leaders) may be trusted generally as witnesses to facts, but not implicitly followed in matters of opinion."[11]

The issue of the circumcision of gentile believers had been settled at the Jerusalem Council, but apparently other issues of Jewish customs and dietary laws had not been addressed. These verses imply that during this time it was already a custom of the church at Antioch for all believers, both Jewish and gentile, to freely eat together in fellowship, having no restrictions or conditions placed upon them. It also appears that when Peter arrived, he found the scene neither unusual or strained in any way. When Peter chose to eat in fellowship with both gentile and Jewish believers, he was, in effect, showing that both were now free from the Law.[12] God had taught Peter the truth of the equality of gentile with Jewish believers and their freedom in Christ by his experience at Cornelius's house (Acts 10), and he had defended his action and that truth on his return to Jerusalem (11:1–18). He had practiced that truth when he came to Antioch until "the coming of certain men from James" (Gal. 2:12). Apparently fearful of the reaction and possible report to Jerusalem of this group, "the party of the circumcision," Peter "began to withdraw and hold himself aloof" from the Gentiles.

Furthermore, his hypocritical actions led other Jewish believers astray, including Barnabas (v. 13). This especially affected Paul, because he and Barnabas had recently carried out a very successful missionary journey together. They had spent much time praying, ministering, and suffering together for the sake of the gospel. They had even journeyed to the Jerusalem conference together. Barnabas was Paul's first real friend (and defender) after his conversion (Acts 9:27), and had heard him preach countless times on salvation by faith alone, yet even he was carried away by this legalism of Peter and the others. Perhaps Barnabas's hypocritical behavior contributed to the rift between he and Paul regarding taking John Mark on their next missionary journey.[13]

People often ask why God allowed such confusion in this early period of church history. Sometimes, out of confusion, more light emerges. The early church and many of its leaders were groping forward, trying and testing what the truth really was all about. They had to lay aside their old prejudices and religious thoughts in order to be able to embrace the revelation of God's grace in the simple message of the gospel. The church was also something new, now comprised of both Jews and Gentiles in a new spiritual body. The Gentiles were not merely attached to Judaism. They were fellow heirs with the Jews of salvation.

When Paul saw that "the truth of the gospel" (cf. v. 5) was being compromised, he confronted Peter publicly. This was proper because it had become a public issue for which Peter was responsible.

When did this episode occur—before or after the public acknowledgment mentioned in verse 9? No indication of time appears. Without a temporal particle to indicate this happened earlier, the natural thing to do is to follow the previous narrative, where one episode succeeds the other in time, and to understand this last as likewise occurring later than the preceding. Yet starting with Augustine, a few writers assume that this event antedates the one mentioned in verses 1–10. They tell us that Peter came to Antioch, then the strict Jewish Christians from James, then the pseudo-brethren who made the Jerusalem conference necessary. This is thought to make the case against Peter and for Paul much stronger. But the reverse is true; for then the matter was still subject to a final decision on the part of the church. Lenski comments on the timing of this event: "Paul follows the chronological order up to 2:10; the natural expectation is that he continues thus in the final episode. If Paul now reversed the order of time, this would necessitate an indication to this effect. Besides all this, it is incomprehensible that Paul could use this episode regarding Peter as the climax of his historical proof if it had occurred at an earlier date. Then, most assuredly, the conference would form the climax."[14]

Paul said that Peter was a Jew but lived "like the Gentiles." He then asked why Peter was forcing "Gentiles to live like Jews." A question exists as to whether Paul's quotation of his statement to Peter ends with this verse or continues to the end of the chapter. Campbell astutely observes that "it would seem that Paul uttered more than one sentence in reproving Peter."[15] Furthermore, the thought flows so naturally, at least through the next two verses, if not to the end of the chapter, that it must be a part of the rebuke.

The tone of the rebuke softens, however, as Paul changes from direct accusation—"you"—to the milder inclusive—"we." He starts by drawing a sharp distinction between the Jews and the Gentiles. To the Jews, the Gentiles were not only sinners because they didn't keep the Law, but did not even possess it; thus they were totally unable to procure any righteousness from it.[16]

Paul points out the truth he shared with Peter as Jews was that justification comes "through faith in Christ Jesus," not "by observing the Law." Both he and Peter had put their "faith in Christ Jesus" in order to be justified— declared just and righteous before God and accepted by Him, in other words, saved. Justification was not received "by the works of the Law," because "by the works of the Law shall no flesh be justified" (v. 16). This is Paul's first reference to justification, one of his main themes in this letter.

Paul's primary purpose is to point out the total inadequacy of the Law to save because *all* have sinned—not only the Gentiles, who never had the Law, but also the Jews, who had the Law and, as such, are God's chosen people. This affirmation of "faith alone" also implies a rejection of any other type of works (aside from the Law), in other words, legalism.[17]

Justification by faith alone was also Martin Luther's main emphasis. Reflecting his own experience in seeking peace with God, he wrote:

> This briefly is our doctrine concerning Christian righteousness. Faith justifies because it takes hold of the treasure of Christ's presence. . . . Therefore, where there is an assured trust of the heart, Christ is present, And this is true formal righteousness, by which a person is justified. Rather than love adorning faith, it is Christ who adorns faith—or rather, he is the true form and perfection of faith. Therefore, Christ, seized by faith and living in the heart, is the true Christian righteousness, for which God counts us righteous and gives us eternal life. This is no work of the law but a quite different sort of righteousness and a certain new world beyond and above the law, for Christ or faith is not the law, nor the work of the law.[18]

Paul had referred to "gentile sinners," the common Jewish designation of all non-Jews, a term used here perhaps to prod Peter concerning a continuing subconscious attitude toward even gentile believers, especially as judged by the Jewish Law. Paul pointed out that the believer's justification—God's viewing him as righteous—is not as seen in himself but "in Christ" and is Christ's righteousness applied to him. It soon becomes evident that the believer, because his old sin nature still resides within him, is a sinner. Neither initial justification by faith nor a second blessing results in a state of sinless perfection. That only comes when the believer stands in the presence of God either through death or the translation of the saints at the rapture. Other believers have insisted that, unless the truth of justification by faith is accompanied by a code of rules and regulations, it results in antinomianism—every believer can live as he desires without any restraints. Paul's immediate, vehement response to both these incorrect ideas was "May it never be!" (v. 17). MacArthur adds: "It must have been painful to Paul to suggest even hypothetically that Christ could participate in, much less promote, sin. But the drastic danger of Judaistic legalism demanded such drastic logic. He knew of no other way to bring Peter and the others to their senses."[19]

To admit that one needs Christ is to confess that one is a sinner. And the human does not like the sound of this confession.

## The Believer, the Law, and Christ (2:18–21)

With verse 18 Paul turns from the first person plural to the first person singular. He also presents the issue as hypothetical, even though it is exactly what Peter had done. After recognizing the equality in Christ and freedom from the law of gentile believers (Acts 10:44–48) and defending his actions (11:15–18; 15:7–11), Peter had progressively withdrawn from fellowship with the gentile believers after "the coming of certain men from James . . . the party of the circumcision." In doing so Peter was rebuilding what he had destroyed—a life controlled and dictated by the Mosaic Law—thereby proving he was a "transgressor." This is true because, as both Paul and Peter knew from their own experience, "a man is not justified by the works of the Law" (Gal. 2:16).

As Peter often ate with the gentile Christians in Antioch, he probably tore down the idea that any Christian needed anything whatever besides faith in Christ for justification by God; he held true to what verses 15–16 say of all Jewish Christians when they come to faith. However, when he separated himself so markedly from all gentile Christians and began to live strictly like a Jew (v. 14), he started to return again to the identical things he had torn down. His actions spoke louder than his words. They made an impression on the entire assembly at Antioch. Peter contradicted all that he had heretofore taught and done. It was as if he had undergone a second conversion. His action proclaimed that some Jewish ceremonial works were probably required and important—of course, also for gentile Christians (v. 14b). Paul loved the figure of building and uses it aptly here.[20]

When Paul and Peter and any Jew recognized that justification "through the Law" was impossible, he "died to the Law" with the result that he "might live to God."

If not before in this passage, certainly by verse 20, Paul was giving his own witness, although it could be repeated by Peter and every Christian. He had been "blameless" according to "the righteousness which is in the Law" (Phil. 3:6b), and yet he "would not have come to know sin except through the Law; for I would not have known about coveting if the Law had not said, 'You shall not covet.' But sin, taking opportunity through the commandment, produced in me coveting of every kind" (Rom. 7:7b–8a). Now recognizing his efforts at self-justification before God as futile, Paul considered them "rubbish, in order that I may gain Christ and may be found in Him, not having a righteousness of my own derived from the Law, but that which is through faith in Christ, the righteousness which comes from God on the basis of faith" (Phil. 3:8b–9).

It is difficult now to fully understand how heavy the struggle was in the early church to get it right. To fully trust Christ was overshadowed by law keeping in the Jewish community. Yet there were hints in the Old Testament that salvation would come about only by the substitutionary death of the Messiah. In prophecy Isaiah wrote about the coming suffering of the Lamb of God: "As a result of the anguish of His soul, He [God] will see it and be satisfied; by His knowledge the Righteous One, My Servant, will justify the many, as He will bear their iniquities" (53:11). In all of the remarkable chapter of Isaiah 53, there is no mention of law keeping! In a larger historical picture, the nation of Israel would reject Christ, though probably thousands of Jews came to Christ initially. In Acts Paul predicts the rejection of the Jews. Quoting Isaiah 6:9–10, he makes it clear that Israel will hear but not understand, will see but not perceive (Acts 28:25–27). God will then send His salvation to the Gentiles, "they will also listen" (v. 28).

The Lord Jesus was the only person who ever lived on earth who could truthfully challenge without response, "Which one of you convicts Me of sin?" (John 8:46). Yet He was put to death according to the law by crucifixion (Gal. 3:13; cf. Deut. 21:23). God the Father accepted that death according to the law as payment for sin and raised Him to new, eternal life, restoring Him to His right hand in heaven. As a result Paul and every person who trusts in Jesus Christ and His work on the cross has "been crucified with Christ" because he is viewed both by God and himself as identified with Christ.

Lightfoot writes concerning the idea of death in Galatians 2:19–20, "A new turn is thus given to the metaphor of death. In the last verse it was the release from past obligations; here it is the annihilation of old sins. The two however are not unconnected. Sin and law loose their hold at the same time. . . . Thus his death becomes life. Being crucified with Christ, he rises with Christ, and lives to God."[21]

This identification by faith continues through Christ's resurrection and, as a result, Paul can say, "I have been crucified with Christ; and it is no longer I who live, but Christ lives in me; and the life which I now live in the flesh I live by faith in the Son of God, who loved me, and delivered Himself up for me" (v. 20). In this confrontation of Peter and rejection of the possibility of anyone securing righteousness before God "through the Law," Paul is not setting "aside the grace of God." Instead, he is emphasizing it, "for if righteousness could be gained through the Law, then Christ died needlessly." The apostle will reinforce the fact that the Law cannot save in 3:1–5, and he will cite Abraham, who was saved by faith alone, "and it was reckoned to him as righteousness."

## Study Questions

1. What was the purpose of Paul's next visit to Jerusalem?

2. What significant fact concerning his companion Titus does he state?

3. What situation in the church where Paul was occasioned his trip to Jerusalem?

4. What was the decision of the church leaders in Jerusalem concerning Paul's ministry and Peter's ministry?

5. What was the only request of the church leaders to Paul for the gentile believers?

6. Why did Paul oppose Peter to his face in Antioch?

7. How serious did this hypocrisy of Peter become?

8. What do Jewish believers know concerning the basis for justification?

# Section Two

# THE GOSPEL OF GRACE BY FAITH

## *GALATIANS 3:1–4:31*

**CHAPTER 3**

# Paul Defends the Gospel through Explanation
# Galatians 3:1–4:7

### Preview:

*At this point in the letter, Paul turns from presenting, defending, and justifying his position as an apostle of the Lord Jesus Christ, especially to the churches God established through him and Barnabas in Galatia. He now undertakes defending and explaining the message he has proclaimed to them—the good news of the grace of God in eternal salvation and the gift of the transforming and indwelling Holy Spirit received through faith in the redemptive, sacrificial death of Jesus Christ on the cross.*

## Paul's Piercing Questions (3:1–5)

Paul opens this section by addressing the Galatian believers in a more formal and a very rebuking manner: "You foolish Galatians" (v. 1). Calling them "foolish" does not mean a lack of intelligence, because ancient Greek philosophers describe these people as very intelligent and astute. Instead, it means irrational, unthinking, a plan of action being considered or taken in the face of all logical evidence to reject it (Luke 24:25; Rom. 1:14). Marvin Vincent observes that the Greek noun on which this adjective is built describes primarily "the faculty of moral judgment," so that Paul speaks of "a folly which is the outgrowth of a moral defect"[1] (cf. 1 Tim. 6:9; Titus 3:8).

*45*

Paul pulls no punches in this section of verses. He wants to dispel quickly any notion of salvation by works or by the works of the Law. Some scholars believe that because Paul says the Galatians saw Christ "publicly portrayed as crucified," there could have been some Galatian Jews in Jerusalem who witnessed the death of the Lord. While this view is possible, it could be that the apostle is saying that others were there and brought back the eyewitness account of Christ's death. Whichever view is correct, the death of the Lord for sinners was firmly established with the Galatians. That issue was beyond questioning.

To soften his rebuke of the Galatian believers, Paul asks, "Who has bewitched you?" This can simply refer to the work of a glib-talking, Judaizing false teacher, as it probably does, or to a spell being cast on them with an evil eye. How could they be bewitched, since, before their eyes, Jesus Christ had been "publicly portrayed as crucified"? That portrayal of the crucified Christ and its significance by Paul had been as clear as if posted "on a public bulletin board."[2]

The perfect participle *estaurōmenos* ("crucified") in this verse does not simply fasten attention on the death of Christ as the culmination and therefore summary of His life as that of "one who took the form of a servant," nor does it imply that Jesus was still hanging on the cross and is to be considered as such even presently; rather, it describes Him in His character as the Crucified and Risen One. The phrase "Jesus Christ crucified" concisely summarizes the decisive event in salvation history and, as such, the fundamental content of the Pauline "kerygma."[3]

Paul continues his rebuke by asking for the response to one question, "Did you receive the Spirit by the works of the Law, or by hearing with faith?" (v. 2). The issue is works or faith, and the answer clearly is faith. Many of the Galatian believers had been Jews and received the indwelling presence and transforming power of the Holy Spirit only by responding in faith to Paul's message of salvation and eternal life through the Lord Jesus Christ. Those who had been Gentiles had been in similar bondage to their pagan deities and had found the Holy Spirit's liberating release only through faith in the gospel (cf. Acts 13:52). As a result Paul asks them, "Are you so foolish [illogical, unthinking]?" He continues to ask, "Having begun by the Spirit," who apparently here is considered responsible for quickening the exercise of faith in the heart and mind of the person who believes in Jesus Christ (cf. John 6:37; 2 Cor. 6:7; Eph. 1:13–14; 2:8–10; 2 Thess. 2:1), "are you now being perfected by the flesh?" (Gal. 2:3). Their goal was growth and maturity in the spiritual life, which would come by walking by faith in the power of and under the direction of the Holy Spirit, just as that spiritual life was received by faith.

It appears unlikely that the Spirit of God is received only by believing what we hear and that nothing else is required of us, that we must set aside all our works and give ourselves only to hearing the gospel. The heart does not really understand or comprehend that such an awesome treasure—namely, the Holy Spirit—is given only by believing in the truth of the gospel. We reason that forgiveness of sins, deliverance from death, the gifts of the Holy Spirit, righteousness, and everlasting life are wonderful blessings, and therefore we must do something that is equally great if we want to obtain these inestimable benefits. In other words, we must work somehow and by some means for our salvation.

Luther reasoned, "The devil approves of this idea [of works salvation] and makes it grow in our hearts. So when our reason hears that we can do nothing to obtain the forgiveness of sins but only hear the Word of God, it immediately cries out, 'Rubbish! You are making the forgiveness of sins too unimportant a matter.'"[4]

The sheer greatness of the gift inhibits a person's ability to believe it. Since it is a totally free gift, it is despised. It is imperative, however, to learn that forgiveness of sins, Christ, and the Holy Spirit are given freely when one simply believes what is preached, despite the depth of one's sins. The focus should not be on the greatness of the gift nor on the unworthiness of the believer to receive it. Instead, the focus should be on the pleasure it gives God to offer this gift freely (Luke 12:32). If the sovereign God of this universe wants to give a person such a gift, that person should receive the gift with great thankfulness and not think of himself and his great unworthiness.[5]

Because of their response to the gospel, the Galatian believers, along with Paul and Barnabas, apparently had suffered opposition and persecution from the Jews in the various cities (see Acts 13:50; 14:2, 5, 19–20, 22b). So Paul asks, "Did you suffer so many things in vain," then quickly adds, "if indeed it was in vain?" (Gal. 3:4). This it most certainly was not, because it brought them eternal life. One specific example of this suffering was Paul's stoning at Lystra after the crowd was won over and incited by Jews from Antioch and Iconium (Acts 14:19). The suffering of these Christians had to come for another reason, and what was it? If they were still law keepers, they should not have been persecuted by the Jews. After all, there were some Jews who had a certain appreciation of Christ who were still "earning" their salvation by keeping the Law of Moses. They were not maligned or suffering for that admiration of Christ. No! The issue had to do with pure faith for salvation—faith plus no law keeping in order to obtain redemption!

Paul's final question to the Galatian believers dealt with the basis of God's bestowal upon them of the Holy Spirit and the power to perform miracles—

observing the Law or believing what they heard, works or faith (Gal. 3:5). It obviously was faith. Before Paul and Barnabas came preaching the good news of salvation through faith in Jesus Christ, the Galatians knew nothing of either the Holy Spirit or of miracles. Response in faith to that message brought awareness of the indwelling presence of the Holy Spirit and a changed life (v. 5). Paul's miraculous healing of the crippled man at Lystra (Acts 14:8–10) and his own rising and walking back into the city after being stoned, dragged outside the city of Lystra, and left for dead (vv. 19–20) are probably only two of the miracles performed that God empowered through the Holy Spirit. Paul does not explain this statement about the miracles worked among them beyond what is mentioned above. But it must be remembered that such miracles and healings were not done in the dark. The word would spread like wildfire when such events took place, for they were irrefutable to those who witnessed them. How could anyone with any spiritual sense deny that God's Spirit was involved in all that was taking place, in regard to the gospel, through Paul and the other disciples?

## The Purpose and Limitations of the Law

The Gentiles have the Law written in their hearts (Rom. 2:15).

The Law condemns all (Rom. 3:19).

The Law gives the knowledge of sin (Rom. 3:20).

Faith establishes the Law (Rom. 3:31).

Abraham was given promises through faith not through the Law (Rom. 4:13).

The Law brings wrath (Rom. 4:15).

Sin is "aroused" by the Law (Rom. 7:5).

Sin takes its opportunity through the Law to kill (Rom. 7:8, 11).

The Law is good but we are unrighteous (Rom. 8:12).

The Law, "the letter," kills, but the Spirit gives life (2 Cor. 3:6).

The Law, engraved in stone, became the "ministry of death" (2 Cor. 3:7).

The Law became obsolete and was replaced by the new covenant (Heb. 8:13).

The Law is called the royal Law (James 2:8).

The expression "who provides you" could read "the Supplier" or "the Provider." It is in the present tense and shows continuous action: "the One who is continually providing you with the Holy Spirit." One of the main functions of the Spirit of God is to maintain believers in their fellowship with God the Father (2 Cor. 13:14), to impart strength (Eph. 3:16), and to give victory over the tendency to follow the fallen nature (Gal. 5:17). For the churches and the assemblies collectively, and in general, there is the need for the Spirit of God to work a spiritual operation among them as a group, a fellowship of committed brothers (1 Cor. 12:4–11).

Paul adds in the present tense, "He who works miracles." It seems that the gifts of miracles were yet in operation in the Galatian congregations. When the apostle says "miracles," he uses the word that could be translated "powers." There is no way to know for certain whether these miracles were physical, moral, or even both together. In other places Paul makes some differentiation between gifts of healing on the one hand and prophecy and tongues on the other (vv. 10, 28). During this early church period, the showing forth of such dynamic power was evidence of the presence of God at work with the apostles. However, it could be that here in Galatians Paul seems to be simply making reference to these issues in the broadest sense, not referring to any miraculous event in particular. Though again, as mentioned, he may have some specific events in mind.

## Paul's Persuasive Example (3:6–9)

The apostle Paul now begins a thorough exposition of the Word of God, especially the Old Testament, which goes all the way to the end of chapter 4. This in effect is his third argument in coming against the threat to the gospel, and also to the converts in Galatia. First, he deals with the agreement on the gospel reached at Jerusalem (2:1–10); then he touches on their own experience with the Holy Spirit (3:1–5); and finally, he discusses the proof from Scriptures themselves (3:6–4:31). Verses 6–9 serve as the initial expression of Paul's case where he cites the crucial text of Genesis 15:6, which gives rise to the thematic statement of verse 7. His second text is Genesis 12:3, with the equivalent summary conclusion drawn immediately.

The first scriptural text links promise, seed, and faith; the second links promise, blessing, and the Gentiles. When he put all of these verses together, they referred to the same promise made to Abraham, with the result that faith and blessing, seed and Gentiles could be seen to belong to one another. This is the "package" of arguments that Paul proceeds to expound in the following verses, in what can be regarded as a Jewish *midrash* (or teaching) on the two texts of 3:10–14—a blessing to the Gentiles that the curse of the Law could no longer prevent; 3:15–18—a promised seed whose extent could not be determined by the Law; and finally, in 3:19–29—a faith restricted for a time by the Law, but now with the coming of Christ, making believers heirs of the promised blessing.

It could be clearly argued that Paul was responding biblically, and by special revelation to him, to arguments he well knew had been put forth by others.[6] James Boice suggests that Abraham is Paul's example of faith instead of works for three reasons: "(1) he had taught concerning Abraham in his ministry to the Galatians, (2) the large Jewish population in southern Galatia made Abraham well-known, and (3) the legalizers had probably been using Abraham to support their position."[7]

Paul quoted Genesis 15:6 here in Galatians 3:6, stating that faith in God's promise was the basis of his being declared righteous, not works (cf. Rom. 4:1–3). Donald Campbell says, "Abraham's faith in God's ability to perform what He promised was accepted by God as righteousness and so the patriarch was justified before he was circumcised ( cf. Gen. 17:24). How then could the Judaizers insist that circumcision was essential to being accepted by God?"[8]

Those who exercise faith are really "the children of Abraham," not those who observe the Law, as the legalizers had probably been saying to lead the believers astray. This includes the justification of gentile believers by faith, because the Scripture "preached the gospel beforehand to Abraham" by stating, "All the nations shall be blessed in you." Since Abraham was the man of faith, all "who are of faith are blessed with Abraham."

Because the Spirit of the living God is the Scripture's primary author, the conclusion is clear that the Lord and His Word are most closely connected. The thing foreseen, because it had been thus ordained before the foundation of the world (Eph. 1:4, 11), was that it was "by faith" and not "by works" that God would justify the Gentiles. If the Galatians would only understand this, they would not allow themselves to be misled by the Judaizers.

Too often the Jews were driven by law keeping and seem to virtually ignore the covenant with their father Abraham. And yet this covenant is in view over and over again in the Old Testament (see Josh. 24:2–3; 1 Kings 18:36; Ps. 105:9). In reality, this covenant is more important than the Mosaic covenant. The promises to Abraham and the fathers are in perpetuity. Yet the moral challenge of obedience to the Lord is tested by the keeping of the Law by the Jews. However, no one can keep the Law. This is why Christ had to die for sinners, both Jews and Gentiles.

"By faith" (Gal. 3:8) means "by trustfully receiving" God's gift that comes forth from His hand. It is only in this way that the nations of the world were to receive pardon, find a right standing in the sight of God and his holy Law, and experience spiritual adoption as God's children. This all comes about because of "justification by faith." This great truth had been previously revealed to Abraham as good tidings of personal joy for the entire world. *Justification* means "to be legally acquitted." Because of Christ, the Lord bangs the gavel and declares His righteousness put to the account of the sinner. This is *imputed, declared righteousness*. It can be seen as promised and coming through the Messiah in Isaiah 53:11. "He would justify the many."

This blessed promise, though always the only way of salvation, was to be realized *on an international scale* with the coming of Christ and of the dispensation of the church age that coming would bring about. The substance of the Abrahamic promise was recorded in words slightly different from what we now know as the gospel of Christ: "In you all the nations of the earth shall be blessed" (Gen. 12:3; 18:18; 22:18). It must be remembered, however, that the dispensation of the church is not now given the land promises that are specifically for the Jews when the messianic kingdom is realized.

> The blessing of which Paul is thinking is that of "justification by faith," as the context indicates; and this, in turn, was basic to all the blessings of salvation full and free. But inasmuch as the fulfillment of this promise, on a world-wide scale, was a matter of the future, it is readily understood that the phrase "in you" must be understood as Abraham himself also certainly understood it, namely, "in the Messiah," "the seed of the woman" (Gen. 3:15), Abraham's seed.[9]

## Paul's Inevitable Conclusion (3:10–14)

The factor that made the difference, in other words, was the Law, the commandments of God. Paul, therefore, turns at once to deal with it. Having expressed the position as set out in the initial statements of the promise to Abraham, he now turns immediately to the position as it is. The jump in thought between verses 9 and 10 simply indicates that he was taking for granted two presuppositions that shaped the traditional Jewish attitude to the other nations.

*The Book of the Law* in the most obvious sense refers to the Torah, the Pentateuch specifically—the writings of Moses, known also as the Law of Moses. Here in Galatians the apostle is referring to the narrower sense. In some passages of Scripture, however, *the Law* is mentioned in a broad or wider use to include other parts of the older testament. It is used this way when referring to the Psalms in John 10:34; 15:25; of the Psalms, Isaiah, Ezekiel, and Daniel in John 12:34; of the Psalms and Isaiah in Romans 3:10–18; of Isaiah in 1 Corinthians 14:21. Therefore, it appears that the expression "the Law" was another reference to *the Scriptures* for the entire book.

Now there is a twist in the book of Galatians. While the Law does not save, the Jews who were trying to claim that it does were not even keeping it themselves. Paul was extremely knowledgeable as to the failure of the Galatians in submitting to the Law of Moses; however, they had not realized that failure themselves. To try to keep the Law would mean that they were professed law keepers and yet would still not attain to salvation. Law is not flexible. It never gives way to weakness; its standards and requirements are never brought down, not even to a hairbreadth. Law refuses to compromise and has no room for grace. It must be remembered that the Law was good; it gave a moral compass to the Jews that the Gentiles did not have, though it was never meant as a means of salvation. Yet the problem was that no one could keep it! James Dunn writes:

> The law was central to God's covenant with Israel; it was law-keeping which marked out the Jew from the (by definition) lawless Gentile. The antithesis was fundamental to Jewish identity, as the Antioch incident had already confirmed (see on ii.14–15). It was the law, then, which prevented the blessing of Abraham reaching out to the Gentiles, by functioning as a mark which distinguished Jew from Gentile, as a barrier between Jew and Gentile. The mind-set is clearly reflected in Rom. ii. 17–20 and Eph. ii.11–16.[10]

When God's blessings are discussed, eventually one must also consider God's curses. This is made clear throughout the Old Testament covenant writings. Blessing and curse were the two ways Moses set before the people of Israel (Deut. 11:26–29): blessings if they kept the commandments, curses if they didn't, and the curses carried the loss of privileges and blessings, those things that distinguished them from the pagan gentile nations around them. These curses could be reversed only if they returned to the Lord and obeyed His commandments. This was the point of the Old Testament Jewish Law— you had to be inside the covenant and keep the Law. You could not be in fellowship with God as a Gentile outside of the Law.[11]

The only logical conclusion from Paul's evidence from the Galatian believers' experience and the scriptural record of Abraham's life is that "for as many as are of the works of the Law are under a curse" (Gal. 3:10). Paul supported that conclusion by quoting its statement in Deuteronomy 27:26. As Paul could testify from his own experience, "that no one is justified by the Law before God is evident" (v. 11), because he had tried and failed. Again quoting Scripture (Hab. 2:4), Paul wrote, "The righteous man shall live by faith." Clearly "the Law is not of faith." Instead, as Paul's final step in his argument states, again quoting Scripture (Lev. 18:5), "He [literally, 'the one,' whether male or female] who practices them shall live by them" (Gal. 3:12).

Since no one can be made righteous by observing the Law but only by believing, what must have been accomplished in order to make belief sufficient for justification (being declared righteous)? This is the work of Jesus Christ on the cross of Calvary. Paul says that "Christ redeemed [literally 'purchased from the market'] us from the curse of the Law, having becoming a curse for us" in being crucified on a wooden cross (v. 13).

Paul does not argue that Jesus was made a curse for Himself, but for us. Christ is innocent, without sin, as far as His own person is concerned, and therefore He should not have to hang on a tree. Yet because under the Law of Moses every thief and criminal had to be hanged, Christ had to die because he carried the guilt of all sinners and thieves. Luther added: "We are sinners and thieves and therefore guilty of death and everlasting damnation. But Christ took all our sins upon him and for them died upon the cross."[12]

The redemptive price God the Father demanded of his incarnate Son, Jesus Christ, was death on a cross, because "Cursed is everyone who hangs on a tree" (v. 13, quoting Deut. 21:23). Elsewhere Paul writes, "He made Him who knew no sin to be sin on our behalf, that we might become the righteousness of God in Him" (2 Cor. 5:21).

Galatians 3:14 gives an extremely important summary to Paul's argument in this section. The Lord Jesus, by His death, made it possible for the "blessing" aspect of the Abrahamic covenant to be applied to "all the families of the earth" (Gen. 12:3). This would be exclusive of the promises of a land. The land promises are given to the natural seed of Abraham and are not promised as an inheritance to the gentile nations. With that blessing would come the gift of the Holy Spirit, though He first was promised to Israel (Ezek. 36:26–28; 37:14; Joel 2:28–29). The church now gets in on the promise of the Spirit through the new covenant (2 Cor. 3:1–8). But to make sure the Galatians understand and do not think they must work to receive the Spirit, Paul adds that the Spirit comes "through faith," as opposed to works! Human flesh cannot earn the great gifts and acts of grace bestowed by a loving heavenly Father!

## The Validity of a Covenant (3:15–18)

Returning to addressing the Galatian believers as "brothers" (v. 15), Paul illustrates with the validity of a covenant made between two individuals. Once "ratified," it cannot be set aside or added to. The same is true of the promises made by God with Abraham (Gen. 12:1–3, 7; 13:14–17), confirmed by a formal covenant with Abraham and his seed (Gen. 15). Paul says that the promise being to Abraham and his seed, not seeds (Gen. 12:7; 15:1), meant one person, "that is Christ" (v. 16). Paul then pointed out that the introduction of the Law "four hundred and thirty years later" did not invalidate the covenant "so as to nullify the promise" (v. 17) and God's declaration of righteousness in response by faith to God's promise. Campbell explains:

> Even if Paul's opponents admitted that Abraham was justified by faith, those Judaizers might have argued that the Law, coming at a later time, entirely changed the basis for achieving salvation. To refute this, Paul declared that just as a properly executed Roman covenant (or will) cannot arbitrarily be set aside or changed . . . so the promises of God are immutable. . . . The blessing of justification by faith is therefore permanent and could not be changed by the Law.[13]

In verse 17 Paul mentions the Abrahamic covenant. He uses the Greek word *diathēkē*, which literally means "a coming together." It describes two individuals, kings or land owners, who come together to make a mutual agreement. But the word itself does not imply two parties, rather one could fulfill the covenant alone. In the Genesis 15:7–18 account of the "signing" of the covenant with Abraham, God put the patriarch to sleep and ratified the covenant Himself (v. 12). The covenant was God's covenant, ratified to be sure, but involving Abraham and his descendants. The covenant did not depend on Abraham's faithfulness, follow-through, perfection, or law keeping (the Mosaic Law is in view).

For the sake of argument, the covenant must be enforced by law or promise, and the priority is with promise. If it had been by law, there would have been no turning back, no restoration for Israel, no salvation. Human weakness would have destroyed all possibilities for grace to be put into action. God has to redeem by His grace because of the weakness of the flesh. All God requires is trust, or faith, in what He did at the cross for our sins. Even Abraham could not receive God's goodness by his own actions. He was an imperfect individual whose sins and weaknesses are clearly spelled out in Genesis. God must act in a sovereign way in dispensing grace and mercy. The Lord would deal with Abraham on the basis of His own integrity and attributes, not on the basis of human merit.

## The Law's Purpose (3:19–25)

If acceptance of the individual by God can come only by his grace through faith in his provision for redemption as Paul has insisted, the logical question becomes, "Why the Law then?" (v. 19a). Paul's immediate response was, "It was added because of transgressions" (v. 19b). If the inheritance promised to

Abraham was the land of Canaan, but that land was given and a numerous posterity promised to populate it only as a means to an end—namely, that the purposes of God expressed in the original promise, "in thee shall all the families of the earth be blessed"—Genesis 12:3 might in due time be fulfilled. In Romans 4:13 the apostle speaks of Abraham as "[the] heir of the world," intending, apparently, to sum up in that phrase the promises made to him and to his immediate descendants, and to give them the widest conceivable scope (cf. particularly Gen. 17:4). In the present passage he uses "inheritance" in the same comprehensive way, but seemingly without any reference to the earthly elements in the promises and having in mind only those spiritual and heavenly blessings of which Canaan was intended to be a type. God, as infinitely moral and righteous, desired such conduct from his people. However, he had not communicated any standard of conduct to the people, who had only their inner conscience to guide them (cf. Rom. 2:14–15). God wanted the people to know their sins were "transgressions," a word that means a stepping aside or violation of the desired standard.

Romans 5:14 points to the period of early civilization and shows how human beings died because of sin. In 2:12–16 Paul further explains how even the Gentiles, who never had the Law given by Moses, have God's Law, even blurred, written in their hearts, their own conscience condemning them. This moral Law, which Moses formulated, was then clarified for the Jews. Romans 7:7–13 shows how this Law brought judgment against Paul and revealed his sin and his subjection to death. This is the Law that still works in sinners. Romans 2 points out that moralism, the effort to keep this Law, is *not* the way in which to escape judgment, but is only the sure way of falling into greater condemnation. R. C. H. Lenski adds: "It is this to the present day. The only escape lies in justification by faith, Rom. 3:20, etc. This escape delivers us from all condemnation of law."[14]

Luther graphically described the purpose of the Law. "Although it does not justify, it is a civil restraint on those who are rebellious and obstinate. Moreover, it is a mirror that shows us ourselves as sinners, guilty of death and worthy of God's everlasting wrath and indignation. What is the purpose of this humbling . . . ? It serves to bring us into grace. So the law is a minister that prepares the way for grace."[15]

In the sacrifices the Law also provided a way to make amends with God for those transgressions. All this was temporary and anticipatory—"until the seed should come to whom the promise had been made" (v. 19).

To show both the inferiority and temporality of the Law to God's promise to Abraham, Paul points out that it was "ordained through angels by the agency of a mediator" (Gal. 3:19c). Although no mention of angels is found in the Exodus account of the giving of the Law (Exod. 19:3—23:19), they are mentioned by Stephen (Acts 7:53) and in Hebrews 2:2 (cf. Deut. 33:2; Ps. 68:17). However, the instructions for the Law are ended in Exodus 23:20-23 with the mention of an angel whom God will send.

The people are to obey God's voice! Paul must have had this angel in view. The mediator obviously was Moses, who represented both God (Exod. 19:3-6, 9) and the people of Israel (v. 8; 24:3) in the covenant in which both parties were involved with commitments and responsibilities. As Paul says, "A mediator is not for one party only" (Gal. 3:20). But he adds, "whereas God is only one," to emphasize that the covenantal promise to Abraham was by God alone and directly. The Law, the Mosaic covenant, was from the Lord. Apparently angelic beings delivered the Law to Moses who then recorded it for the people.

Some critics of the Bible argue that Moses himself simply lifted certain laws that could be found in the legal codes of the various nations surrounding the Jewish people. It must be remembered that even the pagan world can observe certain moral principles that only make sense for a given culture. So there are some laws that sound as if they came from Babylon or Egypt. But the Law of Moses is comprehensive; it is a total way of life that makes those who adhere to it responsible first to God and then to society. The Mosaic Law code was seen as a whole, an entire system, yet was divided into three parts when viewed in context: the moral code, the civil directives, and the ceremonial rules that governed sacrifice. The sacrificial system was a preview of how Christ would bring forgiveness and salvation. Sacrifices could be carried out without sincerity, but God was looking at the heart of the one bringing the offering. Forgiveness followed when repentance accompanied the sacrifice.

This subordinate position of the Law to the promise raises the subsequent question, "Is the Law then contrary to the promises of God?" (v. 21a). For the second time in this letter, Paul uses the strongest phrase of denial—"May it never be!" (v. 21b). He explains that "if a law had been given which was able to impart life," meaning spiritual life, "then righteousness would indeed have been based on law." Lightfoot adds, ". . . in the present, and the glorified life in the future, for in the Apostle's conception the two are blended together and inseparable."[16]

As mentioned before, the scriptural accounts of both the rich ruler (Luke 18:18-25) and the unregenerate Saul (Phil. 3:5b-9) demonstrate that true righteousness cannot be earned through the Law. "The Scripture," to the contrary, "has shut up all men under sin that the promise [literally, 'in order that the promise'] by faith in Jesus Christ" [literally, 'out of faith'] might be given to those who believe" (Gal. 3:22). Human flesh cannot please God. Human effort is offensive to Him because it is but a poor demonstration of human limitation in its attempt to please God. The guilt of sin is an infinite matter. A righteous God must punish sin; He cannot tolerate it in His universe. Only the Second Person of the Godhead, the Lord Jesus Christ, can satisfy His own righteous demands.

Paul continues his explanation by writing, "Before faith came" (v. 23), meaning the faith in God's promise of salvation made available by the sinless life, death, burial, resurrection, and ascension in Jesus, the virgin-born Son of God, "we," meaning all of humanity, "were kept in custody [literally, 'kept under guard,' cf. Phil. 4:7; 1 Peter 1:5] under the law, being shut up to the faith [literally, 'enclosed unto this coming faith'], which was later to be revealed." Paul's concluding explanation was "Therefore the Law has become our tutor to lead us [literally, 'was a child guardian leading us'] to Christ" (Gal. 3:24). The noun *pedagogue* is a transliteration of the Greek noun used here and means "the slave in Greek and Roman families of the better class in charge of the boy from about six to sixteen. The pedagogue watched his behavior at home and attended him when he went away from home as to school."[17]

The specific noun, *paideia*, also refers to discipline, as found in Ephesians 6:4 and Hebrews 12:5, 7, 8, 11. In 2 Timothy 3:16 the Holy Scriptures are said to be profitable for teaching. The giving forth of the knowledge of the will of God ("teaching") produces conviction of mistaken ways ("reproof") and leads to restoration to a proper spiritual state of mind and then to right living ("correction"). Then follows "discipline . . . in righteousness," which is essential to the well-being and to the ministry of service of the man of God.

The verb, *paideuō*, also means to train, either in the schools of men (Acts 7:22; 22:3) or in the school of God (Titus 2:12; 2 Tim. 2:25). The word is used of what takes place in family discipline (Heb. 12:6, 7, 10; 1 Cor. 11:32; 2 Cor. 6:9; and Rev. 3:19). In 1 Timothy 1:20 *paideuō* is translated "teach," but in whatever way the passage is to be understood, it is clear that it is not simply in the impartation of knowledge; rather, severe and specific discipline is meant. In Luke 23:16, 22, Pilate, since he had declared the Lord guiltless of the charge brought against Him, and hence could not punish Him, weakly offered as a concession to the Jews to "chastise" (*paideuō*) Him and then dismiss Him.

What does Paul mean when he says "to lead us to Christ"? (Gal. 3:24). The meaning may have this idea in mind: "We were kept locked up under the law, with, or until, the coming of Christ came in view." The "shutting up" was not an end in itself; it was necessary that they should know and feel the constraints of the taskmaster in order that they might welcome the Deliverer when He appeared.

The Law's ultimate purpose, then, was "to lead us to Christ." The end of Paul's argument is, "But now that faith has come, we are no longer under a tutor [literally, 'under the child guardian']" (v. 25). People in the past, in the Old Testament, were always saved by faith. So what is Paul's point? The point seems to be when *pure faith* comes in opposition to salvation by works through the Law. The Jews could always say they *believed* in God, but now the point is that this trust cannot be mixed with human effort carried out by law keeping! Or, to put it in another way, *faith alone has now been made clear and obvious through Christ!* It can be pretty well substantiated that the Old Testament saints did not hold to law-keeping salvation! They understood, as it was given to Abraham, that justification comes only through trust in what God has said. Through the centuries this fact had been distorted.

## God's Sons and Heirs (3:26–4:7)

Now that faith has come, the Galatian believers "are all sons of God through faith in Christ Jesus" (v. 26). The Greek word translated "sons" means young men (and women, see v. 28) who have matured in every way to be free of the supervision of a pedagogue. Lenski explains further:

> The point is that the Galatians are not in a position that resembles that of the Old Testament believers. Theirs is full Christian liberty. But more than this. The Judaizers were trying to put the Galatians back under the Mosaic regulations, and that not as the Old Testament believers were once under them but in a monstrous way such as God never thought of during the Old Testament period, namely that the Galatians should seek to be saved by observing these regulations. God had appointed the law as a mentor for his children, the Judaizers wanted this mentor turned into a tyrant slave driver for his sons. Paul tells the Galatians that even the mentor is gone, that they are now free sons.[18]

This is true because "all of you who were baptized into Christ have clothed yourselves with Christ" (v. 27). The word "all" is important because it encompasses both Jew and Gentile. All people are leveled at the cross of Christ. Since Christ is God's Son, believers are now identified with Him and are God's sons also. As a result, spiritually speaking, "There is neither Jew nor Greek, there is neither slave nor free man, there is neither male nor female," the reason being "you are all one in Christ Jesus" (v. 28). The gospel has been one of the greatest instruments in the history of humanity to break down social and class distinctions. All social strata are melded into one body. This creates a certain commonality that no other movement has ever brought to the pages of history. This fact brought forth the fruit of democracy from the seed planted in the Reformation, though this reality has never been recognized with absolute perfection! Concerning the oneness in Christ including "male and female," Boice observes: "It is hard to imagine how badly women were treated in iniquity, even in Judaism, and how difficult it is to find any statement about the equality of the sexes, however, weak, in any ancient texts except those of Christianity. Paul reverses this. Indeed, in this statement we have one factor in the gradual elevation and honoring of women that has been known in Christian lands."[19]

| **What It Means to Be a Son of God** |
|---|
| We believe in Christ (John 1:12). |
| We are born of God (John 1:13). |
| We are born again (John 3:3). |
| We are born of water and the Spirit (John 3:5). |
| Everyone "must be born again" (John 3:7). |
| We become adopted as sons of God (Rom. 8:15). |
| The Spirit bears witness that we are children of God (Rom. 8:16). |
| As children of God we become heirs of God (Rom. 8:17). |
| As children our sins are forgiven (1 John 2:12). |
| As children we should "abide," or stay with Christ in fellowship (1 John 2:28). |
| Christ leads the believer as a son of God (Rom. 8:14). |

In the physical realm the differences of ethnicity, status, and sexuality persist, but in Christ believers are one. "If you belong to Christ [literally, 'If you are of Christ'), then you are Abraham's offspring," because Christ is Abraham's seed, "heirs according to promise" (v. 29; see also v. 16). Being Abraham's offspring does not mean that Gentiles in the church become "spiritual Jews." The offspring, or seed, here is a spiritual idea. And with this thought what Paul is saying should never be "spiritualized" or allegorized into something it is not. God still has a plan for national Israel. The church is not a "new" Israel, replacing the Jewish people and their messianic kingdom program.

Paul compares the relationship of the individual and the Law to that of the heir of a Grecian or Roman estate while he "is a child [literally, 'infant,' but frequently used of any minor]." Such a child "does not differ at all from a slave, although he is owner of everything [literally, 'even though he is lord of all']" (4:1). In biblical days, the child held a future promised of preeminence that would be fulfilled when he became mature. But as a child in his youth, he was seen as no better than a slave. "But he is under guardians and managers [literally, 'house-stewards'] until the date set by the father" (v. 2). It was up to the father as to when the youth came into what an older generation called his "majority." But this was determined by the father and by no other outward circumstances. In similar fashion, "while we were children [literally, 'infants'], we were held in bondage under the elemental things of the world" (v. 3). It is sometimes difficult to fully understand how great is the spiritual liberation believers now enjoy. The Law constituted those rudiments of the world designed to prepare and train humankind for spiritual adulthood. "But when the fullness of the time came" (the Greek noun translated "fullness of time" is transliterated in English as *plērōma*) emphasizes the fact that God works on a timetable, because at the proper point "God sent forth His Son, born of a woman." Fausset says: "God does nothing prematurely, but, foreseeing the end from the beginning, waits till all is ripe for executing His purpose. Had Christ come directly after the fall, the enormity of sin would not have been realized fully by man, so as to feel his desperate need of a Saviour. . . . Providence, by various arrangements in the social, political, and moral world, had fully prepared the way for the Redeemer."[20]

He did not suddenly appear like an angel (e.g., Judg. 6:11–12; Matt. 1:20; Luke 1:11–13) to deliver his message and go away again, but identified himself with humanity by being miraculously conceived by the Holy Spirit in the womb of the Virgin Mary, born as a Jewish infant "under the Law, in order that He might redeem [literally, 'purchase out from the market'] those who were under the Law" (v. 4). The goal was "that we might receive the adoption as sons [literally, 'son placement,' i.e., adoption]" (v. 5).

As a result, "because you are sons, God has sent forth the Spirit of His Son [i.e., the Holy Spirit] into our hearts, crying, Abba! ['Father' in Aramaic], Father!" (v. 6). The sending of the Holy Spirit reveals that the Trinity is involved in the work of redemption and salvation. The Spirit is a gift of God to all believers when they become children of God. No sons or daughters are without the Spirit. Further, the Spirit is present in each believer's heart to give testimony of that person's standing in God's family. *Abba* is the diminutive form in Aramaic used by small children in addressing their fathers. It is appropriate to see its similarity to the English word *Daddy*. Used by Christ (cf. Mark 14:36), this familiar form indicates intimacy and trust as opposed to the formalism of legalism.[21]

The end result is that the believer is "no longer a slave," to which the minor child under a guardian was equivalent, "but a son [an adult child]; and if a son, then an heir through God" (v. 7). The Holy Spirit takes up residence in the heart of the believer to bear witness to our sonship relationship to God.

On verse 7 the KJV reads "an heir of God through Christ," while the NASB reads "if a son, then an heir through God." The NASB seems to be the better textual reading. In 1:1 the plain statement is that sonship involves heirship and that all sons are heirs. This is certainly further confirmed by these added words, for people become sons and heirs of God by no efforts of their own but completely by the acts of the sovereign God and Father, who sent forth His only Son (v. 4) who went to the cross to free us from slavery to sin and the Law (v. 5). And it is through the Spirit working in believers' hearts that all this is accomplished (v. 6). Neither the human birth in the flesh nor meritorious works of law keeping can bring about salvation.

What Paul was saying in these passages was explosive to the believers to whom he was writing, but the concept of sonship was also profound to those living in that culture. Few could move from slavery to heirship or sonship! It was also a remarkable concept that Paul says that the believer can now call out to the Lord as the heavenly Father. Such a change of position was a miracle, a marvel, and a wonder to his generation. All three persons in the Trinity are involved in these verses. The Spirit is performing a "spiritual" work, and He is related to God's Son! The Father can now be addressed in this new and intimate way—as indeed the heavenly Father!

It is more than obvious from these words that the apostle not only enjoys the blessedness of his own redemption, but that he assumes his readers are to be experiencing a similar assurance in their personal relationship with the Lord. To know Him is to acquiesce to His Fatherhood; to be known of God is to be acknowledged as His children.

All this is set out here and elsewhere in Scripture, not simply as a future anticipation, a possibility of the position in eternity, but as a present fact, an actual and gracious experience for present-day comfort and encouragement of all who believe in Christ. "By this we know [*ginōskō*, 'have come to know'] that we abide in Him and He in us, because He has given us of His Spirit" (1 John 4:13).

## Study Questions

1. How does Paul describe the Galatian believers?

2. How did the Galatian believers receive the Holy Spirit?

3. What was the basis for the Galatians receiving the Spirit and working miracles?

4.  What example of a person of faith did Paul present?

5.  How did Christ redeem us from the "curse of the law"?

6.  Who is the seed of Abraham in whom God's covenantal promise is fulfilled?

7.  Why was the Law inaugurated 430 years after the promise to Abraham?

# CHAPTER 4

# Do Not Turn Back to Enslavement
# Galatians 4:8–11

### Preview:
*Paul confronts the Galatians with their behavior—a behavior as old as Lot's wife turning back to look at Sodom. Now free in the Lord, the carnal side of the Galatians yearns to return to their old ways and pagan beliefs.*

## The Galatians' Former State (4:8–11)

At this point Paul reminds the Galatian believers of their former unsaved state. At that time they "did not know God," but "were slaves to those which by nature are no gods" (v. 8). To help them better understand new position, Paul writes: "You were slaves to those which by nature are no gods." These Gentiles were most miserable slaves; they slaved for idols. Note the likeness that was similar under the Mosaic regulations. Even the Old Testament believers were in a position that was no better than that of a slave (v. 1); the Gentiles, who were ignorant of God, were outright servants under the influence of idolatry.

There was, therefore, a difference: the Mosaic Law was divinely given while the false gods were mere human inventions. Jewish believers had sonship; pagans had nothing. Yet there is a certain likeness existing regarding this position of slavery. The terrible and awful condition of the slavery of the Gentiles was demonstrated in the fact that "they slaved [constative aorist, expressing the entire action as a unit] for those who by nature are not gods." They were imaginary beings, fictitious gods.[1]

The same condition applies to the unsaved today. For the Galatians these gods were idols controlled by Satan and his demons. Today's false gods are fame, pleasure, and wealth—also under Satan's control (cf. Eph. 2:1–3). Paul reminded the Galatian believers that now they "know God," or, more important theologically, are "known by God" (v. 9).

In light of that blessed spiritual state, Paul properly wonders why the Galatians would "turn back again to the weak and worthless [literally, 'beggarly'] elemental things." He asks if they wish "to be enslaved all over again." This slavery was in observing "days and months and seasons and years" (v. 10), characteristic of their pagan religions as well as Judaism (cf. Col. 3:16–23). Paul writes, "I fear for you, that perhaps I have labored over you [literally, 'toiled fruitlessly'] in vain" (v. 11). Paul's fear was well founded. He knew there would be failure for those who attempted to combine some other philosophy, or some other religious zealousness, with their claim to Christ. Paul would accept no other approach except for embracing the pure gospel. God had done it all at the cross for lost humanity. The redeemed can do no other but trust the salvation contract that put total confidence in Christ's death and resurrection. Anything else was self-effort. And law works are a form of self-effort for obtaining salvation.

While the reference to "years" (v. 10) could be referring to pagan yearly festivals, it may also have in mind the Sabbath years, or the Jubilee years (Lev. 25:1–8). This seems to be the best interpretation. If Paul's readers were so caught up in law works, this would only make sense. While it is more than likely these were the occasions in the thinking of the apostle Paul when he penned these words, still they must not be taken too literally, as though the Galatian Christians had actually been observing a year of jubilee. If they observed just some of them in a legalistic way, they were acknowledging the principle of law keeping as though they were keeping all of them. Again, it must be remembered that the law in itself is good; the problem is human ability to carry through with law keeping.

Paul will later mention circumcision only to show that they could not draw the line on this law or that rule. Once they place themselves under the law, they become debtors to do all the whole law (5:3). While circumcision in itself has hygienic value, the Jews were not thinking of it that way. To many, circumcision was a great sign of faithfulness, of ritual practice that to a degree automatically made one a child of God! Circumcision, then, and religious observance of special days is inconsistent with the spirit of the gospel. To keep one day to show some form of "self" sanctification is a tacit admission that that day is, in some form, holier than other days; whereas, to the Christian, every day is holy.

This legalistic problem is dealt with from another point of view in Romans 14. In that chapter the apostle sets forth his counsel as to the treatment of fellow Christian brothers who may be still tied to certain aspects of legalism. Plainly, therefore, they are not to be denied the privileges of believer fellowship (15:7), even though they have weakness of faith and are unable to share the full burden of Christian responsibility (14:1). They are not to be held in contempt or otherwise grieved (v. 15) or judged (v. 13). Instead, they are to be encouraged and given consideration that they might be edified (v. 19). The Lord Jesus in His strength bears with the weaknesses among His people; likewise, they are to bear with the weak in their midst (15:1–3).

The apostle also speaks of these matters in Colossians 2:16, though he approaches it from yet another viewpoint. Paul warns the believers against permitting anyone to judge them in respect of these very things, meaning, "Let no one act as your judge." Liberty is either liberty for all or is not liberty at all.

William Hendriksen notes that the apostle was shocked and horrified to learn that men who had been so enriched with the gospel of God's free and bounteous grace in Jesus Christ would now, under the influence of false teachers, be turning back again to those "elemental things of the world" (Gal. 4:3). In verse 9 they are described as being "weak and beggarly." What makes matters far worse is that they are doing this by their own choice and personal decision. Such a mixture of law and grace was never first introduced to them. Previously, they had been enslaved by the childish teachings of pagan priests and ritualists, so some believe. They had been taught to try to discover the will of the gods by means of omens or by afflicting the body or to submit to blind fate. Now moral stipulations had been derived from observing nature, religious custom, and arbitrary and foolish practices. Having been delivered from all of this darkness, did they now wish to become enslaved all over again, this time by Judaistic laws and Old Testament regulations?[2]

Paul refers to these "elemental things" as "weak and worthless" (v. 9) because they do not possess the power to help people in any way. Hendriksen notes that Luther commented on this verse and applied the lesson to his own day, observing that some monks were zealously laboring to please God for salvation. However, the more they worked the more miserable, uncertain, and fearful they became.[3] Hendriksen adds: "People who prefer the law to the gospel are like Aesop's dog who let go of the meat to snatch at the shadow in the water. . . . The law is weak and poor, the sinner is weak and poor: two feeble beggars trying to help each other. They cannot do it. They only wear each other out. But through Christ a weak and poor sinner is revived and enriched unto eternal life."[4]

# The Galatians' Care of Paul (4:12–16)

In his exhortation and pleading to the Galatians, the apostle has now come back around to the same point his argument from Scripture had reached in 3:29, both by drawing out the analogy of a son and heir (4:1–5) and by tying it in to their own experience of the Spirit (vv. 6–7). But in verses 1–5, Paul had also provided a valuable before-and-after analogy, that is, the transition from minority to majority, from slavelike childhood to adultlike sonship. This is a firm analogy that could refer equally to the before and after of the Christian Gentile as well as to the Christian Jew. It is in this aspect of the analogy that he now takes up, that is, as the rebuke of 1:6–9 and of 3:2–5, which becomes a passionate appeal.[5]

Paul begged the Galatians to "become" (Greek present tense, "keep on becoming") like him (v. 12). In the immediate context this means to live free of the bondage of the law in the liberty of Christ. In the broader sense, Paul presented himself as a model of Christian faith and life, something he does elsewhere as well (1 Cor. 4:16; 11:1), because he introduced them to the Christian faith (v. 13). Paul's life motto was "For to me to live is Christ" (Phil. 1:21), which should be the life objective of every Christian. Paul did not think he had achieved sinless perfection in his mortal life, however (3:12–15a), as some Christians do now. Usually the quickest way to reveal that a person who claims to have achieved sinless perfection has not is to question that claim. Paul based the validity of his claim for the Galatians to become like him on the fact that he had become like them. Evidently this means that he had put aside the strict Pharisaical restrictions of his heritage to fellowship with and minister to the Gentiles as well as the Jews in the Galatian cities. James Boice explains that Paul "became like them, in order to win them to Christ. . . . This is a principle of great importance for all who are trying to win other people for Christ. Our goal must be to make them like us, while the means to that end is to make ourselves like them. Witnessing involves doctrine, but it also involves the most personal involvement of the witness with those to whom he or she is witnessing."[6]

Evidently the believers had a deep affection for Paul as a result, because he writes, "You have done me no wrong." He points out, "It was because of a bodily illness [literally, 'weakness of the flesh'] that I preached the gospel to you the first time [literally, 'formerly']." We do not know what that illness was. Because he wrote, "If possible, you would have plucked out your eyes and given them to me" (v. 15b), some think the illness may have caused his very poor eyesight. As a result he evidently dictated his letters (Rom. 16:22) and then wrote a closing greeting in his own hand (1 Cor. 16:21; Col. 4:18;

2 Thess. 3:17), with the possible exception of this letter to the Galatians (6:11). Many think this also suggests that it might have been "an attack of malaria on coming up from Perga." Nothing is mentioned by Luke in Acts 13:13, but a malaria prone area may explain why "John left them and returned to Jerusalem."

Paul continued, "And that which was a trial to you in my bodily condition [or 'testing,' cf. James 1:2, 12], you did not despise or loathe [literally, 'to spit at' in disgust)" (Gal. 4:14). Paul's physical illness probably was a literal physical trial for the Galatians, but it certainly was an ethical and spiritual test to accept someone claiming to come with a message from God being incapacitated with a disability or illness. Instead, the Galatians received Paul "as an angel [literally, 'sent one'] of God, as Christ Jesus Himself" (v. 14b).

It is important to point out that Paul was fully aware that he, like the Galatians, was a sinner, and though he had been careful when among them not to allow any conduct on their part that suggested worship of him (see Acts 14:8–18), nevertheless, he does not suggest here that their respect for him as a messenger and an anointed apostle of God was in error. Just the opposite. They were quite right to receive him in this manner. For he came among them as the appointed apostle and messenger of the Lord Jesus Christ. Today there are no apostles. But to a similar degree that ministers and teachers of the Word of God do teach the Word, in a certain sense they should be received as the Galatians received the apostle Paul. Ministers of the gospel do not have that same authority or power. But they are commissioned to set forth the truth. Ministers should not be received and evaluated on the basis of their personal appearance, intellectual attainment, or winsome manner, but as to whether they indeed are God's messengers bearing the word of Christ.[7]

After describing the Galatians' reception and care of him, Paul asks, "Where then is that sense of blessing you had [literally, 'declaration of blessedness']?" (v. 15). Evidently they had considered themselves blessed by God when Paul brought them the gospel, but now their attitude had changed. Paul says that he could bear witness that they would have given him their eyes if possible, the clearest indication that his illness involved his eyes. He pointedly asks, "Have I therefore become your enemy by telling you the truth?" (v. 16). Telling the truth sometimes alienates people, at least temporarily, but that possibility is no excuse for withholding the truth. The truth of the gospel will always be under attack. There will always be those who want to change it, distort it, and repudiate it, along with the one who brings the message. By this, nothing has changed since the days of Paul and the apostles. Satan is the father of lies (John 8:44), and he works hard to deny and ruin the message along with the messenger.

Luther wrote: "It is the role of friends to admonish freely if we go wrong; and when we are thus admonished, if we are wise, we are not angry with our friends for telling us the truth, but we thank them. We often see that truth produces hatred in the world and that anyone who speaks the truth is regarded as an enemy. But it is not like that among friends, much less among Christians."[8]

It needs to be noted in this section that the motives and the tactics of the Judaizers were neither worthy in themselves nor were they intended to further the rightful spiritual growth and interests of the Galatian believers (see also 1 Thess. 5:21). The apostle Paul has proven his love for them in a way that cannot be misunderstood. How could those who were enforcing the law among the people of the Galatian churches prove that they cared for them?

There is a distinct difference between proselytizing and evangelizing. Proselytizing holds a zeal for a creed, in this case a zeal for legalism embedded in Judaism. Evangelizing involves concern for true repentance and salvation and the true following of Jesus Christ as Savior.

Another factor in the acceptance of truth is the manner in which it is told, whether bluntly from an attitude of superiority or in an attitude of concern and love, as Paul shows (Gal. 4:19–20).

## Paul's Superior Desire (4:17–20)

Paul now describes the seduction of the Judaizers for the Galatian believers. They did not have a Christ-centered desire, but rather a selfish one. They wanted to convert these new Christians to rethink their salvation and make them return to legalism. They wanted to isolate those who were trusting in Christ. This is generally the practice of cults—to make their followers exclusive, to keep them from talking with others. Paul writes, "They eagerly seek you, not commendably, but they wish to shut you out"—that is, they wanted to keep the Galatians from the company or influence of Paul, or from the companionship of others who might think the same way, to the end that the Galatians "may seek them" (v. 17). In other words, they wanted to make the Galatians dependent on their exclusive views and plant fear in them that this was the only way to believe. Paul says, "It is good always to be eagerly sought in a commendable manner," and he encourages the Galatians to be zealous always, "and not only when I am present with you," evidently their initial attitude and action in response to hearing the gospel (v. 18). There is no problem with "being wanted," but it must be done in the right way and for the right reasons. But this was not the case with the Judaizers. They could not tolerate their views being exposed and scrutinized. Paul was not jealous in what was happening. He cared not that others may be influencing these young believers, as long as that influence was based on the truth of the gospel of the grace of God and not bowed down by a system of legalistic works.

Paul expresses his deep concern and love for the Galatian believers as he addresses them as "My children [literally, 'born ones']" and says that he was once again experiencing "labor until Christ is formed in you" (v. 19). He declares his strong wish to be with them at that time instead of writing, indicating that he would "change [his] tone." Paul realized how difficult it was to communicate his true feelings in written instead of spoken words, which are accompanied by physical presence with eye contact, gestures, and tone of voice. Luther, who had his own problems with the effects of harsh words, wrote: "The apostle wishes he were with them, so that he might temper and change his tone as he sees necessary. If he saw any of them troubled, he could temper his words so they would not be oppressed by them with more heaviness; conversely, if he saw others high-minded, he could reprehend them sharply, lest they should be too complacent and careless and eventually despise God."[9]

Being absent from them and learning of their spiritual problems, Paul was "perplexed" about them, which could be relieved if not eliminated if he were present with them (v. 20).

The apostle Paul was also laboring to have Christ brought forth fully in the spiritual life of the Galatians and was at a disadvantage by being so distant from them, unable to come to them when needed. If he were there, he could change his voice so as to meet their need in the most perfect way. As it was, he worked to correct them under a handicap and had to secure his doctrinal information about them at secondhand. Paul probably struggled to be absolutely certain of meeting all their inmost thoughts and had to resort to writing, which is rarely as effective as face-to-face communication. Paul was prompted by his intense love, which had already been openly put forth.

Paul's purpose in writing was to induce the Galatian churches to cling to their liberty in Christ since they were born spiritually to freedom. He wants them to reject the yoke of legalistic slavery the Judaizers were trying to force on the Galatians. This is why he keeps asking in so many words: "What does the Scriptures say? Are you supposed to place yourselves back under the Mosaic Law?" Paul did not like to speak so harshly. He wished he could communicate with these believers without scolding, but he admits he was stymied by their change of doctrine and by their departure from the simplicity of the gospel of the grace of God.

## Analogy from Abraham's Wives and Sons (4:21–31)

Paul now attempts to argue from the Old Testament with the story of Sarah and Hagar. He "creates" an allegory to try to explain the difference between law and grace.

As Paul changes his focus, and after having made his personal appeal, he returns again to Scripture. The argument he had already established on the basis of the promises to Abraham was already well enough established (3:6–29) and its corollaries pressed home (4:1–20). What follows then could be regarded not so much as an additional or independent argument, but as an illustration or documentation of the point he has already set forth, in which he demonstrates and shows how well the actual prophetic fulfillment of these truths exemplifies or foreshadows what was now happening through his ministry. By the simple example of the faith of Abraham, the gospel now made manifest through Christ would give freedom from the law and justification, as it did to Abraham, and by means of which he can reintroduce the key theme of freedom (4:22–3, 26, 30–1).[10] It is important also to remember that Abraham was saved by grace through faith way before the Mosaic Law was given.

This also gives Paul the opportunity to exhibit his skills as an exegete and to showcase the elegance with which he documents his case from Scripture. His imagery of birth in verse 19 makes for an effective transition to his discussion of two child-bearing covenants.[11]

Paul begins this lengthy section with the question, "Tell me, you who want to be under law, do you not listen to the law?" (v. 21). J. B. Lightfoot makes a point that the word "law" in the first clause of this sentence is without the article. It means just law in general or bondage and refers to Paul's comments on Galatians 2:19 and 4:4–5.[12] The Judaizers emphasized their relationship as Jews to God, based on their descent from Abraham, and made obeying the law appealing by providing rules and regulations for godly living and pleasing God. As a result the Galatian believers did not know the true message of the Law, which Paul now explains with an analogy based on historical facts. But he challenges them as if they did know something of the legal requirements in this system. When he asked if they had listened to the Law, he meant by this, "Did they fully grasp the heavy burden of trying to keep it?" Why did they think they could keep it when others could not?

The phrase "it is written [literally, 'it stands written']" (v. 22) describes Scripture quoted or referred to as authoritative (e.g., Matt. 4:4; Mark 7:6; Luke 4:8,10; Rom. 1:17; 1 Cor. 1:19, 31). The scriptural record in Genesis states that "Abraham had two sons, one by the bondwoman (Hagar) and one by the free woman (Sarah)." Paul pointed out that Abraham's "son by the bond woman was born according to the flesh [by natural conception]"), but "the son by the free woman through the promise" when Sarah was past the age of conceiving a child (Gen. 18:9–14; Gal. 4:23–24). In these verses Paul shows that he is a master of interpretation. He understood well the issues that come out of the story of Sarah and Hagar.

After presenting the history, Paul now draws the analogy (the Greek word provides the English "allegorization," v. 25). Donald Campbell explains, however, that "this 'allegorizing' is a far cry from the practice of 'allegorical interpretation'—followed by Origen, Augustine, and many others down through the ages into the present day—in which the historical facts are relegated to a lower, less significant level and fanciful, hidden meanings unrelated to the text, are considered vastly more important."[13]

Paul says that "these women are two covenants, one proceeding from Mount Sinai bearing children who are to be slaves; she is Hagar" (v. 24). Hagar "is in slavery with her children" and represents "the present Jerusalem" (v. 25), the center of Judaism and spiritual legalism. This is the only allegory stated as such in the Bible. It is all right to use allegory as long as it is identified as such. This is far different from saying that allegorical interpretation is used to interpret the whole of the Word of God. Luther wrote astutely concerning this:

> Abraham, a figure of God, had two sons; that is to say, two sorts of people are represented by Ishmael and Isaac. These two are born to him by Hagar and Sarah, who signify the two covenants, the old and the new. The old Hagar is of Mount Sinai, begetting slavery. (In Arabic Hagar is the name for the mountain the Jews call Sinai; it seems to get this name for the brambles and thorns.) It is very appropriate that Mount Sinai in Arabic means a handmaid. . . . Just as Hagar the slave gave Abraham a son, yet not an heir, but a servant, so Sinai, the allegorical Hagar, gave God a son, that is, a carnal people. Again, as Ishmael was the true son of Abraham, so the people of Israel had the true God as their Father, and he gave them his laws, oracles, religion, true service, and the temple (Psalm 147:19). The only difference was that Ishmael had been born physically of a slave woman, without the promise, and could not therefore be the heir.[14]

Drawing the contrast, Paul says that "the Jerusalem above [represented by Sarah] is free; she is our mother" (Gal. 4:25–26). To support his argument authoritatively ("it is written"), he quotes Isaiah 54:1, which prophesies that the "barren woman" will have more children than the one "who has a husband." Paul concludes that his "brethren" in Christ, "like Isaac, are children of promise" (Gal. 4:28). Historically, descendants of Ishmael have persecuted descendants of Isaac, but Scripture directs, "Cast out the bondwoman and her son," because they "shall not be an heir" (v. 30), a quotation of Genesis 21:10. Paul concludes by writing, "brethren, we are not children of a bondwoman, but of the free woman," allowing them to draw the application to their own situation (Gal. 4:31).

Paul, in quoting this passage from Genesis 21, shows himself to be a master logician, one who is able to grasp the full implications of what was going on in the Old Testament. His argumentation cannot be equaled. One would think that if the Galatians had read carefully, they quickly would have gotten the point and seen the error of their ways. By using such a telling story about Abraham the patriarch, admired by believing Jews and Gentiles alike, they would have changed their minds.

## Study Questions

1. To what does Paul compare a believer before he trusts Christ?

2. What does the Holy Spirit do in the believer to identify him as a son of God?

3. What position does God give the believer in addition to sonship?

4. How were the Galatian believers compromising their faith in Christ?

5. How did the Galatians treat Paul when he first ministered to them?

6. What does Paul now finding lacking in their attitude and behavior?

7. What did the false teachers intend to do with the Galatian believers?

# Section Three

# THE LIFE OF GRACE BY FAITH

## GALATIANS 5:1–6:18

# CHAPTER 5

# Be Free in Christ and Walk by the Spirit
# Galatians 5:1–26

## Preview:
*Paul begins his closing instruction to the Galatians, drawing the inevitable con-clusion: true faith in Christ negates the bondage of the Law. Do not seek to return to the bondage of the Law. Instead, use your freedom to walk by the lead-ing of the Holy Spirit.*

## Paul's Opening (5:1)

To open this section of the letter, Paul states its basic truth, in fact, the basic truth of the entire letter: "It was for freedom that Christ set us free" (v. 1a). Christ sets the believer free from sin, but here in the case of the Galatians, they had bound themselves to the law system as a proof of their sanctification. By law keeping they could keep themselves looking good before others in their communities. They even may have strutted about as was typical of the Pharisees who boasted in the Law. Paul follows this by giving his basic com-mand of the section and the letter: "Keep standing firm, and do not be sub-ject again to a yoke of slavery" (v. 1b). Here he is urging them not to fall back into a form of slavery as was the case of so many Jews. Why should gentile Christians put themselves under a system that even the Jews could not follow? The gentile Galatian believers had been freed from a yoke of slavery to pagan religions, and placing themselves under the law would be taking on another yoke of slavery. Some Jews sometimes referred to the law as a yoke, although obviously not using the word in the same sense Paul did.

James Boice observes: "To the Jews taking up the law's yoke was the essence of religion; to Paul it was assuming the yoke of slavery. He may also be remembering Jesus' reference to Christians taking his yoke upon them (Mt 11:29–30), but his yoke was 'easy' and 'light.'"[1]

When the apostle says, "Keep standing firm," he means, *"Be firm and unwavering."* This verse clearly belongs to the previous chapter and should not have been separated from it. The sense is, "They were to be firm and unyielding in maintaining the great principles of Christian liberty." They had been set free and released from the bondage of rules and laws of legalism, and from ceremonies that could be deadening. They should by no means and in no form yield to them again. The idea is, do not again allow such a yoke to be put on you; do not again become slaves to that which is imposed by men; and certainly do not yield to any rites, customs, or habits, that is, the yoke of bondage. This would be plainly a servitude to the Jewish laws (see Acts 15:10). It is "religion" that brings about servitude, but Christianity is emphasizing a relationship with the Savior and with the heavenly Father. In this sense, Christianity is not a religion, a human ritual meant to appease God. This lesson is hard for some believers to fully grasp, and it certainly was a dilemma for the Galatian believers.

## Paul's Final Warning (5:2–6)

Jewish men who became believers in Christ, like Paul, had been "circumcised the eighth day" (Phil. 3:5), but gentile Galatian believers were uncircumcised. The performance of this rite and the observance of Jewish rules and regulations were being presented by the Judaizers as necessary to be truly saved. In other words, in addition to faith in Christ, a Gentile had to become like a Jew to be saved. Paul very sternly says, "Behold I, Paul, say to you," and tells them that, if they fall for this false teaching, "Christ will be of no benefit to you." He explains that the person "who receives circumcision . . . is under obligation to keep the whole Law" (v. 3). The person who tries "to be justified (declared righteous) by law" has been "severed from Christ" and has "fallen from grace" (v. 4). God's free and undeserved declaration of righteousness is received through faith alone. The same truths apply today to people who seek to win God's acceptance through their good works or performance of rituals.

At this point, Luther, thinking of his own experience, wrote that this passage is like a touchstone by which we can and should evaluate all human doctrine, practice, religion, and ceremony. The pastor who teaches and preaches that anything besides faith in Christ is necessary for salvation or who devises any practice or religion or observes any rule is proclaiming false doctrine. Or if he teaches any tradition, ceremony, or ritual whatsoever with the idea that these things will provide forgiveness of sins, righteousness, and eternal life, he is wrong and is misleading the flock. "This passage contains the Holy Spirit's sentence against them: Christ is of no value to them at all. If Paul dares to pronounce this sentence on the law and circumcision, both of which were ordained by God himself, what might he do against the chaff and dross of human traditions?"[2]

With verse 5 Paul turns from writing to the Galatian believers who were tempted to turn to circumcision and the law to include himself in presenting the true Christian hope. This is the "through the Spirit, by faith" eager awaiting of "the hope of righteousness." This is not the righteousness of justification—the declaration of us as righteous as viewed in Christ by God the Father when we believe and are indwelt by the Holy Spirit; it is the final, perfect righteousness we receive when we stand before Him in heaven. Donald Campbell says: "At the coming of Christ believers will be completely conformed to all the requirements of God's will. The inward and forensic righteousness which began at justification will be transformed into an outward righteousness at glorification."[3]

When by faith the believer stands "in Christ Jesus, neither circumcision nor uncircumcision means anything [the Greek word literally means 'strength' or 'force'], but faith working [literally 'being energized']) through love" (v. 6). William Hendriksen adds:

> This declaration concerning the eager forward look of Spirit-imparted faith is true, **For in Christ Jesus neither circumcision nor uncircumcision is of any avail, but faith working through love.** As far as Christ Jesus is concerned—or, as one might say, in the sphere of Christian religion—*being circumcised* will be of no benefit toward salvation. But here as always Paul shows excellent balance by immediately adding, *nor being uncircumcised.* The circumcised person must not boast about the fact that his foreskin was removed, nor should the uncircumcised put on airs because he still has his. Cf. the similar statement in I Cor. 8:8 regarding food. What *is* important, however, is "faith working through love." Compare Rom. 14:17, "For the rule of God does not consist in eating and drinking but in righteousness and peace and joy in the Holy Spirit."[4]

There has long been a controversy between Protestant and Roman Catholic interpreters as to whether Paul intended to say "faith wrought through love" or "faith working through love." With the first view, favored by

Rome, love precedes faith. A believer's works of love, or "charity," give substance to faith. This view, however, gives too much weight to "works" and comes dangerously close to making them basic in the effectuation of salvation. This theory therefore contradicts the thesis Paul is trying to establish, that justification is by faith alone; works are not involved. So, as to which is first in order: love or faith, the priority must be given to faith. The works are fruits, not roots (cf. Eph. 2:8–10; 1 Thess. 1:3).[5]

Paul showed by his own life what he wanted of the Galatians: "Circumcised the eighth day" (Phil. 3:5), he now calculates "all things to be loss in view of the surpassing value of knowing Christ Jesus my Lord" (3:8).

The apostle convincingly declares that being circumcised is no advantage, nor is being uncircumcised a disadvantage. To be "in Christ Jesus" is all that really counts. To be circumcised before conversion (as Paul was) accounted for nothing before God, and to be uncircumcised (as the Galatians) was likewise of no account. To be accepted before God in Christ and to be united to Christ were the things that carried eternal value. This union with Him is expressed in faith working through love. So then trust is the energy that brings forth love, and love is the fruit of faith. The genuine character of faith is demonstrated in actions of love. This is the first mention of love in the epistle. Note too that verses 5–6 bring together faith, hope, and love. The three-fold nature of these graces in the Christian walk is presented in such passages as 1 Corinthians 13:13; 1 Thessalonians 1:3; and Colossians 1:4–5.

In concluding these verses, Paul emphases the dynamic work of God's Spirit in aiding the believer to understand that our final righteousness comes only through faith. The Holy Spirit must convince the child of God of this fact. The "hope of righteousness" is important in Paul's argument. The word *hope* (*elpida*) is almost always used in an eschatological or prophetic way. Our "hope" is not "Well, I hope this will happen!" Hope here is a certainty, an assurance that the believer will receive the final state of righteousness by faith. Human works are out. Salvation is a gift and not brought about by law keeping or works.

## Paul's Final Indictment (5:7–12)

Paul likes figures of speech (2:2; 1 Cor. 9:25; Phil. 2:16). He here describes the Christian life as a race, telling the Galatian believers, "You were running well" (Gal. 5:7). Then he asks, "Who [singular pronoun] hindered you from obeying the truth?" By using the singular he punctuates the fact that their efforts at law keeping were personal. It is possible that the Judaizers had a prominent leader. Some commentators surmise that the apostle may be pointing the finger at someone specific who was misleading the entire group of believers, though this theory seems unlikely. Carrying forward Paul's figure of speech of life as a race, Boice says, "This probably refers to the illegal interference of a runner who cuts in ahead of another and thereby disadvantages that runner. Thus, the situation in Galatia was one in which the Galatians had already ceased, in some measure, to obey the plain truth of the Gospel."[6]

Paul frankly says that their "persuasion," or point of view (v. 8) is not from the one calling them, who is God (cf. 1:6). Paul then quotes a proverb— "A little leaven leavens the whole lump of dough" (v. 9; cf. 1 Cor. 5:6)—with the implication at least that leaven (yeast) is an evil substance.

Because it is possible that someone would feel that the apostle was making too much of the problem, he quotes a familiar proverb to the effect that false teaching, and false doctrine, like yeast, spreads and permeates throughout the whole loaf. The Judaizing converts may be few, but the believers must be on guard because the error would destroy the entire church, or all the congregations being persuaded by this false idea of salvation by works. The apostle's point may also have been that one small variation from the truth could destroy the entire doctrine of redemption. If circumcision, for example, were made necessary for salvation, the whole grace system would fall.[7]

Presenting a challenge as well as a commendation, Paul then writes of his confidence "in the Lord" that the Galatians will hold to the true message he has proclaimed. Still writing of a single false teacher, Paul declares that he "shall bear his judgment," judgment from God, possibly here, certainly hereafter.

Evidently the false teachers (or teacher) had been supporting their position by saying that Paul preached circumcision (v. 11). Certainly he had been a devout Jew before the ascended Christ appeared to him. Circumcision was a sign of the Abrahamic covenant, and it was also commanded in the Mosaic Law. Addressing the Galatian Christians as "brethren" with irrefutable logic, he asks them why he is "still persecuted" if that is true. If he were still preaching circumcision, then "the stumbling block of the cross has been abolished." Paul's somewhat joking desire for the false teachers was that they "would even mutilate themselves" (v. 12). Because even Abraham was justified by faith (3:6–16), what does circumcision have to do with salvation? The Jews over time had come to the mistaken view that this sign of the covenant made them saved! This was far from the truth.

The Jews may try but they could not be convincing about this issue if Paul could prove that Abraham was redeemed in the mind of God only by his faith. How could they justify adding circumcision to the salvation equation? By saying that the ones troubling these believers might go out and be circumcised, "mutilating themselves," may give an indication that some of them were Gentiles who had converted to Judaism and were zealous for all of the rituals and ceremonies prescribed in the Old Testament. "Circumcision under the law and to the Jews was the token of a covenant. To the Galatians under the Gospel dispensation it had no such significance. It was merely a bodily mutilation, as such differing rather in degree than in kind from the terrible practices of the heathen priests."[8]

It would make one think that those opposed to Paul were claiming that Paul still held to circumcision, possibly basing their claim on the fact that he had circumcised Timothy. He had circumcised Timothy, a young man of mixed parentage, of both Jew and Gentile, so that his witness among the Jews in regard to the gospel would be more acceptable. But that was not making circumcision a requirement for salvation.

Paul mentions this charge and raises the questions: "If it were true, then why was he still suffering persecution? Would it not stop immediately? Why would his Jewish enemies persecute him if he was proclaiming their own doctrine?" He now sets forth the case that if he preached circumcision, he would no longer be preaching the cross. The cross was a stumbling block or offense to the Jews. The preaching of the cross set aside and made null and void all in which they found glory.

The cross set aside both circumcision and law keeping. It took away their legalistic monopoly in the realm of spiritual issues. It broke down forever the wall of separation between Jew and Gentile, and the cross proclaimed that Christ was the essence and the completion of all the types and shadows. The cross and the death of Christ were altogether completely offensive to them, arousing deep hatred, which was expressed in their persecution of Paul.

Circumcision and the cross clash together in contrast. To advocate circumcision was popular; to preach the cross was to bring on persecution, opposition, vile hatred and abject malice and envy. To preach circumcision was to tell the sinners, especially among the Jews, that they could save themselves; to proclaim the death of Christ on the cross and to point out all that He did with both His death and His resurrection were to declare their total and complete inability to save themselves. It was clear and certain that only Christ could save, and that through the cross. The Jews hated this message, and they detested to be told that their self-efforts and works were to no avail, that salvation had been provided by God and procured by Christ on the cross. This message only increased the hatred of the Jews. It was this hatred that cost Stephen his life (Acts 6:13–14; 7:51–60).

# Liberty Not License (5:13-15)

Again addressing them as "brethren," Paul restates his basic theme, that in Christ they are "called to freedom" (v. 13). A. R. Fausset says: "Gospel liberty consists in three things: freedom from the Mosaic yoke, from sin (1 Thess. iv.7; John 8:34–36), and from slavish fear."[9] Freedom, however, is not equivalent to license to do as you please. The Christian still has a sin nature within him (cf. Rom. 7:17–18, 20, 25) to be controlled, a sin-dominated world around him (Eph. 2:2; 1 John 5:19) to be ignored, and a Satan-directed host against him (Eph. 6:11–12) to be controlled. To the contrary, the Christian is commanded, "through love [the preposition also means 'through the means of'], serve [literally, 'keep on being a slave'] one another."

It is a bit of irony that, having urged the Galatians not to become slaves to law, the apostle should now encourage them to become slaves of one another. It is a paradox, but the paradox is instructive and it teaches a powerful message. The Galatian Christians are to be slaves to each other, though this servitude is not at all like the first. In fact, this is the paradox. It is the Christian form of being free. Slavery to sin is in itself involuntary and terrible; a person is born into sin (Ps. 51:5) and cannot escape it (Rom. 1:18). It becomes the master over every aspect of a person. Slavery to the Mosaic Law, which now comes by choice and not by Scripture, is foolish and burdensome. On the other hand, slavery to one another is voluntary and a source of deep and lasting joy. This is possible only when Christians are delivered through the presence and power of the Holy Spirit from the necessity of serving sin in their lives.[10]

Paul in effect writes that, if the Galatian believers so desire and need to follow a law, he will give them one. After stating that "the whole Law is fulfilled in one word," he quotes Leviticus 19:18: "You shall love your neighbor as yourself" (cf. Matt. 22:39; Luke 10:27; Rom. 13:8–10). The verb translated "fulfilled" is used in the sense "that Christian love is the 'fulfillment' or 'carrying out' of the Law" Paul warns, "If you bite and devour one another, take care lest you be consumed by one another" (Gal. 5:15).

The attitude toward "one another" that is so stressed in this passage is in contrast with what was urged upon those addressed in verses 13 and 14. Here, in verse 15, the people in the church are pictured in the act of rushing at each other like savage animals. They are pictured as biting each other—"gulp each other down"—and if they keep it up, will in the end be totally consumed by one another. They obey the sinful urges of their old man and, with natural inclinations, tear at each other "tooth and claw." It seems to be a pattern of human nature, even for believers who should know better, that when doctrinal error is allowed, the worst of attitudes and habits come forth. These believers should be loving each other and continually expressing that love in concrete ways. But instead, they are fighting and clawing over issues of law keeping. Paul had to return to the great principles found in the Old Testament Law itself, that those who follow God are to love each other as themselves (v. 14). Carnality can be a subtle thing. Those not listening to God's Word seem to forget so quickly what it says!

One might expect such acts of terror and violence from the enemies of God's people, the pagans, in their violent slashing at the righteous (Pss. 35:25; 79:2, 7; 80:13; 124:3), but could those who call themselves believers in the Lord Jesus Christ, and Christians, and members of the spiritual body of Christ be accused of such evil practices? Even though one may be born again by the work of the Spirit of God, the old nature is still present. And nothing works its evil more than "religious" zeal. It brings on destruction, envy, and even hate. Legalistic Christians completely miss the point of how to be living in the Christian walk.

The question might come up, just what does Paul mean in his accusation? Is he merely warning the Galatians against certain sins that they might be considering, without in any way implying that such evils as "biting" and "devouring" already existed in their midst?

It seems apparent from this letter, especially from 1:1–5:12, that a considerable segment of the membership here addressed was in the process of yielding to the wishes of the Judaizers. It is also clear from verses 19–21 that there were others who leaned in the exactly opposite direction and were abusing the doctrine of grace, using God's mercy as a license to sin as they pleased. The apostle then surely must have had a reason to hammer away on the vices mentioned in the verses that follow. And finally, does not the fact that he knew so much about the conditions that prevailed in these churches indicate that he must have had close friends there who shared his thoughts? Were they also infected either with legalism or with the belief that they had the license to sin? And were his informers infected as well? It appears then that to some extent there were factions and divisions in the church. Spiritual rivalries came about with believers being split in their loyalties.

It is certainly not necessary or even reasonable to believe that every individual Galatian Christian was engaged in such overt carnality. There is no doubt that many, but not all, of those in these churches were engaged in the heavy strife Paul is so concerned about. If we accept the theory that at least *some* of the addressed were thus engaged, and that Paul writes as he does not only to prevent these quarrels from becoming more extensive and/or intensive, but also to put an end to them completely by urging the contending parties to adopt "the more excellent way" of love, what a terrible plight and sorry witness these believers were having among those who were not saved. They are not only destroying themselves, but their testimony was clearly tarnished with all the troubles that were aired out in each community for all to see.

> ## The Work of the Holy Spirit in the Believer
>
> *He regenerates and renews the believer (Titus 3:5).*
>
> *He baptizes the believer into the spiritual body of Christ (1 Cor. 12:13).*
>
> *He imparts spiritual gifts (1 Cor. 12:12).*
>
> *He is the Helper of the believer (John 14:16).*
>
> *He is the "Spirit of truth" to reveal spiritual things (John 14:17; 16:13).*
>
> *He comes to abide within (John 14:17).*
>
> *He is sent by Christ from God the Father (John 15:26).*
>
> *He leads the believer as a son of God (Rom. 8:14).*
>
> *He bears witness that we are the children of God (Rom. 8:16).*
>
> *He intercedes for the believer (Rom. 8:26).*
>
> *He illumines the believer (1 Cor. 2:12–13).*

## The Spirit's Leading (5:16–18)

In view of their calling to freedom in Christ, Paul now gives the Galatian believers a mild command: "Walk [literally, 'keep on walking,' the word that transliterates as 'peripatetic'] by [or 'in'] the Spirit, and you will not [Greek double negative, implying adding in English 'by any means'] carry out [literally, 'fulfill, bring to its end or goal'] the desire of the flesh [which is identified in the Scriptures as the sinful nature]" (v. 16). J. B. Lightfoot says, "Throughout this passage the pneuma is evidently the Divine Spirit; for the human spirit in itself and unaided does not stand in direct antagonism to the flesh."[11] The reason is that the desires of the sinful nature and the Spirit "are in opposition to one another, so that you may not do the things that you please" (v. 17) (cf. Rom. 7:14–25). Paul concludes this section by writing, "But if you are led [present tense, 'keep on being led'] by the Spirit, you are not under the Law" (Gal. 5:18). Boice writes: "Paul reminds the Galatians that, though he is now talking of the need to live a godly life, he is not therefore reverting to legalism. Life by the Spirit is neither legalism or license—or a middle way between them. It is a life of faith and love that allows a person to be led by the Spirit."[12]

How does Spirit leading work? Starting out with verse 18, Paul's thinking about "spiritual leading" can be traced backward to a specific point he has in view. Those led by the Holy Spirit are the same ones who walk in the Spirit (v. 16). Going back even to 4:31 and 5:1, it includes those who belong to the Lord Jesus (3:29) and are in "faith" as they trust Him for salvation (3:9). Spirit leading in this context means to be born again, and all true believers in Christ then are led by the Spirit of God.

Furthermore, the deep influence exercised by the indwelling Holy Spirit is not a sporadic influence. It is working, continually *leading* the child of God in a progressive and firm manner. Carnality can of course blunt His work. Believers can grieve and quench the work of the Spirit. Even though the child of God can disobey the Holy Spirit, as often happens, He does not leave them alone and progressively works repentance and conviction in the heart.

This representation is in keeping with the only other truly parallel passage in Paul's epistles, namely, Romans 8:14: "For all who are being led by the Spirit of God, these are sons of God." Here, too, being led by the Spirit is set forth as the indispensable characteristic of God's children. If a person is a child of God, he is being led by the Spirit. If he is being led by the Spirit, he is a child of God. Usually, a child walks with his parent in a certain passive mode. He allows the parent to lead, and he follows without argument but also with complete trust. Wherever his father or mother goes, he follows along with complete obedience. Only when the spirit of rebellion raises its ugly head does the child balk at being led. This is a perfect analogy for the Christian experience. Trust in God subdues the attitude of defiance and rebellion. "Where He leads we will follow!"

How does Spirit leading work? Carnality means being governed by one's own lusts and sinful attitudes and impulses. The Spirit works within, directing the inclinations and aiding the believer in overcoming the tug of the old man. To be "led" by the Spirit means more than to be *guided* by Him; though, to be sure, the Spirit is also truly the Guide of the child of God (John 16:13). According to Galatians 5:18, the enslaving power of the law has been broken for all those who are being "led" by the Spirit. This shows that this *leadership* the Spirit provides implies more than simply a "pointing out the right way." Merely showing the right direction does not help the Christian. When the Holy Spirit *leads* believers, He becomes *the controlling influence* in their lives. He remains within until He has brought all of the children of God to glory.

Being led by the Holy Spirit implies that one allows himself to be led. This is a great mystery—this interrelation of these two factor—the believers' responsibility in his own Christian walk and the leading of the Holy Spirit. Paul's own Spirit-inspired statement cannot be added to: "Work out your salvation with fear and trembling; for it is God who is at work in you, both to will and to work for His good pleasure" (Phil. 2:12–13).

## The Flesh's Products (5:19–21)

Describing them as "evident [literally, 'in plain sight']" (Gal. 5:19), Paul gives a list of the "deeds [literally, 'works'] of the flesh." Luther wrote, "Paul does this because there were many hypocrites among the Galatians who outwardly claimed to be godly people . . .; nevertheless, they did not live by the Spirit but according to the sinful nature, doing its works."[13]

A. T. Robertson classifies them under four headings: "Sensual sins, idolatry, personal relations, and drunken excesses."[14] In the first group are "immorality" (literally "fornication," the basis of the English word *pornographic*), "impurity" of a moral nature, and "sensuality" ("licentiousness, wantonness") (v. 20). It is the flesh, not the Holy Spirit, that produces such practices. Believers in Christ are capable, when following the dictates of flesh, to do that which is morally reprehensible. Paul does not come up with this list simply as filler. This is a reminder of what can happen when self leads rather than the Holy Spirit!

Joined with "idolatry" (literally, "idol worship") in the second group is "sorcery." The Greek word transliterates into English as "pharmacea" and is mentioned because drugs were widely used in sorcery (witchcraft) as a part of idolatry. It is hard to imagine how far some believers had to go to conform their walk with the moral imperatives found in Scripture. The struggle must have been overwhelming for many. But being a new person in Christ, those things that really mattered took on new light and a new dimension.

Although in their unregenerate state the Galatians undoubtedly were guilty of the sins in the first two groups, the list of eight sins in the third category must have hit them right between the eyes, just as they often do modern Christians. They are often called the lesser sins in contrast to the grosser. Luther observed: "Every age, even among believers, has its peculiar temptations. Sinful desires assail a man most of all in his youth; in his middle age, ambition and vainglory; and in his old age, greed. There was never yet any of the faithful whom the sinful nature has not often provoked to impatience, anger, vainglory, and so on."[15]

Some of them, such as enmities (hatred), jealousy, disputes, and envying, sometimes exist only in the heart and mind of the sinner, but they are known to God (Pss. 139:1–4, 23–24). This list of sins falls short of completeness, as evidenced by Paul's adding "and things like these" (v. 21). A. R. Fausset points out that "'works' (plural) are attributed to the 'flesh,' because they are not necessarily connected—nay, often mutually at variance—and are man's *doings.*"[16] Apparently, as in his ministry when he was with them, so now again Paul writes: "I forewarned you that those who practice [literally, 'continually practice'] such things shall not inherit the kingdom of God." A true Christian may fall and sin, sometimes grossly, but it is no longer the practice of his life.

This brings up the important issue of a believer's *position* in Christ and *experience* in the Christian walk. In the category of position, believers are considered "saints" (1 Cor. 6:2), and as "brethren" in Christ (v. 5). The position of the lost is that they are "unrighteous" (v. 1) and "unbelievers" (v. 6). People in this position "shall not inherit the kingdom of God" (v. 9). Again, in position in Christ, the believer is "washed," "sanctified," and "justified in the name of the Lord Jesus Christ, and in the Spirit of our God" (v. 11). Concerning *experience*, the unrighteous can do some good things, and the righteous can do some evil things. But those who are in the position of being unrighteous cannot reach heaven.

It is quite obvious from Paul's words to the Galatians that during his visits he must have given them a considerable amount of instruction, and this was not only doctrinal but also moral, the two being very closely related and coming from each other. This gives the lie to the charge of his enemies that he was teaching, "Let us do evil, in order that good may come" (Rom. 3:8; cf. 6:1). Furthermore, according to Paul's argumentation, it is not possible to gain entrance to the kingdom of God by means of what were deemed to be *good* practices of legalism; however, it is definitely possible to shut oneself out by lack of trust in Christ, leaving one to live and finally be judged by one's own *evil* practices. A person must bid farewell to *all* the works of darkness, and if he does not, he demonstrates that he is not as yet walking in the light (1 Cor. 6:11; Eph. 4:17–24; 5:7–14). The Christian must realize that even though he is *in* the world and has a mission to fulfill, he is not *of* this world. He is only a stranger or pilgrim on the earth (Ps. 119:19).

The apostle Paul, then, has a message for every generation in this dispensation, including this present generation. Those who confess Jesus Christ as their Savior and Lord must bear in mind that far more worldly people "read" *them* than read the Bible (2 Cor. 3:2–3).

## The Spirit's Fruit (5:22-26)

The flesh, or "sinful nature," has desires (Gal. 5:16) that can be controlled, but the Holy Spirit produces fruit that flows naturally from its source when its production is not hindered (v. 22a). A. R. Fausset writes, "The 'fruit of the Spirit' is singular; because, however manifold the results, they form one organic whole springing from the Spirit."[17] What a difference between the two lists! How could anyone complain or kick against Paul's second list? Who would not want to experience these inner characteristics that change the entire demeanor of the individual? Here Jesus' illustration of the vine and the branches fits (John 15:1-8, 16). In the final analysis, Jesus Christ is the tree or vine to whom the believer is attached as a branch by the Holy Spirit at the moment of faith. Then the Spirit takes up permanent residence in the believer and becomes the avenue, if unhindered, for the production of His and Christ's fruit. The nine qualities listed are divine in nature and were displayed supremely in the incarnate life of our Lord Jesus Christ.

Campbell organizes these nine qualities into three triads.[18] The first group has to do with inner personal virtues that mark the spiritual Christian. Love is mentioned first (Gal. 5:22b) because it characterizes the nature of God (1 John 4:8). Joy is the settled attitude that rests in the assurance of one's relationship to God in Christ and God's ultimate control of all things in the accomplishment of His plan. It contrasts with happiness, which is controlled by circumstances and is Christ's gift (John 15:11). Peace is the inner calm in spite of adversities that Christ bestows (John 14:27). Lightfoot pictured this triad as a building: "Love is the foundation, joy the superstructure, peace the crown of all."[19] While on one hand it is easy to appropriate these qualities for Christian living, on the other hand, the old man, the power of the flesh, is ever present to trip up the walk of the child of God.

Building on these three is the second triad of qualities expressed in interpersonal relationships. Lightfoot says these three spiritual qualities are "again arranged in an ascending scale."[20] First is patience, either in the sense of forbearance with other persons or long-suffering with circumstances. Second is kindness, which signifies benevolence toward others whether deserved or not. Third is goodness, which can be either active or passive. The third group involves attributes of personal character.

Faithfulness signifies reliability or trustworthiness. In the Greek text this is the simple word usually translated "faith," of which Lightfoot writes: "seems not to be used here in its theological sense 'belief in God.' Its position points rather to the passive meaning of faith, 'trustworthiness, fidelity, honesty' as in Matt. xxiii. 23; Tit. ii. 10; comp. Rom iii. 3. . . . Possibly, however, it may here signify 'trustfulness, reliance' in one's dealings with others."[21]

Gentleness implies sensitivity in dealing with others in times of discipline (Gal. 5:23). It is related to self-control, which involves mastery of both one's emotions and actions. Paul says that against such qualities "there is no law." When the fruit of the Spirit is expressed in your life, you are living on a higher level than the law. Conversely, when your thoughts or actions violate one or another of the commandments of the law, you are not being "led by the Spirit."

The spiritual reality is that when you "belong to Christ Jesus," you "have crucified [once for all] the flesh with its passions and desires" (v. 24). In light of varied misunderstandings, Campbell explains:

> This does not refer to self-crucifixion or self-mortification. Rather, it refers to the fact that by means of the baptism of the Holy Spirit, Christians were identified with Christ in His death and resurrection. . . . While co-cruci-fixion took place potentially at the cross, it becomes effective for believers when they are converted. This does not mean that their sin nature is then eradicated or even rendered inactive but that it has been judged, a fact believers should reckon to be true.[22]

Therefore, when fleshly passions rise up, you can rebuke and reject them as dead. The spiritual reality is that, as a believer in Jesus Christ, you "live [literally, 'keep on living'] by the Spirit" (v. 25). Therefore, you are commanded to "walk [this is a military parade word] by the Spirit." Paul's final command here is "Let us not become [literally, 'cease becoming'] boastful," something at least some of the Galatian believers were doing; and as a result, "challenging one another, envying one another" (v. 26).

By this Paul is saying, "Let us not go about bragging about what we have or might think we possess, bringing out equally pretentious swagger on the part of the person to whom we are making bold statements; nor should we grudge that other person as to what he has." Haughtiness and conceit, a "know-it-all" attitude, brutal aggressiveness—these show forth a carnal spirit that is the opposite of Christ's nature (Isa. 42:2; Zech. 9:9; Matt. 11:29; 20:28; John 13:5; 2 Cor. 10:1; Phil. 2:8). The Holy Spirit does not want us to act puffed up. The apostle's main thought, then, is: "Allow the fruit of the Spirit to replace the works of the flesh."

It is a sad fact that the carnality expressed in these verses is part of what happens to believers in Christ as they walk through life. Carnality raises its ugly head and begins destroying what should be loving relationships between brothers in the Lord. It seems that often carnality just appears out of nowhere and brings about destruction. Sometimes, no matter how much this fact of carnality is talked about, it will inevitably happen. Verse 25 seems to be the key to the problem, but how to give oneself totally to the leading of the Holy Spirit can be allusive to many in the Christian family.

## Study Questions

1. Why has Christ "set us free," and what then should believers do?

2. What is the one thing that counts in Christ Jesus?

3. To what does Paul liken this false teaching?

4. What does Paul ask the Galatians to do to avoid using their faith as a license to do evil?

5. What spiritual conflict takes place in the life of the believer?

6. Why does Paul list the "acts of the sinful nature"?

7. Why does Paul list the "fruit of the Spirit"?

# CHAPTER 6

# Responsibilities of Christian Fellowship
# Galatians 6:1–18

## Preview:

*Paul ends his letter to the Galatians with practical applications of the doctrine he has just taught. Walking in the Spirit should give us a burden to help our fellow Christian and to support those who teach the Word, that we may mature as believers. Finally, Paul makes one more appeal to avoid those who mix the Law with salvation by grace.*

## Mutual Ministry (6:1–6)

Paul's addressing the Galatian believers as "brethren" points to the introduction of a new subject with this chapter, that of ministering to one another as fellow Christians (v. 1a). Paul presents someone being "caught in any trespass" (6:1b) as a hypothetical case, but, unfortunately, it happens all too often. Luther explained: "The Apostle is not speaking here about errors and offenses against doctrine, but far lesser sins into which people fall not deliberately but through weakness. The words "is caught in" imply being tricked by the devil or by the sinful nature."[1]

Luther would not want to imply that the child of God is helpless and has no power given by the Lord to resist temptation and sin. Christians cannot say, "The devil made me do it!" Yet the devil's power and influence are indeed great. Christians, and all human beings, are personally responsible. People do not sin in a vacuum, or as if they are mindless robots. It is true that the heart is dark and sin can suddenly rise to the surface and snare one in its evil clutches, but this still does not remove responsibility for one's actions. While sin can come on quickly, it still can be called a blunder!

The word "trespass" here literally means "a misstep, blunder," but nevertheless refers to a deliberate, willful sin. It must be a public act, however, because the spiritual ones are directed to "restore such a one in a spirit of gentleness." "Restore" means "to make fit, mend." There is restoration on the other side of sinning, though consequences may last a lifetime. The Bible indicates that there can be both (1) restorative grace and (2) preventative grace. Every believer in the Lord has experienced both from God's hand.

While restoring others, the spiritual believer is commanded to be "looking to yourself" to avoid also being tempted. Paul commanded the Galatians to "bear [literally, 'keep on bearing'] one another's burdens [literally, 'weights']" (v. 2). They had done so for Paul (see, e.g., 4:14) but apparently were unwilling, or at least hesitant, to do so for each other. If they do that, Paul wrote, they will "fulfill the law of Christ," which is to "love one other just as I have loved you" (John 15:12, 17).

---

### Spiritual Restoration

*Confession of sin brings restored fellowship with God (1 John 1:9).*

*Forgive and comfort the repentant (2 Cor. 2:7).*

*Reaffirm love for the repentant (2 Cor. 2:8).*

*Admonish the wayward as a brother, not as an enemy (2 Thess. 3:15).*

*Do not allow a root of bitterness to come up (Heb. 12:15).*

*Confess sins to one another (James 5:16).*

---

What can hinder the Christian from helping to carry other believers' burdens? Paul suggests first of all conceit, thinking "he is something when he is nothing." That person "deceives himself [literally, 'leads his mind astray']" (Gal. 6:3). "The implication seems to be that if Christians neglect or refuse to bear another's burdens, it is because they think themselves above it. But this is to be self-deceived, for, measured by God's standards, no one amounts to anything."[2]

Second, Paul writes, "But let each one examine [in the sense of prove like a precious metal] his own work" (v. 4). "And then he will have reason for boasting [literally, 'have basis for glorying'] in regard to himself alone, and not in regard to another." If honestly done, on one hand this will destroy conceit. On the other hand, however, if a person has low self-esteem, it might prompt him to help a fellow believer carry his burden or encourage him to "bear his own load [literally, 'ship's cargo']" (v. 5). Explaining the apparent contradiction, Donald Campbell writes: "In this verse a different Greek word (*phortion*) is used to designate the pack usually carried by a marching soldier. It is the 'burden' Jesus assigned to His followers (cf. Matt. 11:30). There are certain Christian responsibilities or burdens each believer must bear which cannot be shared with others. Jesus assured his disciples that such burdens were light."[3]

Related to ministering to one another is the responsibility to provide for those who devote themselves to teaching the word of God. Henry Alford says: "From the mention of bearing one another's burdens, he naturally passes to one way, and one case, in which those burdens may be borne—viz., by relieving the necessities of their ministers."[4]

Paul writes, "Let the one who is taught (from this Greek verb we derive the English *catechism*) the word share all good things with him who teaches" (v. 6). Apparently by this early date more men than the apostles were ministering the word full-time, and both our Lord Jesus and Paul declared that "the worker deserves his wages" (Luke 10:7; 1 Tim. 5:18). He discusses at length the right of the minister, together with his wife and family, to be supported by those to whom he ministers in 1 Corinthians 9:3–18. This included his own right to such support (vv. 4–5, 12). Paul, however, purposely did not exercise that right but worked as a tentmaker to support himself and his party for two reasons: (1) because his ministry was largely in virgin territory and (2) to have the joy and reward of preaching "the gospel without charge" (v. 18). Paul did not write this discourse on ministerial support to the Corinthians "that it may be done so in my [Paul's] case" (v. 15), but he did on occasion graciously accept unsolicited gifts (see Phil. 4:10–11, 14–18).

## God Keeps Accounts (6:7–10)

Undoubtedly with the false teachers in mind, Paul warns the Galatian believers, "Do not be deceived [literally, 'Stop being led astray']" (v. 7a). The reason is because "God is not mocked." The Greek word translated "mocked" has the idea of turning up one's nose. A person can mock God, but he cannot get away with it. Paul explains that "whatever a man sows, this he will also reap" (v. 7b). "The principle of sowing and reaping is especially true of Christian living. Those who spend their money on what gratifies their fleshly nature will reap a fleshly harvest. And, since the flesh is mortal and will one day pass away, the harvest will pass away also."[5]

Our omniscient, omnipresent, omnipotent God knows and sees everything (see Heb. 4:13), and he keeps accurate accounts. The person who gratifies his "flesh" (sin nature) will reap "corruption." The Greek word for "corruption" can refer to physical and moral corruption. Contrariwise, the person "who sows to the Spirit shall from the Spirit reap eternal life," beginning at the moment of faith in Christ and for eternity (v. 8).

The idea of sowing and reaping points to the fact that a good farmer pays careful attention to his seed and the fields he is working in. He is looking for abundant returns and manages his resources well, keeping in mind his future and that of his family. Sowing and reaping also imply work and effort. How sad for anyone to become so blinded about their Christian walk that they focus all their attention on seeking a harvest of perishable fleshly produce. When the farmer fails to seek the guidance of the Master Harvester, believing that he is self-sufficient and all-wise in managing his life, he reaps failure.

Paul closes this section of warning with a message of encouragement, speaking to himself as well as to the faithful Galatian believers, which he signifies by changing to the first person plural—"Let us not lose heart in doing good" (v. 9). This verse makes it clear that there is pain in what the Christian does in this life. There can be moments of short-sightedness and times of doubt and discouragement. Even with the best of actions and the purest of motives, disappointment still comes. The war of the believer is with the world, the devil, and unfortunately, even with Christian brothers who try to destroy other brothers. This verse promises a glimpse of hope that God will have the last say in the results of our efforts. Growing weary implies discouragement and fosters the attitude of, "Oh, why even try to do what is right in serving the Lord?" At this moment the child of God has to fall back on the truth that God is sovereign; He is not passive or impotent in carrying out His plans. Campbell observes that undoubtedly "Paul included himself as he no doubt contemplated his sometimes frustrating labors on behalf of the Galatian Christians."[6]

In farming the harvest is several months after the sowing, with many difficulties during that time; the same rule applies in the spiritual realm. The truth is that "a harvest" will be reaped "in due time . . . if we do not grow weary." Paul's concluding principle for all believers is to "do [literally 'work'] good" to everyone "while we have opportunity," but above all to those of "the household of the faith" (v. 10). The old saying, "We must keep on keeping on!" applies here. The believer does not stop seeking every chance for serving the Lord. And what is done surely must first bless the believers. The Christian community is like a fraternity, a family, a household, not of strangers, but of brothers and sisters who may have needs of every sort.

The lost should also be cared for when the moment presents itself. The "all men" certainly refers to those who do not know Christ. So often on the mission field charity has gone before the presentation of the gospel. To give to others shows care and concern. Then when the gospel is presented, the lost are given a glimpse of the fact that the child of God is living out what he or she believes. The greatest act of love was exhibited when God sent His Son to die for the lost (John 3:16), but that love is transmitted through acts of kindness for the needs of humanity.

## Conclusion (6:11–18)

Paul begins his conclusion by calling his readers' attention to the "large letters" he writes "with my own hand" (v. 11). This was done, first, to authenticate the letter as from Paul and, second, to emphasize the fundamental truth of the letter in the final paragraph. General agreement exists among Bible scholars that this statement applies only to this concluding section with the majority of the letter transcribed at Paul's dictation by a stenographer (cf. 1 Cor. 16:21; Col. 4:18; 2 Thess. 3:17). A. T. Robertson gives a good discussion of the significance of the phrase "large letters," questioning whether they were the result of Paul's impaired eyesight, were used for emphasis like capital letters or underscoring, or were simply his ordinary writing in contrast to the careful, polished script of a professional stenographer.[7] Perhaps Paul was making reference to his handwriting because he could write only with ill-formed letters like the poor script of a child. Or he may have wished to call specific attention to this closing paragraph by placarding it in big letters. Another argument cites the fact that intellects often do not write neatly but instead with large, clumsy letters.

The two most cogent arguments would be that Paul had a problem with his eyesight or that he was writing with large letters for emphasis. Maybe he wanted to catch the attention of his readers by using large letters just as someone today may use bold type or underscoring. If one must settle on a reason for this verse, the eyesight theory may make the most sense, though the issue cannot be settled definitively.

The apostle now comes back to his main concern for writing this letter. He sums up his letter's message by saying that the Judaizers, who "desire to make a good showing," seek to get the believers to be circumcised in order "that they may not be persecuted for the cross of Christ" (v. 12). Those who think this way cheapen the sacrifice of Christ on the cross. They are willing to sell out as to its eternal value in bringing salvation. They wish to escape the shame and the pain of persecution. They do not want to be ostracized by their family or community. Those who think this way reveal their true cowardly motive: they want to be accepted and not criticized. They want to do what is more human, more fleshly, in order to receive praise and possibly even honor.

Paul points out that "those who are circumcised" do not "keep the Law"; nevertheless, they try to get other believers circumcised in order to "boast [or 'glory'] in your flesh" (v. 13). He reminds his readers again that those who want to live legalistically cannot even keep the Law themselves. Nevertheless, they want to have those they influence brought back under the Law. Paul's argument sounds very similar to what Peter said at the Jerusalem Council. Why would anyone want to put the Law on the neck of the gentile disciples, a yoke "which neither our fathers nor we have been able to bear," for we Jews are "saved through the grace of the Lord Jesus, in the same way as they also are" (Acts 15:10–11). Christians are saved by faith through grace and must live by faith through grace as well! Luther summarized Paul's just attack against the Judaizers as follows: "These false teachers, being accused by the apostle for dreadful enormities, were to be avoided by everyone. . . . Your teachers are vain. Because they are afraid of the cross, they preach circumcision, in case they should provoke the Jews to hate and persecute them."[8]

By way of contrast, Paul says that his only source of boasting (glorying) would be in "the cross of our Lord Jesus Christ" (v. 14). Through his identification with Christ on the cross by faith, he writes, "the world has been crucified to me, and I to the world." This should be the attitude of every Christian. The believer has no more claim on the world, and the world should have no more claim on him! The life of the child of God centers around the work of the Savior on the cross. Everything else fades in importance. As a result, "neither is circumcision [a male Jew] anything, nor uncircumcision [(a male Gentile]" (v. 15). With this verse Paul destroys all distinctions of race and entitlement. Before God all peoples stand equally, either as sinners or as the redeemed. This idea gave many Jews trepidation because they were for so long God's earthly and privileged nation. Now all of humanity was "leveled" before the foot of the cross. In the dispensation of the church, no one can claim racially to have special consideration or status. The only thing that counts is "a new creation," being a new person with eternal life in Christ.

Paul concludes this summary of his letter's message by praying "And those who will walk by this rule, peace and mercy be upon them, and upon the Israel of God" (v. 16). Paul has been speaking throughout this epistle to the Galatians both to Jews and Gentiles who are now one in Christ. Yet because of his special love for the Jewish believers, he gives them a special and separate reference in this passage. "The Israel of God" is not a reference to the church in the broad sense, or to the Gentiles. Some believe the church has replaced Israel, so such a reference would have to be to those in Christ, the church itself. However, nowhere is the church ever called *Israel*. This term is used exclusively for the physical descendants of Abraham, Isaac, and Jacob.

Paul finally desires that no one will cause him trouble. He writes, "I bear on my body the brand-marks of Jesus" (v. 17). Paul had paid the price. No one could say his zeal came from any personal or selfish motive. His conviction about his calling was above all human recognition. He had never received, nor ever would receive, earthly acclaim for being a messenger of the gospel. In addition to the physical marks of the natural hardships he endured was the evidence of persecution for his faith, such as the stoning at Lystra (Acts 14:19–20), which had already occurred before this letter was written. Paul closes this letter to the Galatian believers, as he did most of his letters, with a benediction, pronouncing, "The grace [unmerited favor] of our Lord Jesus Christ be with your spirit" (v. 18). With his final word—"brethren"—Paul reminds them of his kinship with them in Christ. To confirm his prayer for them, he ends with "Amen."

A closing thought about verse 18: Some have pointed out the brevity that characterizes this benediction. The theory is that Paul was under stress because of the crucial issue of legalism. There is no doubt that this terse salutation stands in contrast to the rich parting words the apostle uses in his other letters (Rom. 16:25–27; 2 Cor. 13:14; Eph. 6:23–24). Nevertheless, it can certainly be argued that the apostle wanted to nip the issue in the bud and indeed meant to be blunt and not flowery.

Galatians can be said to be a tough book. Paul minces no words, because by revelation he is given an understanding of the gracious nature of salvation in Christ. He writes elsewhere that believers are saved by grace alone (Eph. 2:8), by which those now in Christ "have boldness and confident access through faith in Him" (3:12). This leaves no room for works as a method of deliverance. This undeserving grace has brought about atonement for sins, made possible the operation of God's Spirit in the hearts of believers, made sinners children of God, and made them heirs of redemption and eternal life. This grace sustains, equips for living, fills the heart, and brings about peace and unspeakable joy and a hope of eternal glory with God the Father and the Lord Jesus Christ.

## Study Questions

1.   How should a brother caught in a sin be treated and by whom?

2.   When helping a sinning brother, what should the spiritual one be doing concerning himself?

3.   What action fulfills the "law of Christ"?

4.   For what is the individual believer responsible?

5.   How do you reconcile verses 2 and 5?

6.   What is the responsibility of those being instructed to their instructors?

7.   What is God's law of spiritual planting and reaping for the individual?

8.   What encouragement does Paul hold out for himself and the Galatians?

# EPHESIANS

EPHESIANS

INTRODUCTION

# Background of Ephesians

The book of Ephesians gives a magnificent sweep of God's saving grace. Here the doctrine of predestination and election is clearly set forth. Believers are called before the foundation of the world to God's summing up of all things in Christ. Christ is exalted and shows how the believer is purposely called of God to eternal life. The book also explains God's plan for the church during this dispensation.

Peter O'Brien understands well what is happening in Ephesians. He points out that the letter has not only had a significant impact on the lives of men and women in the past, but it also speaks with great power to our contemporary situation. To a world that seems to have lost all sense of direction and a society that for all its great achievements is in a mess, the divine analysis of the human predicament along with God's gracious and comprehensive salvation, such as is found in Ephesians 2:1–7, ultimately provides the only hope for a world that stands under divine judgment. The understanding of the gospel in Ephesians challenges and redefines the superficial understanding of the gospel prevalent in our day.[1]

Repeatedly within Ephesians one finds the contrast drawn between the "former" lifestyle of believers and their new life as reborn children of God, now in Christ. This contrast is accentuated by use of the "once–now" form. Ephesians 5:8 clarifies the fundamental distinction between the unsaved and those in Christ: "For you were formerly darkness, but now you are light in the Lord; walk as children of light." This verse and other examples were given to emphasize the new life and privileges given to believers to encourage them to pattern their lives on God's character and not to be conformed to the pagan world around them.[2]

101

O'Brien points out how Ephesians speaks to an increasingly postmodern world. The book is refreshing in its strong affirmations that *truth* is important, especially the truth of God and his gospel. Salvation in Christ stands over against all sham and lack of reality. The letter, however, does not focus on truth at the expense of ignoring love. Just the opposite. The love of God and of Christ is regarded as foundational throughout Ephesians, while believers, who are urged to *imitate God,* are to do this by living a life of love (5:1–2). This thought summarizes much of the exhortatory material in the second half of the book (chaps. 4–6). In fact, it has been pointed out that, apart from 1 Corinthians 13, Ephesians has more references per page to love, or at least to believers living *in love,* than anywhere else in the Pauline letters. Furthermore, this concern for truth and love in relationship is tied in with unity. In the light of God's magnificent saving purposes (spelled out in chaps. 1–3) and his plan to bring all things together in unity in Christ, those who are recipients of "every spiritual blessing in the heavenly places in Christ" (1:3) are urged to live a life worthy of the calling they have received (4:1). At the heart of this exhortation is the urgent and powerful admonition, "[Be] diligent to preserve the unity of the Spirit in the bond of peace" (4:3). The strong motivation for this appeal is presented through a series of seven acclamations (vv. 4–6), in which the readers are reminded of the fundamental unities on which the Christian faith and life are based.[3]

O'Brien goes on and notes that after the theological affirmations of chapters 1–3, the exhortatory material of chapters 4–6 is both lengthy and significant (i.e., the teaching on marriage in 5:21–33). However, Ephesians does not provide the believer with a set of rules to follow or a set of easy solutions to our fundamental needs before God and others. Rather, based on our union with Christ and thus our relationship with God, Ephesians urges us to radically change our inner self and our character. Life now is to be lived with reference to Christ. Believers are to give thanks in everything to God the Father in the name of Christ (5:20). Christians are to continually grow in their understanding of God, to know Him better (1:17–19). This can only be accomplished through divine enablement, because God's desire and will are for believers to be filled to all the measure of the fullness of God (3:19).[4]

# The City of Ephesus

Strabo, a geographer of the first century, described Ephesus as being a seaport city located at the mouth of the Cayster River, at the middle of the western coast of the Roman province known as Asia at that time.[5]

Although Ephesus was past its prime as a commercial and business center by the time of the apostle Paul's visits (Acts 18:19–21; 19:1, 8–22, 29–31; 20:1), it was still a great tourist attraction as the location of the temple of the Greek goddess Artemis (Acts 19:24, 27–28, 34–36), also known by the Roman name Diana. Alexander the Great had built the temple and, although burned and rebuilt several times, in New Testament times it was still an attraction.

Harold Hoehner offers these additional details:

> Over the years there were renovations and additions. According to Pliny (A.D. 23–79), the temple in the first century measured 69 by 130 meters (225 by 425 feet) with 127 columns 18 meters (60 feet) high and 2 meters (6 feet) in diameter. Some think that the breadth and width refer to the temple platform and that the temple itself was 55 by 110 meters (180 by 361 feet), which is an area slightly larger than an American football field (160 by 360 feet including end zones). It was built of marble, Cyprus wood paneling, and cedar roof beams. It was the largest building known in antiquity and was considered one of the seven wonders of the world. For centuries much of life in Ephesus revolved around the temple of Artemis.[6]

Although the worship of Artemis dominated the city of Ephesus, to assume that this was the only religion practiced would be incorrect. Emperor worship was also very prominent in Ephesus. In fact, in 26 A.D. Ephesus was in the running with many other cities to be named temple warden of the emperor (during the reign of Tiberius). To be named temple warden was a great honor for a city. However, Ephesus was not chosen, primarily because of the dominance of Artemis worship in the city.[7]

Also prominent was the practice of magic and sorcery. Ephesus was known as being very hospitable to practitioners of this type. In the book of Acts (19:18–19), Luke speaks of those in Ephesus who had recently been saved as coming together and burning their magic books. According to Luke, the total value of the books destroyed was fifty thousand pieces of silver. This was in a day when the wages for one day's work was one piece of silver![8] Truly, a monumental conversion.

E. J. Banks writes that "Ephesus was the most easily accessible city in Asia, both by land and sea,"[9] even after silt from the Cayster River made its harbor inaccessible to larger vessels. The Greeks had made it an emporium (the word means "a way in" to the interior) and proconsul's seat, and it boasted of its title, "The Landing Place." The marble street, the "Arcadian Way," that lead to the harbor and was lined with buildings with impressive colonnades made the name Ephesus, which possibly means "desirable," appropriate.[10]

As for political influence, "Ephesus was the provincial capital of the senatorial province of Asia (Asia Minor)."[11] This meant that it was ruled by a proconsul, a very powerful official who lived in the city. We also know from Acts 19:35 that Ephesus had a town clerk, another important official, who was in charge of certifying, storing, and copying official documents. It was this official who quieted and chastised the uproarious crowd before dismissing them (Acts 19:35–41).[12]

Commercially, according to Strabo, Ephesus was "the largest trading center in Asia Minor west of the Taurus, which is on the eastern side of Asia Minor."[13] In addition to its ample harbor, Ephesus connected shipping routes with Italy on the west, as well as Egypt and Syria on the east. It was also at the western end of the "Royal Road," which started at Susa. This road was of Persian origin and was still a major transportation artery during the Roman period.[14] Hoehner adds, "Ephesus was regarded as 'the first and greatest metropolis of Asia.' With an estimated population between 200,000 and 250,000, its importance ranked only behind Rome and Athens."[15]

The apostle Paul first visited Ephesus on his second missionary journey. "With him were Priscilla and Aquila" (Acts 18:18), whom he left there after he "reasoned with the Jews" (18:19) in the synagogue. "When they asked him to stay for a longer time, he did not consent" (18:20), because he was desirous to return to Syria before Pentecost to fulfill a vow he had taken at Cenchrea, but he promised to return "if God wills" (18:21). He did return on his third journey, coming through the interior (19:1) from Galatia and Phrygia (18:23). After three months of ministry in the synagogue, opposition by some of the Jews occurred, so Paul "took away the disciples, reasoning daily in the school of Tyrannus. And this took place for two years, so that all who lived in Asia heard the word of the Lord, both Jews and Greeks" (19:9–10). Without doubt this extended and extensive ministry by Paul and his associates and converts was the basis for the evangelization of the province of Asia and the founding of the seven churches there (Rev. 1:4), among many others. Paul left Ephesus after the riot of the craftsmen led by Demetrius, a silversmith (Acts 20:1), and did not return except to call on "the elders of the church" from Miletus as he passed by on his way to fulfill his vow at Jerusalem before Pentecost (vv. 16–17).

## Authorship

Staying consistent with the convention of his time, the author begins by announcing himself as the apostle Paul (Eph. 1:1; cf. 3:1). Further, the letter contains many personal notes: the writer has heard of the readers' faith and love (1:15); he gives thanks and prays for them (1:16); he calls himself "the prisoner of Christ Jesus" (3:1; 4:1), and he asks for his readers' intercessions on his behalf (6:19–20). The man who claims to be Paul was known to the traders and was confident that his claim would not be overthrown. We should hold anyone who claims to be the author of any letter coming to us from antiquity to be just that unless there is very strong evidence to the contrary.[16]

Because of this close association with the founding and early development of the church at Ephesus, as well as the fact that he identifies himself twice as the writer (Eph. 1:1; 3:1), Paul's "authorship was never called in question till very recent times."[17] O'Brien comments:

This affirmation of the Pauline authorship of Ephesians was universally accepted in the early church, and was not challenged until the late eighteenth and early nineteenth centuries. The letter was referred to early and often, apparently from Clement of Rome (A.D. 95) on. It is quoted by Ignatius, who shows familiarity with the armour of God (6:11–17), and by Polycarp, who cites Ephesians 4:26 along with Psalm 4:4 as Scripture.[18]

Ireneus, as well, quoted Ephesians 5:30, stating "as blessed Paul declares in his epistle to the Ephesians." He also attributed Ephesians to Paul in *Adversus Haereses* 1.8.5; 5.2.3; 8.1; 14.3; 24.4. Marcion also considered Ephesians to have been written by Paul, although he thought it was intended for the church at Laodicea (Tertullian, *Adversus Marcionem* 5.17). Ephesians is attributed to Paul in the Muratorian Canon (c. AD 180), and in the third century was regularly attributed to Paul by both the orthodox and their heretical opponents.[19]

Denial of his authorship was led by De Wette and Baur and focused on the language used in the letter and its impersonal tone. On one hand, attention was called to the many words and phrases found also in Paul's other letters, especially Colossians and, on the other hand, the many unique words and phrases found only in Ephesians. You can't have it both ways, and furthermore, reasonable explanations exist for both situations. When otherwise reliable manuscripts were discovered that had a blank space instead of the words "in Ephesus" in the salutation, suggesting that the letter was intended to be read in several churches in the province of Asia and simply ended up in Ephesus, and providing an explanation for the impersonal tone, both arguments rejecting Paul's authorship were answered. Further support of the letter's circular nature is the fact that Marcion, although recognizing it as written by Paul, called it the letter to the Laodiceans, evidently acquainted with a copy that remained in Laodicea. Also, Paul wrote the Colossians to ask them to send their letter to "the church of the Laodiceans" and to "read my letter that is coming from Laodicea" (Col. 4:16). This could be what we know as the letter to the Ephesians and explain Marcion's identification of it with Laodicea, or it may refer to still another letter that God saw fit not to preserve.

Hoehner concludes with these thoughts: "The impersonal nature of this letter does not prove that it was not from Paul. In fact, Black thinks that the impersonal character of Ephesians is not out of character with the rest of Paul's epistles and it should not be even considered as an encyclical letter. Furthermore, it seems that the better Paul knew the church, the fewer personal greetings were given."[20]

A good example of this is the epistle to the Romans, which has the most extensive greetings even though Paul had never been there. Conversely, the Thessalonian epistles have no greetings, and Paul had been there a few weeks earlier. Possibly Paul used greetings to strengthen his credibility, which means they would be of greater necessity in cities he had never visited. A greeting would be least needed in letters to cities where he was well known. Thus the impersonal tone of Ephesians in no way necessitates the denial of Pauline authorship.[21]

Paul identifies himself as "the prisoner of Christ Jesus" (Eph. 3:1; cf. 4:1) when writing, a fact he mentioned also as true when writing his letters to the Philippians (1:7, 13–14), Colossians (4:10), and Philemon (vv. 1, 9–10, 13, 23). For this reason the four are called the Prison Epistles. At least Ephesians, Colossians, and Philemon were written at the same time, because all three were sent with Tychicus (Eph. 6:21; Col. 4:7), who also brought Onesimus, the converted runaway slave, back to his owner, Philemon, in Colossae (Col. 4:9; Philem. 10–17).

While fulfilling his vow in Jerusalem, Paul caused a riot by mentioning his ministry from God to the Gentiles (21:27—24:27) and ended up spending two years in custody in Caesarea (Acts 25:27). He did not write the letters during this imprisonment, however. At his appeal as a Roman citizen (25:10–12), his trial was transferred to Rome, where he also was under house arrest for two years (28:30–31). It was during these two years, probably toward their close, as indicated by the fact that he was anticipating release (Philem. 22), that the letters were written, and the "whole praetorian guard" had learned that Paul's imprisonment was "in the cause of Christ" (Phil. 1:13). Paul was in prison in Rome a second time (2 Tim. 1:16–17) when he was not expecting release but death and glorious entrance into God's presence in heaven (4:6–8). The writing of Ephesians and the other Prison Epistles occurred, therefore, approximately AD 61.

J. Llewelyn Davies sees the letter to the Ephesians as showing forth lofty and grand truths. No one can read the epistle to the Ephesians without being awed by the particular eloquence, by the grandeur of conception, by the profound insight, by the blessedness of its inspiration. It would take heavy arguments to persuade anyone that it was written by someone else who wished it to pass off as Paul's. Within the lifetime of Paul, such a fraud would not have been attempted. Within a few years after his death, the difficulty of deceiving his friends and the church in such a matter would have been very great. At a later time, the high esteem in which Paul's writings were held would have ensured the careful scrutiny of any previous unknown work put forth in his name. And there are no signs that the genuineness of Ephesians was ever doubted in the church.[22]

## Theme

The overall themes of Ephesians are God's establishing the church and the believer's walk as part of it. The church is always seen as Christ's spiritual body. Certain facts of the life of Christ are taken for granted in Ephesians, including Christ's incarnation, death, resurrection, and ascension. His incarnation is hinted at in 4:9, and the cross receives relatively little attention. The ascension, however, is brought much more to the front (1:20–21; 2:6; 4:8–10).

In Galatians, the apostle spoke of believers being crucified or dying with Christ; this idea is still present in Colossians but is not found in Ephesians: here being raised with Christ is taken as already accomplished (2:6; so also in Col. 3:1) rather than as an event of the future. The soteriology of Ephesians is thus more realized than Galatians. In Galatians Paul appears to set himself up as the sole recipient of the revelation that God intends Gentiles as well as Jews to be redeemed; this stress on his position is continued in Ephesians, but the apostles and prophets are introduced as apparently equal recipients of that revelation.[23]

In previous letters of Paul, it is evident that he saw the whole cosmos as the object of God's redeeming love (Rom. 8:19–21; Phil. 2:9–11). This is more clearly revealed and presented in Ephesians. Thus, Christ is given a greater cosmic role in the book than in Paul's earlier epistles. It is interesting that the worldview presented in Ephesians is without a mention of a future judgment of the lost, whereas this is customary with Paul in other writings (e.g., Phil. 2:10). Paul's essential teaching on salvation through God's grace and not achieved by self works is presented in 2:8–10, but the terms used to express this are recast, and at one point "works" is used with a good sense and does not refer to any self effort for salvation.[24]

## Purpose

Earnest Best believes that because of the letter's general nature and the inability to tie it to any particular situation, the answers to the question of purpose have been many and diverse. Occasion and purpose are normally related, though there are exceptions. For example, Sunday requires a sermon from a minister; that is its occasion. The occasion remains the same throughout the year, yet the purpose of the sermon will vary from Sunday to Sunday, and at times its content and purpose will be determined by the Christian year.

Content and purpose can certainly be related. Concerning the book of Ephesians, lacking clues to its occasion, we have only its content from which to work and speculate. Different elements in the content are emphasized, making it possible for different purposes to emerge. As far as content goes, Ephesians contains two main elements: the first three chapters have a high theological content; the second three are largely practical. Ephesians 4:1 brings the two together with a change here from a prevailing indicative section to a *commandment* section with the implication, "God has been good to you; therefore be good to him and to your neighbor."[25]

Most commentators have emphasized the first, or theological, part. This may be due to their training, which leads them to think of theology as being more important than conduct. Exegesis, however, shows that the relation between the two parts points to a clear relation between the content of the doctrine and the content of living out of the Christian life. There is a tying together between how one lives the Christian experience as it relates to one's doctrinal belief system. Thus, there is an intimate connection between the two parts of this epistle. This factor is most important to keep in mind when considering the purpose of the letter.[26]

The behavioral emphasis of which Best speaks is a unity of believers through love, a topic emphasized in Ephesians. The noun and verb forms combined appear 20 times in the epistle. In all of Paul's epistles combined, the noun and verb forms of love appear 109 times, which means that about one-fifth of all appearances of this word occur in Ephesians.[27] Hoehner concludes: "This frequent use of love seems to furnish the key to the purpose of the book. Apparent are both God's love for people and the believers' love for one another within the new community. Love in action within the community of believers fosters unity, the other prominent theme. Unity without love is possible, but love without unity is not. Love is the central ingredient for true unity, laying the foundation for internal and external unity."[28]

# The Apostle Paul

Paul's life and ministry are also integral elements in the purpose of Ephesians. O'Brian points out that, on the one hand, Paul was well aware of the awesome privilege that had been given to him as the apostle to the Gentiles. His role as an apostle and as an accredited representative of Christ depended on the revelation of the Lord Jesus to him on the Damascus road (Gal. 1:15–17). And according to 2 Corinthians 3:7–4:6, this glorious ministry, with its revelation in the gospel, was an outreach of God's love to the entire world. Paul had been "called as an apostle, set apart for the gospel of God" (Rom. 1:1). As one who had received revelation and God's "grace and apostleship," his task was to bring about the obedience of faith among the Gentiles (Rom. 1:5; 15:18; 16:26), a role that held a significant place within the saving plan of God and had its warrant within the Old Testament Scriptures (notably Isaiah).[29]

With this in mind, it is not surprising, then, that in Ephesians, where the saving purposes of God are so magnificently presented, particularly regarding His "mystery" (Eph. 1:9–10), Paul's ministry to the Gentiles, should be a point of focus in relation to that same "mystery" (in 3:2–9 the term appears four times).[30]

# Section One

# ALL ONE IN GOD'S PLAN

## EPHESIANS 1:1–2:22

**CHAPTER 7**

# Blessings Obtained through Redemption
# Ephesians 1:1–23

## Preview:
*After greeting the Ephesians, Paul immediately launches into doctrine concerning the blessings believers receive through redemption in Christ. Then, after acknowledging their love for the saints, Paul details his prayers for the Ephesians, which leads into more doctrine.*

## Paul's Salutation (1:1–2)

Paul opens his letter by stating his name, something he does in all his letters with the exception of Hebrews if he was its author. He also identifies himself as "an apostle" (v. 1)—literally "sent one" but used here in the technical sense of one of those called and commissioned by Jesus Christ who had seen him after his resurrection (Acts 1:1–9, 13)—because of his encounter with the ascended Christ on the road to Damascus (Acts 9:3–6; Gal. 1:1) and his instruction in his message by revelation from Christ in Arabia (Gal. 1:12, 15–17). His commissioning was "by the will of God" (v. 1), a statement made in several other letters as well (1 Cor. 1:1; 2 Cor. 1:1; Col. 1:1; 2 Tim. 1:1).

The Greek word for "will" is *thelēma* and is used for either God's will or man's will.[1] God's will is infinite. His will does not vacillate or change direction. God is not reactionary, simply responding to what people do. This is a mystery, and it is impossible to fathom or fully grasp with the human mind.

This authority given to Paul is from the source of all authority. It has not been given by any earthly monarch or religious body, but by the Creator and Sustainer of the universe. God's will calling Paul forth as a servant began well before his birth (Gal. 1:15). He testified, "[God] had set me apart, even from my mother's womb, and called me through His grace." The Lord is the omniscient, omnipotent *Theos*, God. John Eadie writes: "For his was no daring or impious arrogation of the name and honours of the apostolate; and that 'will' according to which Paul became an apostle, had signally and suddenly evinced its origin and power. The great and extraordinary fact of his conversion involved in it both a qualification for the apostleship and a consecration to it."[2]

In the address of the letter, the phrase "in Ephesus" (v. 1) is missing in a couple of the earliest Greek manuscripts (B, Aleph). However, many scholars believe that "the inclusion of "in Ephesus" is supported as the best reading. Externally, it has excellent support in the date and character, geographical distribution, and genealogical relationships of the manuscripts. Internally, the inclusion of "at Ephesus" has good support in both the transcriptional and intrinsic probabilities.[3] If "at Ephesus" is omitted, the address reads, "To the saints [literally, 'holy ones'] . . . faithful in [or, 'ones believing in'] Christ Jesus" (v. 1). "The *sanctification* by God is put before man's *faith*."[4]

Every person who believes in Christ Jesus is a saint, or holy one (Gk., *hagios*), because he or she is viewed by God the Father as cleansed from all sin—past, present and future—by the shed sacrificial blood of Christ. This is the Greek word from which we get "holy," "sacred," and "saint." It means "dedicated," "consecrated," "set apart."[5] In this case, to be set apart, means to be set aside for God, for His use, for His glory, and for His purposes. All those in Christ are considered holy because of their relationship to Him and are thus to live holy lives. All Christians are saints and are to live in that reality. Hoehner says:

> With reference to believers the term [*hagios*] is used in three senses in the N.T. First, very few passages refer to the believer's personal sanctity (Rom. 12:1; Eph. 1:4; Col. 1:22; 1 Pet. 1:15–16). Second, a few instances refer to the believers as members of a spiritual community (1 Cor. 6:2; Eph. 1:18; 2:19; 3:18; Col. 1:12; 3:12; 1 Pet. 2:5, 9). Third, the overwhelmingly predominate use refers to members of a visible and local body (e.g., Acts 9:13, 32, 41; 26:10; Rom. 1:7; 15:26; 1 Cor. 1:2). The context determines its usage. Normally the term is in the plural and is one of the most frequent designations of the believers. When used of believers, it is always in the plural.[6]

Paul's opening benediction pronounces "Grace [unmerited favor] to you and peace [calmness of heart and mind] from God our Father and the Lord Jesus Christ" (v. 2). This is a standard greeting of the culture in Paul's day, but here the apostle is not simply being polite and formal. He really wants these qualities to bless the believer. They are aspects of the love of God that comes to each child of God. These qualities become the experience of the believing person through the ministry of the Holy Spirit, the third member of the tri-une Godhead.

## United in God's Choice (1:3–14)

Brooke Foss Westcott described verse 3 as "man's adoring response to God for the manifestation of his love. . . . The word *eulogētos* expresses the claim to be blessed as of right. In this respect it stands in contrast with *eulogēmenos*, which is used of a person who has been visited with blessing."[7] Hoehner says: "Praise to God was a characteristic component of Jewish prayer which became fixed toward the end of the first century A.D., in the *Shemoneh Esreh* or Eighteen Benedictions. They were recited three times daily in the synagogue, and each ended with the refrain, 'Blessed are you, O Lord.' Therefore, blessing God or calling God blessed is not something new to the people of the NT era."[8]

Paul began the doctrinal portion of his letter by pronouncing praise to God, who is the "Father of our Lord Jesus Christ" (v. 3) and our heavenly Father by faith in Christ as well. The reason for this is because he "has blessed us with every spiritual blessing in the heavenly places in Christ" (v. 3). Some have suggested that this should be translated "every blessing of the Spirit" to complete reference to the Trinity, but T. K. Abbott writes: "That these blessings proceed from the Holy Spirit is true, but that is not the signification of the word, which characterizes the nature of the blessings, not their source"[9]

The Greek words translated "blessed, blessing" are cognate with the word translated "praise," which could be translated "pronounce blessing on." The child of God can only give back to God a limited blessing. God does not need our accolades and pronouncements. He is sufficient in Himself, but He gives us the privilege of honoring Him for who He is. We are to in turn bless God because He blesses us. Charles Hodge observes:

> God is here designated as the God and Father of our Lord Jesus Christ. That is, he is at once God and Father, sustaining both these relations to Christ. Our Saviour used a similar form of expression when he said, "I ascend unto my Father and your Father; and to my God and your God." John 20:17. The God in whom the Israelites trusted was the God of *Abraham*, Isaac, and Jacob; their covenant God. This designation served to

remind the ancient people of God of his promise to their fathers, and of their peculiar consequent relationship to him.[10]

Two important aspects of this verse are: (1) that all believers have been given "every" spiritual blessing which God has to offer. This list cannot be comprehended by the human mind. It includes redemption, eternal life, freedom from pain, suffering, and so much more. Yet, believers today do not, and in Paul's day did not experience all of these blessings. This is because (2) all of these spiritual blessing reside in the "heavenly *places* in Christ." Two locational aspects are addressed here. The first concerns the position of believers before God. As Paul pointed out earlier, these Ephesian saints are "in Christ."

Positionally, before God, this is where believers reside, already redeemed in Christ, before God. This differs, of course, from the practical day-to-day working out of faith while sanctified here on earth. Just as believers are "in Christ," so too are all of the spiritual blessings God has for believers. Not that those in Christ don't experience blessings now, just that the full complement of blessings from God cannot be received this side of heaven. Once in His presence, the manifold blessings that are anticipated will be showered on every believer at the moment of final redemption.

Verse 4 starts with a Greek adverbial conjunction translated "just as." This conjunction is usually used in a comparative manner, suggesting that the way in which God conveys His blessings to believers is through all of the members of the Trinity. These spiritual blessings would be the Father electing, the Son redeeming, and the Holy Spirit sealing. Another consideration is that this conjunction sometimes has a causal sense, especially when used as a sentence introduction. This would give it a translation of "because" or "since." If taken in this sense, then, the Trinity would be the cause for every blessing stated in the previous verse.[11]

We bless or praise God because "He chose us in [Christ] before the foundation of the world [the Greek word *kosmos* means the world and the earth, though sometimes it refers to the world system], that we should be holy and blameless before Him" (v. 4). God had in his mind the goal of the plan from its beginning. From eternity past He had a plan that included our redemption carried out in time. This has to do with God's mysterious operation and plan in history. He chose the believer before this world was put into place. The expression "the foundation" means "the casting down of the earth." Hoehner rightly observes: "First, in most instances in the OT and NT, as it is here, God is the subject. Second, the subject did not choose in a vacuum but in the light of all known options. God chose 'us' from the whole human race. Third, there is no indication of any dislike towards those not chosen. It is not a rejection with disdain. The choice of Levi for the priesthood does not imply anything negative about the other tribes."[12]

When speaking of election, the Bible never contrasts it with reprobation. It only ever speaks of the ones who are chosen. It does not speak of those not chosen.[13] There is no indication in the New Testament of a "double predestination." In fact, just the opposite seems to be true. Paul, when speaking of the idea of election in Romans 9:14–24, indicates that God is waiting patiently for the lost to come to Him. But because of the power of sin and the rebellion of the human heart, none will come by their own accord. Paul writes that God "endured with much patience vessels of wrath prepared for destruction" (v. 22). He adds that God "prepared beforehand for glory" the elect (v. 23), but he never says that God "prepared beforehand" the lost for perdition. Hoehner continues: "Fourth, it is in the middle voice, as it is in almost every instance, indicating a personal interest in the one chosen. Hence, God chose with great personal interest rather than a random impersonal choice. Fifth, the one who is chosen has no legal claim on the one who chooses."[14]

Scripture makes it clear that no human being ever seeks God and that all fall short of His glory (Rom. 3:10–11). God was under no compulsion to choose any. There are none that are holy, thus having any type of legal claim which God would be required to honor.[15] Hoehner concludes: "On the contrary, all people are sinners and deserve rejection. There was no obligation on God's part to choose anyone, but he freely chose some, and this is evidence of his great grace. The point is that if God had not taken the initiative, no one would have his everlasting presence and life. The real problem is not why he had not chosen some, but why he chose any. No wonder God is to be praised."[16]

The manner in which God chose was unconditional. There were no conditions placed on God by which He had to make a decision or act in a certain way. He freely chose to bless all believers "with every spiritual blessing" in the same way that He freely "chose us in Him before the foundation of the world" (v. 4). In Greek the word for *"chose"* is *eklegō* and means to "call forth, speak forth," or "elect." He did this purely because it was His prerogative to do so. There is nothing in those who are saved that commended them by their own good deeds, or merits, that would cause the Lord to bring them to Himself. God did not look down through the ages and see decisions made by people to accept His Son as Savior and, on that condition, choose them before the foundation of the world. If that were so, if such an important point as a person's involvement in his or her own salvation were part of the salvific process, wouldn't Paul have made mention of it? Instead, he places salvation totally within the purview of God. This is an unconditional act on His part for His greater glory. Klyne Snodgrass says: "This is one of the most important texts on election in the Bible. Election is not some strange, unnecessary doctrine, but merely another way of speaking of God's grace and salvation. Words like 'chose' and 'predestined' underscore God's activity in setting apart a people for himself."[17]

"Before the foundation of the world" (v. 4) designates the time at which this election took place. As already mentioned, the Greek noun translated as "foundation" is actually a compound of two words that together mean "to throw down." To say that God "threw down" the earth, in the same sense that farmers throw down seed into the ground, or stones are thrown down to form the foundation of a building, speaks of His omnipotence,[18] the power that also supports His right to choose.

And God chose believers unconditionally so "that we should be holy and blameless before Him" (v. 4b). "Holy" means to be "set apart," "reserved for God and His service."[19] "Blameless" means to be unblemished morally, in the same manner as an animal was to be unblemished physically in order to be an acceptable sacrifice. Only a decision made by a holy, and pure God could result in a sinful man becoming "holy and blameless before Him." This holiness and blamelessness here is positional in nature. This is how He will present us in glory. A blemished man, an unsaved sinner, is unable to make himself clean before a holy God. As Job says, "Who can make the clean out of the unclean? No one!" (Job 14:4).

For the Christian, this must be viewed in two ways. First, positionally, in heaven before God, through Christ, believers stand as holy and blameless. However, practically, we are "working out" our salvation daily (Phil. 2:12). This is the process of sanctification that starts at salvation and continues in time as the child of God lives out his Christian life. This glorious election, a sovereign choosing by God, is not to be taken as license to live in any way imaginable. "Holy and blameless" should be the life objective and goal of every believer because of this great gift. "Holiness is the very purpose of our election. So ultimately the only evidence of election is a holy life."[20]

Greater clarification is given concerning God's intent and practice at the end of verse 4, carried over into verse 5, "In love He predestined us to adoption as sons through Jesus Christ to Himself, according to the kind intention of His will" (Eph. 1:4b–5a). Love is the cause of His predestination. The question is always asked, "But why those who never seem to care about God?" No one can answer why God's grace has come to them. No one is worthier than anyone else.

Once again, evidence is given of God's sovereignty. God's love qualifies His unconditional choice. "Predestined" (Gk. *Proorizō*) means "to decide upon beforehand."[21] Technically it means to "before encircle." In love, God decided which individuals would be adopted as sons, and this was done "according to the kind intention of His will" (v. 5b). No outside forces affected God's decision. It was His will and His will alone that made the decision. The vehicle used to accomplish this act was His Son, Jesus Christ.

"And the reason?" is a question that is often asked. If a holy, righteous, infinite, self-contained, and complete triune God was under no compulsion to effect this act of election, then why would He do so? The answer brackets the very act described. Verse 4 ends with the beginning of a new sentence that reads, "In love. . . ." First John 4:8, 16 tell us that "God is love." Everything God does, even His righteous judgments, involves His love. No requirements were placed on God to act. His first motivation was His love. The apostle gives the second reason in Ephesians 1:6: "to the praise of the glory of His grace." The genitives used in this phrase have generated much discussion as to their proper classification. The most consistent, is that which views the first as an "objective genitive of praise and the second . . . a genitive of quality . . . 'to the praise of the glory of his grace' . . . or 'to the praise of God's essential being for his gracious quality.'"[22] God here is being praised for His essence, His glory, for the graciousness shown in His choice to elect and predestine.[23] It is difficult for the finite human mind to see love in the act of predestination. The reason is that people cannot see their own spiritual lostness before a righteous and holy God. Humans are so self-satisfied in their sins that they cannot fully comprehend how a holy God is offended by sin and evil. God would be perfectly just to judge all people and offer none the blessedness of eternal salvation.

Most important for believers regarding this grace is that "He freely bestowed [the grace] on us in the Beloved" (v. 6). The Greek word for "bestowed" is *charitoō*, from *charis*, meaning "grace." In other words, God "graced" believers in the Beloved. *Charitoō* means to "grace, highly honor, or greatly favor."[24] Believers have been both "highly honored" and "greatly favored" by being placed in Christ, and also for continuing to be "in Christ."

Several things seem clear. God's election of people and His flowing grace for salvation are inseparably connected with God's warm and personal relation to Jesus Christ. And election cannot be separated from love—or else another election is spoken of than the one discussed in the overture to Ephesians.[25] Believers are now tied to the Lord Jesus Christ. They have an intimate spiritual relationship with Him. What is said of Him is in a certain sense passed on to the elect, though they certainly do not become deity or divine!

This position is a major theme in this first chapter of Ephesians. Paul emphasizes the many blessings of being "in" Christ (referenced eight times), not only in this age, but in the one to come (referenced three times).

"In Him we have redemption through His blood, the forgiveness of our trespasses, according to the riches of His grace, which He lavished upon us." (vv. 7–8a). Paul now states the spiritual mechanics, which once performed on the elect, make them "holy and blameless" before God. The opening phrase of verse 7 is not "In Him," as the NASB translates, but "In whom," a direct reference to "the Beloved," from the previous verse. Only through being "in" the sinless, perfect, Son of God, by God's grace, through the act of redemption, having their sins forgiven, may believers exist in the presence of God. Our Lord Jesus Christ is the center and circumference of God's eternal plan of salvation.

The basis for God's freedom to bestow his grace in love is the redemption that has been purchased through the sacrificial death of the blameless Lamb of God, the Lord Jesus, fulfilling the pattern of the Old Testament sacrifice without blemish, defect, or spot. The word "redemption" has the idea of deliverance upon payment of a price. The price for the payment of our sins was the shedding of Jesus' blood, securing "the forgiveness of our trespasses," which we have as a continuing possession. Hoehner observes: "The cost of Christ's blood is the measure of God's unmerited favor to every believer. It was accomplished not 'out of' but 'according to' (*kata*) the wealth of His grace (cf. Phil. 4:19). Six times in Ephesians Paul referred to God's riches (1:7, 18; 2:4, 7; 3:8, 16)."[26]

---

### *The Blessings of Redemption*

*Redemption is found only in Christ Jesus (Rom. 3:24).*

*Redemption is for the forgiveness of sins (Col. 1:14).*

*There is a future redemption of our bodies (Rom. 8:23; Eph. 1:14).*

*Final bodily redemption takes place at "the day of redemption" (Eph. 4:30).*

*The new covenant provides the redemption for transgressions (Heb. 9:15).*

---

The word translated "trespasses" is not the singular word, which means a sin nature, but a plural one, which means false steps or trespasses that are the expression of the sin nature. All this is "according to [not out of] the riches of His grace which He lavished [literally, 'made to abound'] upon us" (vv. 7b–8a). God also abundantly gave us "all wisdom [in the sense of intelligence or skill] and insight" (v. 8b) (in the sense of practical wisdom or prudence). The word "lavish" is important. It means "made to abound" or "to overflow." God pours forth His grace. It is more than enough to redeem and bring about forgiveness. Again, the key has to do with the fact that believers are now "in Christ," related to Him by the work of God. Believers are part of His spiritual body and draw their source for the new spiritual life from Him. This is a spiritual work and a mysterious work but not a mystical happening as that word often implies.

God also "made known to us the mystery of His will, according to His kind intention" (v. 9). In Scripture a "mystery" is a truth that has not been revealed in the past that is now revealed (see 3:3–6, 9). Henry Alford explains that "St. Paul ever represents the redemptive counsel of God as a mystery, i.e., a design hidden in his counsels, until revealed to mankind in and by Christ."[27] The work of Christ on the cross and the redemption that takes place in time was fashioned by the Lord as a plan to rescue lost human beings. We know this only by divine revelation. No one could have plotted or planned out such a blessing. God's justice concerning sin is not violated, and His grace is poured forth. But it is not cheapened nor commonplace. It is a costly grace. It required the death of the righteous Son of God. This truth was "purposed" in Christ in God's eternal plan "with a view to an administration suitable to the fulness of the times" (v. 10).

To more literally translate the Greek text, "When the dispensation [*oikonomian*, 'household management time period'] of the fullness [the word from which the English 'pleroma' is transliterated] of the seasons [time periods] are to be headed up in Christ." Salvation through the revelation of Christ came at just the right time. It was revealed when God was ready to accomplish redemption. But this redemption is large and expansive! It has universal consequences. This includes "things in the heavens and things upon the earth" (v. 10). God will set forth to the created heavens believers as His trophies of grace. Heavenly intelligence will have to ask, "How could God love and save such rebellious creatures?" This great show of mercy and grace will take place in Christ's millennial kingdom of righteousness and peace. John F. Walvoord explains: "The word *dispensation* does not in itself involve the concept of time, but the fact that one dispensation replaces another dispensation at a certain time suggests it. Thus dispensationalism refers to the view that God has administered the world in various stages of revelation and according to various principles or standards. Four times Paul used *oikonomia* of a divine stewardship or administration (Eph. 1:10; 3:2, 9; Col. 1:25)."[28]

At its beginning, the Beast and the False Prophet will be cast into the lake of fire (Rev. 19:20), all their unbelieving followers will be slain (vv. 17–18,

21), and Satan will be bound in the abyss for a thousand years (20:1–3a). Then believing martyrs of the Great Tribulation will be resurrected (v. 4) who, together with believers who live to the end of the Great Tribulation, will join the returning Christ and His church who were resurrected and caught up in the air at the Rapture (1 Thess. 4:13–18) to enter Christ's millennial kingdom. The millennial kingdom is the pleroma of the seasons, the period of time when "things in the heavens and things upon the earth" (Eph. 1:10) are headed up in Christ. At its close, Christ will "deliver up the kingdom to the God and Father, when He has abolished all rule and all authority and power. For He must reign until He has put all His enemies under His feet. The last enemy that will be abolished is death" (1 Cor. 15:24–26). "And when all things are subjected to Him, then the Son Himself also will be subjected to the One who subjected all things to Him, that God may be all in all" (v. 28). This will begin the eternal state. All things that are now happening in history are going toward that end. God will have the last say. A bright sinless day will dawn. The patterns of time will then make sense. Presently, there is sin and pain in the realm of humanity. But the promises of final and complete redemption will transpire.

In Ephesians 1:11 Paul returned to the theme of God's choice first mentioned in verse 4, but here he used a verb used only once in the New Testament, which means "chosen as an heir" instead of the normal verb that means simply "to choose." This verb is *klēroō* in Greek and means "to be appointed by lot."[29]

Since this is the only occurrence of this word in the New Testament, and its appearance in classical literature has various renderings, four differing views have been promoted concerning its meaning here in Ephesians. (1) This passive form of *klēroō* is actually functioning as if in the middle voice, being expressed as "we have obtained an inheritance" (e.g., NASB). This, however, does not agree with the other passives being used in this passage. (2) This is viewed as a simple passive, postulating that God chose in a manner as if He were using lots. This is expressed as "we were obtained by lot" (e.g., RSV). Words in the Greek language must be used in context. While the idea of "lots" is implied in the word, "chance happening salvation" is really not in view. While we never fully know why God does what He does, this does not mean that redemption is capricious, though from our limited human perspective we may think so. However, revelation will not let us go there!

Chrysostom addresses the meaning of *klēroō*, attempting to show that God did not choose by chance, since the following passage speaks of God's predestination of believers, which is also "according to . . . the counsel of His will" (v. 11). This view falls short, however, because it makes *klēroō* mean "to choose," and does not include the sense of a "part," or "lot," or "portion," as it should. One has to be clear that this passage isn't concerned with how the "lot" or "portion" was obtained, but with the substance of the portion. (3) The passive conveys the idea that believers are receiving a share of what God possesses, and could be expressed as "we were made partakers of the inheritance" (e.g., NEB). This view works well with the context regarding the believers receiving redemption and also having their sins forgiven, as well as where they receive the Holy Spirit's seal. (4) This passive form of *klēroō* views the believer as God's inheritance and could be expressed as "We were made a heritage [of God]" (e.g., ASV). This view draws its strength from the Old Testament references to Israel being God's possession or heritage.[30] Moses writes, "But the LORD has taken you [Israel] and brought you out of the iron furnace, from Egypt, to be a people for His own possession, as today" (Deut. 4:20), "to be His people, a treasured possession" (26:18).

Views 3 and 4 appear the best, with a few reasons giving preference to view 4. First, the usage is more consistent, because the topic regards being "assigned something." Second, it fits better with the following participle, translated as "having been predestined" (Eph. 1:11). With this use it is more sensible for believers to be predestined as God's possession than as their own possession (as would be recommended by view 3). Third, if this term is a referring to believers' possessing redemption, then having sins forgiven and being sealed by the Holy Spirit is redundant.[31]

Paul also uses the first person plural "we" with reference to himself and the other Jewish Christians in distinction from the second person plural "you" in verse 13 to identify the Ephesian and other gentile believers. The Jewish Christians were "predestined according to His purpose who works all things after [literally, 'according to'] the counsel of His will" (v. 11). The objective was that "we [Jewish believers] who were the first to hope in Christ should be to the praise of His glory" (v. 12). The Jews were the first to have salvation in Christ presented to them. Christ "came to His own, and those who were His own did not receive Him. But as many as received Him, to them He gave the right to become children of God" (John 1:11–12a). The Jews had the Old Testament revelations and prophecies that the Messiah would come, and that He would even die for their sins (Isa. 53). They had all of the evidence that He was the Promised One! Hodge adds:

> There are two sentiments with which the mind of the apostle was thoroughly imbued. The one is a sense of the absolute supremacy of God, and the other a corresponding sense of the dependence of man and the consequent conviction of the entirely gratuitous nature of all the benefits of redemption. . . . In the present instance, having said we have in Christ

obtained a glorious inheritance, the question suggests itself, Why? His answer is: *Having been predestinated according to the purpose of Him who worketh all things after the counsel of his own will.* It is neither by chance nor by our own desert or efforts, that we, and not others, have been thus highly favoured.[32]

The Ephesian and other gentile believers also were included in God's eternal purpose and plan centered "in Him . . . after listening to the message of truth, the gospel of your salvation" (Eph. 1:13). Paul takes them back to their starting point, their rebirth and the process by which it took place. First they had to hear and listen. Divine election and predestination are God's mysterious works, yet those who are saved are not robots. There is the reaching up by faith, prompted by the Spirit of God, that activates salvation (2 Thess. 2:13). Believers can truly say that they are chosen by God; but they also can say they exercised personal faith in Christ by a conscious decision. There is a process, an order, a sequence in time that brings about salvation in the individual. Some have put it this way: one side of the door says, "Whosoever may come," and the other side says, "Chosen before the foundation of the world." Both are true and both are absolute in the Scriptures. "So faith *comes* from hearing, and hearing by the word of Christ" (Rom. 10:17). Then, having heard, they need to believe: "Believe in the Lord Jesus, and you shall be saved" (Acts 16:31).

When the lost believe, they are "sealed in Him with the Holy Spirit of promise" (Eph. 1:13). This seal (4:30) is evidence of ownership and insures protection (2 Cor. 1:22). Sealing occurs the moment a person trusts in Christ. Both Peter and Paul make it clear that, although the Jewish believers had priority over gentile believers in trusting Christ and receiving the seal of the Holy Spirit, they did not have superiority, only equality: we are all one in Christ (Gal. 3:28; Eph. 4:4–6).

The work of salvation is a miracle of history. It changed the course of world events. The coming of Christ and His death, resurrection, and ascension brought history into another chapter. By the thousands men and women came to Christ, especially throughout the Roman world and known civilization. Many Jews, too, initially believed in Christ, though many rejected God's grace revealed through Israel's Messiah. The course of the world was set in another direction. This work could not be stopped. The "sealing" accomplished by the Holy Spirit (who is the seal Himself) would transform individuals and produce a new class of humanity—those who are in Christ. "The word 'seal' . . . is often used figuratively for the act or token of authentication, confirmation, proof, security or possession. . . . In the NT the main ideas in the figure are those of authentication, ratification, and security. . . . God by His Spirit indicates who are his, as the owner sets his seal on his property."[33]

Hoehner adds:

> In this context the sealing refers to ownership. . . . Many think this refers to baptism (or possibly confirmation), denoting identification. This idea is derived from Rom. 4:11 where it refers to Abraham's circumcision as a seal of his righteousness. It is thought that this is transferred to baptism for the Christian. Although there may have been some church fathers who made this deduction, it is a great leap and really foreign not only to this context but to the whole NT.[34]

In this closing statement, Paul returns to the first person plural, identifying for all believers the Holy Spirit as "a pledge of our inheritance, with a view to the redemption of God's own possession" (Eph. 1:14). Once again, as in verse 10, Paul uses the phrase "with a view." This is an appropriate translation of the preposition *eis*, as denoting time. *Eis* is a Greek preposition that speaks primarily of movement toward something, thus "with a view," Paul is speaking once again of the future. In this case, however, it is the future of every believer, both Jew and Gentile, when their redemption is fully realized and the inheritance is gained, that is, when the seal of promise through the Holy Spirit is no longer required. The seal secures the guarantee of salvation. The seal cannot be removed or changed. It is a "governmental" sign of what God is going to do. His "property," the believer, is secured and belongs to Him.

This also, as all of God's plan and its execution, is "to the praise of His glory" (v. 14). Always, and in all things, especially in salvation, God receives the glory! He is the author of redemption. He conceived of the plan, sent His Son to carry out the plan, and then applies its gracious effects to the elect. No expenditure of human effort or energy could bring about salvation. It is totally the work of a sovereign God. And no human beings could have devised such a perfect master plan. This is why He alone receives the glory and the honor.

Although the NASB divides this section into six sentences, Hoehner points out that verses 3–14 form "one sentence . . . considered by some scholars to be the most cumbersome sentence in the Greek language!"[35] He continues to observe that "Ephesians has eight lengthy sentences (1:3–14, 15–23; 2:1–7; 3:1–13, 14–19; 4:1–7, 11–16; 6:14–20)."[36] Paul obviously was impressed with the marvelous expressions of the details of God's eternal plan and its outworking centered in Christ. The apostle could not stop his thoughts about the wonderous workings of the Lord in redemption and just kept on writing. It is as if he did not know where to end the flow in describing the blessings of God to lost humanity. God's work of grace is an eternal work and requires special and unique thoughts to try to communicate what He has done.

All commentators agree that this section is one of the most complete and comprehensive parts of the Word of God describing the work of salvation. The human side of faith is hardly mentioned. The work of God is amplified and explained with as much detail as the human mind can grasp.

## United in Paul's Prayers (1:15–23)

The apostle opens this section of verses with arguing for a purpose for his writing. He gives the introductory *berakah,* or eulogy. He then reports his thanksgiving (vv. 15–16a) and intercession for his readers (vv. 16b–19). Paul mentions his unending gratitude to God for the good news he has received about the Ephesians, and he assures them that he constantly intercedes for them. Peter O'Brien says: "The thanksgiving is linked syntactically with the eulogy: *For this reason it* probably refers to the whole of the eulogy, but especially to vv. 13 and 14, where mention was made of the gentile readers ('and you') being drawn into the sphere of God's saving purposes. Paul, 'for his part' ('I also'), has painted the broad sweep of God's magnificent plan; now he turns to offer thanks to God for what he has heard about the readers."[37]

God's choice of the Ephesian believers and their response in faith to the gospel was the basis for Paul's continuing thanksgiving and prayer for them. This faithful intercession also was motivated by the report Paul received not only of their faith but also of their "love for all the saints" [literally, 'holy ones,' i.e., as viewed by God in Christ]" (v. 15). His statement that he was not stopping his thanksgiving and prayers for them does not mean he was constantly praying but only that he had not dropped them but remembered them in his frequent daily prayers (v. 16). Paul really had this church on the top of his prayer list. The believers there were strategic to that region and to the continual spreading of the gospel. Ephesus was an important city, and whatever came out of it would have a social and spiritual impact. The apostle knew this and was counting on their faithfulness in sending for the truth. Eadie explains: "The apostle gave thanks, and his thanks ended in prayer. As he blessed God for what they had enjoyed, he implored that they should enjoy more. He *thanked* for their faith and hope, and he *prayed* as he looked into the future."[38]

He made a similar statement of continuing thanksgiving and prayer for the receiving groups in many of his letters (Rom. 1:8–10; 1 Cor. 1:4; Phil. 1:3–6; Col. 1:3, 9; 1 Thess. 1:2–3; 2 Thess. 1:11–12; 2 Tim. 1:3; Philem. 4–6). A significant part of Paul's ministry was his prayers for his churches and undoubtedly for all Christians of his day. It must have been satisfying for him to see how quickly the gospel was moving forward. Of course there was pain involved because of the deep opposition of both the Jews and the Gentiles. This was part of the reason he was praying so consistently and diligently. O'Brian adds: "The apostle's rich intercessory prayer is directed to *the God of our Lord Jesus Christ*, who is also called 'the Father of glory.' This full title, which has a liturgical ring to it, is a variation on the opening address of the eulogy (v. 3), with the notion of the divine fatherhood being expanded and emphasized. The first predicate, *the God of our Lord Jesus Christ*, seems specifically intended to recall the similar address in the *berakah*."[39]

Paul is directing his petition to the God who has *already* blessed all believers in the Lord Jesus Christ (Eph. 1:3). This means that any prayer then offered to Him, asking that those blessings be realized in the lives of believers, may be done so in full confidence and expectation.[40] O'Brian continues: "Since the apostle's usual designation is 'the God and Father of our Lord Jesus Christ' (v. 3), the second title 'the Father of glory' breaks the sequence and is specifically emphasized. This suggestion finds support in the closely related prayer of Ephesians 3:14–19, where God is humbly addressed as 'Father' and then identified as the one 'from whom every family in heaven and on earth derives its name' (vv. 14–15)."[41]

Hoehner adds:

> Paul's petition for the Ephesian believers was *"that the God of our Lord Jesus Christ, the Father of glory, may give to you a spirit* (literally, "a spirit" in the sense of an attitude) *of wisdom and revelation."* All Christians have the Holy Spirit from the moment of faith in Christ and, therefore, Paul does not need to pray for God to give them the Holy Spirit. Not all Christians, however, have a spirit or attitude of wisdom and revelation; therefore, a prayer for them to receive such a spirit is appropriate. For only through the Holy Spirit can a person obtain such a spirit.[42]

The reason for having such a spirit is that the believer in Ephesus may have "knowledge of Him" (v. 17). To have such a spirit should be the desire and goal of every child of God. By *spirit* Paul is referring to one's deportment, attitude, and mental frame of mind. But more, what does it mean to have a spirit or attitude of wisdom and revelation regarding the knowledge of God? A spirit of wisdom gives one insight into things—in this case, the knowledge of God. The Holy Spirit will give a believer a spirit that can deeply understand God as revealed through His Word. But what does Paul mean when he speaks of this "revelation"?

The Greek *apokalupsis* means to uncover, disclose, or unveil. As a believer grows in the knowledge of God through His Word, the Holy Spirit reveals more, and more insight is gained. This is not revelation or knowledge about secular issues such as chemistry or physics! This has to do with spiritual issues, about what God is doing with the believer—even a knowledge of Himself! Also, as the believer grows in knowledge, he is enabled to reveal more truth to others. This is a continual process that causes some commentators to place the revelation before the wisdom in their analysis of this verse. Whichever way this is interpreted, the process continues and the believer grows in the knowledge of God. To grow spiritually is what the Lord is after. He wants maturity and insight to flourish and blossom. The believer needs to be in close fellowship and in touch with His God and His Savior.

Therefore, Paul prays and asks that God would give the Holy Spirit's insight and disclosure in the realm or area of the knowledge of God Himself. This lines up with 1 Corinthians 2:10–16, where the Holy Spirit searches the deep things of God and reveals them to the believer. The deep things of God are God's wisdom and power to change individuals through the crucified Christ. This should not be something theoretical but real and practical. Hoehner adds:

> In the present context he believer is to come to know him intimately and as a result the believer will become acquainted with God's actions described in the following verses. Hence, it is not facts about God that are most important but knowing him personally and intimately. . . .

> Thus, one acquires this knowledge of God not only by facts from the Bible but by the Holy Spirit's giving insight and disclosure in the knowledge of God himself. In the end, philosophy says, "Know yourself," whereas Christianity says, "Know your God, through the Holy Spirit."[43]

What follows is a continuation of Paul's prayer. Literally translated it reads "the eyes of your heart having been enlightened unto your knowing the hope of his calling, what is the fullness of the glory of his inheritance in the saints and what is the surpassing greatness of his power unto us, the believing ones" (vv. 18–19a). "Not merely God's calling in the past, and God's inheritance in the future," J. Armitage Robinson notes, "but also God's power in the present. Of the first two he has said much already; on the third he will now enlarge."[44] While this is Paul's great desire, that believers truly have a deep spiritual understanding about their relationship with the Lord, this is rarely achieved by the average Christian. The world gets in the way, sin does its dirty deed, and carnality and strife and bitterness can rule. But what a high and lofty ideal the apostle sets forth. He wishes this knowledge of God would impact the minds and hearts of every child of God. R. C. H. Lenski adds:

Now the power which guarantees the final bestowal of this inheritance in the fulfillment of our hope. This power is beyond question God's omnipotence, but it is viewed by Paul, not abstractly, but concretely in regard to what this omnipotence has already done in the exaltation of Christ. It is well to remember that, as the humiliation pertained to Christ's human nature, so also does his exaltation. He who has so exalted Christ, he guarantees our inheritance, the fulfillment of our hope of glory.[45]

It is essential to Paul that the Ephesians understand the "surpassing greatness of His power," which is effective "toward us who believe" (v. 19). God's power is greater than anything which may seek to nullify the hope of believers, or that may seek to stop the bestowing of "the riches of the glory of His inheritance" (v. 18).[46] Lenski continues: "When we know the excessive greatness of this power, nothing will ever disturb our hope. Other men also hope; alas, their hopes are built on air, there is no power to fulfill their hopes, to bestow that for which they hope. God's power is only 'for us the believing ones,' for us who trust him and in that trust hope."[47]

The example of this power of God is what He demonstrated in the resurrection of Christ. It also involved God's seating Christ at his right hand in the heavenly realms "far above all rule and authority, power and dominion, and every title that can be given not only in the present age, but also in the one to come" (vv. 19–20; Ps. 110:1–2). This rule will be over all human agencies and governments as well as angelic and demonic forces (Eph. 1:21). God the Father will bestow this authority in its completeness when the Lord Jesus returns to earth to establish the Daividic kingdom.

---

### Christ Is Now Seated in Heaven

*After His sacrifice for sins, Christ was seated by the Majesty on high (Heb. 1:3).*

*He was seated at the right hand of the Father (Ps. 110:1).*

*He was seated after enduring the cross (Heb. 12:2).*

*He was seat in the heavens as a high priest (Heb. 8:1).*

*Stephen, before being martyred, saw Christ standing at the right hand of God (Acts 7:56).*

*Believers are to seek the things above, where Christ is seated (Col. 3:1).*

*Believers are seen as having been raised up and seated with Christ in the heavenlies (Eph. 2:6).*

*From His seat in heaven, will someday come in the clouds with power (Matt. 26:64).*

After having conceptually described God's power, Paul in these last verses is now giving examples of this power in operation.[48]

The first example given of God's power is Christ's resurrection from the dead. This is the ultimate expression of power. While Scripture gives examples of God's awesome power to destroy and defeat, human beings also exhibit certain great abilities. Resurrection power, however, belongs to God alone. This power is from God and takes no notice at all of obstacles, just as Jesus rose from the dead, paying no attention to the stone, to the decrees of Caesar, to the fulminations of the Jewish priests, nor to the guard in front of the tomb. Resurrection authority does not pay any attention to obstacles. It surges on ahead and leaves the problems to God. From the earthly perspective there is no greater work than Christ's resurrection from the dead. And this power will someday work in the lives of all believers to bring them forth from the grave. There is nothing so marvelous in the natural realm than resurrection from the dead. It defies all logic, all natural laws, but it is the absolute promised miracle from a miracle-performing God! The Lord Jesus Christ is the first from the grave and is the pattern and the hope for all trusting in Him! Ray Stedman says: "Resurrection power requires no outside support. It doesn't rely upon someone else, nor upon something else. It doesn't need a vote of confidence. It doesn't require any kind of undergirding expressions of support from anybody. It can operate alone, completely alone, if necessary. And it makes no noise or display. It doesn't try to arrest attention by some publicity stunt. It effects its transformation quietly, bringing life out of death."[49]

The second example given of God's power follows the resurrection, when God seats Jesus at His right hand, "far above all rule and authority and power and dominion" (Eph. 1:20–21) as prophesied in Psalm 110:1–2 and Daniel 7:13–27. This was understood by Paul's audience as being a position of power and complete trust, as it was the practice of reigning earthly monarchs as illustrated in history for centuries. Since most people are right-handed, whoever a monarch chose to sit at his right hand, that person had control over the monarch's movements with that hand. In other words, if a traitor was sitting at the king's right hand, he could reach over to stab the king while stopping the king's hand from defending himself by blocking the attack or grabbing his own sword or knife. This is why only the most loyal and trustworthy person was allowed to sit at the king's "right hand."

The complementary verse to this passage in Ephesians is, as already mentioned, Psalm 110:1, where God says to Jesus, the coming Messiah, "Sit at My right hand, until I make Thine enemies a footstool for Thy feet." This prophecy is fulfilled at the victory of Armageddon and the beginning of the millennial reign of Christ (Rev. 19:12–16, cf. Matt. 25:31–46). Presently, however, Jesus is sitting at the right hand of the Father, acting as the Intercessor for the child of God. Christ is now the High Priest in heaven for the believer. He holds this priesthood forever and permanently (Heb. 7:24). "He is able to save forever those who draw near to God through Him, since He always lives to make intercession for them" (v. 25). John the apostle adds that He is the believer's Advocate, the Righteous One, who stands before the Father continually pleading our case (1 John 2:1).

Although there are many spirit beings now in the heavenlies (deceased believers and angelic beings), only Christ has been given the exalted position to sit at the Father's right hand. This position "displays sovereignty at the present time and indicates his authority over the world and the church."[50] By His providence He is leading all things to their final conclusion. Yet this authority now is not absolute because of the manifestation of sin. But someday it will be total and absolute. The writer of Hebrews continues on: "We do not yet see all things subjected to him" (Heb. 2:8b). Someday soon that will change!

Christ now holds the preeminent position described in Ephesians 1:21. Four different levels of authority are listed in this verse: "rule," "authority," "power," and "dominion." The first, translated "rule," is a Greek word that always indicates primacy, being in first place. It is used in the New Testament to speak of both spiritual and secular leaders, as well as angelic leaders, which is most likely the meaning in this context.[51]

The second term, translated "authority," speaks in the Greek of having the right or the freedom to act. In the New Testament, it is singular in form and often refers to "governments," while its plural form speaks of secular or spiritual leaders as well as evil spiritual powers. In the context of verse 21, angelic authority is considered its most likely meaning.[52]

The third word, translated "power," is in Greek the word from which we get "dynamite." Hoehner says: "It consistently has reference to the abstract sense of power; although the present context seems to be a bit more concrete and thus could refer to human power, although more likely it is a reference to angelic power that is subject to Christ's power."[53]

The fourth word, translated "dominion," is a rarely used Greek word. It is hardly used outside of the New Testament, and within the New Testament occurs only four times (Eph. 1:21; Col. 1:16; 2 Pet. 2:10; Jude 8). It refers to the "essential nature" of a ruler, his "majestic power."[54] In this context, once again, the best reference is to a specific angelic power.[55] By such references the apostle is going beyond the earthly realm and is telling readers that there are universal powers and forces they cannot see. This is the unseen realm of angelic beings. They operate in ranks and legions. They are not seen by the human eye, though often their work (even the evil deeds of the realm of the fallen angels) is made manifest. The sinfulness of humans is seen openly, but behind the dominion of evil, wicked spiritual beings are at work.

Some commentators do not believe that these forces are angelic only. Thus there is much debate over the specific nature of these four authorities, whether they are human or angelic and, if angelic, whether they are good angels, evil angels, or both. Taken within the context of Paul's message to the Ephesians, it appears most likely that these are all references to angelic beings, specifically those of an evil nature.[56] Hoehner concurs:

> These powers most likely are angelic and evil and wish to rob us of our spiritual benefits. The point is clear that Christ is over these authorities and they will not have the final victory. The struggle between God and these evil powers is real, and in the present day the battle rages between these angelic powers and believers, individually and corporately. The central point of this passage is that believers have the power that raised and seated Christ far above every power: We are to appropriate that power in light of the spiritual warfare that is portrayed in chapter 6.[57]

After discussing these four types of angelic authority, Paul ends Ephesians 1:21 with the statement, "and every name that is named, not only in this age, but also in the one to come." Since God is the subject of the verb in this entire passage, He is the One designating the names and placing Christ above each name. We see examples of this in Scripture. In the Old Testament, God changed the names of Abram (Gen. 17:5) and Jacob (Gen. 32:28), as well as giving names to the stars (Ps. 147:4). So, here in Ephesians, Paul is basically saying that any and every name which God cites (including the previously named angelic authorities), will be under the authority of Christ.[58]

Paul sums up by saying that God "put all things in subjection under His feet" (v. 22). This includes Christ's appointment as "head over all things to the church, which is His body," (vv. 22–23a), which in turn is "the fullness of Him who fills all in all." Later, and in other letters (e.g., 1 Cor. 12:12–27), Paul will develop this truth of Christ as the head of the church and the church as His own spiritual body. Once again the entire section (vv. 15–23) in the Greek text is one complex sentence, because the truths are interrelated as part of Paul's prayer.

In the lengthy paragraph that follows Paul's magnificent eulogy (vv. 3–14), he reports his thanks to God for the readers (vv. 15–16a) and his intercession for the realization of the blessings in their lives (vv. 16b–19). The apostle employs confessional thoughts in which God is praised for exercising His mighty power in raising Christ from the dead and exalting Him to be head over all things for (concerning, in regard to) the church (vv. 20–23). O'Brien concludes: "Once again, there is a theological, christological, and ecclesiological focus in the passage. Paul wants his readers to understand and appreciate the divine salvation, and in particular the place which they as God's people have in the divine purposes."[59]

Paul wants it to be clear that what has been done in Christ is beneficial to his readers. The availability of God's power, in Him, for those who believe (v. 19), as well as Christ's rule over the universe, is for their benefit (v. 22). This knowledge should allow these predominantly gentile Christians in Asia Minor, living with the pressures of their pagan surroundings, to take heart because of what God has done, graciously and powerfully, through His Son on their behalf.[60]

In the final verse in this chapter, what does the apostle Paul mean when he says that the church "is His body, the fullness of Him, who fills all in all" (v. 23)? The best explanation is that God fills the church with the fullness of moral excellence and power. Christ is the agent who fills the church as opposed to the relationship of God to the saints or to the church. Thus it is that the apostle's prayer is founded on the basis that God has now enriched all believers with every spiritual blessing for spiritual well-being. Paul asks in his prayer that every child of God have a deeper walk with these spiritual benefits.

## Study Questions

1. Where are the blessings the believer has already received located?

2. What did God purpose believers to be when He chose us in Christ from before creation?

3. What quality of God's character is preeminently displayed through His redemption in His Beloved One?

4. In these verses what is described as the "mystery of His will"?

5. What happened to the Ephesian believers upon believing in Christ?

6. What caused Paul to ceaselessly give thanks and pray for the Ephesian believers?

7. What requests did Paul make for them in his prayers?

# CHAPTER 8

# From Death to Life in Christ
# Ephesians 2:1-22

### Preview:

*Paul explains how we are saved by faith alone, through grace given to us as a free gift from God. This gift came through His Son, Jesus, to those who were yet enemies of God—those who had no hope and were separated from Christ.*

## United as God's New Creation (2:1-10)

After his glorious report at the end of chapter 1 of the position and role of Jesus Christ, now seated in the heavenlies at the right hand of the Father, Paul returns with a chilling blow of experiential truth for the Ephesians: "And you were dead in your trespasses and sins" (v. 1). The importance of this verse cannot be underestimated, for many today teach that all unsaved people possess enough grace to make their own choice regarding salvation. They may choose "for" or "against" it. They are not totally dead in their sins but have just enough life to grab the offer of salvation by their own strength.

Contrary to this teaching, Paul states, "and you were dead" (v. 1). This Greek phrase, *ontas nekrous*, is a present, active participle. It draws its reference as occurring in the past from the first phrase of verse 2. Here it is saying, "continually existing in a state of being dead" (spiritually). This is not an occasional state or one occurring with great frequency. It is a continual state for unbelievers—one from which they cannot break free. Why? Because they are dead, *nekros*. This does not mean "almost dead" or "barely alive." This means "dead," as in, "on the slab, in the morgue," dead. A dead person cannot reach for anything and does not understand or seek anything (Rom. 3:11). Harold Hoehner explains: "Death signifies absence of communication with the living. One who is dead spiritually has no communication with God; he is separated from God"[1] This is why God's election of believers in eternity past was His free choice. He did not look down through the ages and see anyone making a choice for His Son. All He could see was what was there—total, spiritual death; physically animated humans with no ability, no understanding, and no desire to know Him or His Son. Only by His love, through His grace, would some be chosen for eternal life.

Humankind is in such a state because they are dead in "trespasses and sins" (v. 1). This harks back to Adam in Genesis 2:17 and following. With sin came total, spiritual death. This death separates man from God, man from other men, man from himself, and man from the rest of creation. The unsaved world has tried to create answers, even entire fields of study, to address all of these issues, but their solutions cannot provide the answers needed. Only a restoration of the proper relationship with God will answer all of humankind's needs. This issue of the deadness of humanity is often debated. Certainly, physical death is not in view except in the sense that people are under the curse and finally face biological death at some point. Does it refer to spiritual and moral death only? Does it mean that people cannot make choices that bring them to God? Deadness here seems to mean just that—a complete and total inability to respond to spiritual things.

In these violations of God's commandments and expressions of their sinful nature they "formerly walked [literally, "to walk around," transliterated into English as 'perambulate']" (v. 2), according to "the course [literally, 'periods of time', transliterated into English as *'eons'*] of this world" (v. 2).

This phrase, "according to the course of this world" (v. 2), addresses two interlinking thoughts. This actual "age" is one of evil and darkness. This "world" is the secular culture that has structured itself apart from God, wanting no relationship with Him. So both of these words refer to an entire societal system foreign to God.[2] And it is energized by Satan himself. Christ said that Satan is the father of those who practice gross evil. He is a murderer from the beginning "and does not stand in the truth, because there is no truth in him" (John 8:44). John Stott observes about the world:

> It permeates, indeed dominates, non-Christian society and holds people in captivity. Wherever human beings are being dehumanized—by political oppression or bureaucratic tyranny, by an outlook that is secular (repudiating God), amoral (repudiating absolutes) or materialistic (glorifying the consumer market), by poverty, hunger or unemployment, by

racial discrimination, or by any form of injustice—there we can detect the sub-human values of "this age" and "this world."[3]

Ephesians 2:2 continues, "according to the prince of the power (literally, "areas of authority") of the air," the Greek noun signifying the lower air immediately surrounding the earth in distinction from the word that signifies the atmosphere of the moon and stars. The devil is the *"spirit* [angelic being] that is now working [literally, 'energizing,' the Greek word transliterating into English as 'energy'] in the sons of disobedience" (v. 2) (which began with Adam's disobedience in the Garden of Eden). There is a sense in which an unsaved person can say, "The devil made me do it," because with cunning he energizes every unregenerate person. But the Bible never allows human beings to simply pass the buck, to deny personal responsibility. Sinners sin willfully and wholeheartedly. People enjoy sinning. It gives power and authority to the self and elevates the personal will over and against God's will.

Humanity is culpable for wrongdoing. In the final analysis, people know when they sin. At the end of World War II, both the Japanese and German leaders knew they would have to face an accounting for their crimes. Some tried to justify their evil actions but in the end had to face their just punishment.

This evil ruler Satan is in control of *the kingdom of the air*. Here, as in Colossians 1:13, the word rendered *kingdom* denotes the "realm" or "sphere" of the devil's influence rather than his personal authority. That realm is further defined as the "air." According to the ancient worldview, the air formed the intermediate sphere between earth and heaven. Peter O'Brien adds:

> It was the dwelling place of evil spirits (as the magical papyri and the literature of Judaism attest), not an atmosphere of opinion with ideas, attitudes, and the like, which is a more recent Western understanding. The "kingdom of the air," then, is another way of indicating the "heavenly realm," which, according to Ephesians 6:12, is the abode of those principalities and powers, the "world-rulers of this darkness" and "spiritual forces of wickedness," against which the people of Christ wage war.[4]

There is a notion that has its antecedents in the Old Testament and Jewish thought that hostile powers inhabit the heavens (cf. Eph. 3:10; 6:12). If any distinction is to be made between the expressions "kingdom of the air" and "the heavenly realm," it is that the former speaks of "the lower reaches of that realm and therefore emphasizes the proximity of this evil power and his influence over the world."[5]

Paul then offers a confession that was undoubtedly hard to make (see Phil. 3:4–6). A literal translation of Ephesians 2:3 reads, "Among them we too all formerly lived in the lusts of our flesh (the word signifies the sinful nature of unregenerate humankind), indulging the desires of the flesh and of the mind and were by nature children of wrath even as the rest" (cf. Rom. 2:1–3:20). Some believe that here Paul is making a distinction between himself and his companions as Jews, and the Ephesians as Gentiles. A. Skevington Wood points out: "Paul has been depicting the former lifestyle of gentile Christians. Now he admits that Jewish believers were no better, for they too once 'lived' an earth-bound life in the grip of sin. Nor does he exclude himself from this general indictment (cf. 'all of us'), despite his claim to have been technically blameless under the law (Phil. 3:6; but cf. Rom. 7:7–11)."[6]

However, others believe that Paul is not striking a comparison of Jew and Gentile, but is rather contrasting himself as the writer, with the Ephesians as his audience. Hoehner says:

> The addition of "all" creates an insuperable objection against "we" as referring only to the Jews. All humans in the unregenerate state are in the same condition of rebellion against God. Furthermore, does the use of the first person plural in verses 4–7 and 10 mean that only Jews are the objects of God's love and workmanship? Moreover, the use of the second person plural in verses 5 and 8 "does not imply that only Gentiles need to be saved by grace!" It is best, therefore, not to make this distinction between Jews and Gentiles on the basis of pronouns. It is not until verse 11 that Paul makes a distinction between Jews and Gentiles.[7]

Paul points out that he, before being saved, lived as the others, "in the lusts of our flesh, indulging the desires of the flesh and of the mind" (v. 3). The Jew was no better than the Gentile, except he could cover his sins with religion and outward morality. This is what the story of the woman taken in adultery is all about (John 8:1–11). The Jews pretended "perfection," but Christ revealed their sin when He told the leaders, "He who is without sin among you, let him be the first to throw a stone at her" (v. 7). Guilt came to the surface and one by one, beginning with the older leaders, they departed and left the woman alone (v. 9).

Paul clearly points out in Ephesians 2:3 that "living" in the lusts of the flesh is carried out by "indulging" those lustful desires. The Greek word translated as "indulging" is a participle that literally means "doing." The participle speaks of an action that is continually ongoing. This is what differentiates the unregenerate sinner from the believer who sins. The believer may sin, but his sin is not of a continual ongoing nature. The unregenerate person's sin is continually ongoing because he can do nothing but sin unless or until the Holy Spirit changes his life. Hoehner concludes:

Hence, the unregenerate does the wishes of the flesh and of the reasoning processes, showing that it is more than an occasional lapse but rather a deliberate or premeditated activity of flesh and the mind. The participle "doing" is the outward manifestation of the inward wishes of the flesh and thoughts. This coincides with Paul's assertion that human beings used the reasoning processes to reject God and consequently they became futile in their thinking and their senseless minds became darkened. Though they thought they were wise, they became fools (Rom. 1:21–22) and used their reasoning process to rationalize their sinful activity (2:15). Hence, unbelievers were not only confronted by the external satanic powers but also the internal powerful desires of the flesh.[8]

Paul then sums up his argument by concluding that all of this sinful behavior was due to his nature as an unregenerate sinner, the nature shared by all who are unsaved, that of being "children of wrath" (Eph. 2:3). This is not referring to some type of inherent wrath boiling up in the life of the unregenerate sinner. This means children existing under the wrath of God because of their unregenerated sin nature. However, it can actually mean more. The thought from the apostle is that human beings by birth are solely characterized and constructed as sinners. Their physical humanness comes from God. That is, all who are born come forth because God is their creator. But the sin tendency within comes from the fall of Adam when he revolted and disobeyed Him.

Hoehner, however, puts it another way and believes that this genitive form of "wrath," rather than being descriptive, is to be considered like a genitive of direction or purpose, being understood as, "The unregenerate are children destined to God's wrath." This could be the case. Hoehner then concludes with this powerful insight: "What a horrible dilemma. It is saying that unbelievers have a close relationship to God's wrath rather than to God himself."[9]

After painting the dark picture of humankind's lost state in their sinful nature under the devil's dominion, Paul turns on the light of God's love and grace in salvation through Jesus Christ. A literal translation reads, "But God, being rich in mercy, on account of his great love with which he loved us, even when we were dead in trespasses, made us alive together with Christ" (Eph. 2:4–5). This is the turning point in the apostle's argument. Grace now comes into the picture. God becomes the Savior of humanity by sending His Son to be the Savior! That is, God is the Savior in that He is the One who fashioned the salvation plan. Christ came into the realm of humanity, took on flesh, and died for the race. This sacrifice is then applied to the elect. T. K. Abbott comments that Paul's "view then is that God has made believers alive with Christ;

that is, by virtue of the dynamic connection of Christ with His believers as the Head with its body, their revivification is objectively included in His. . . . The apostle therefore views this as having already taken place, although the subjective individual participation remains future."[10]

God's motivation was purely His own sense of mercy and love. There was (and is) nothing within humankind that deserves any kind consideration from a just and holy God. Humankind is totally depraved and deserving of only condemnation. It is only God's intentional and undeserved mercy and love that brought us salvation. The word translated here in verse 4 as love is *agapē*, the highest form of love. It is the type of love in which one considers another before considering himself. God "chose" to provide a solution for sinful humans when He was under no compulsion to do so. Jesus "chose" to suffer and die as that solution for sinful humans when He was under no compulsion to do so. Salvation is all of God and is an expression of His gracious mercy and love.

The apostle Paul writes about this love in so many places in his letters. He writes in Titus 3:4–6: "But when the kindness of God our Savior and His love for mankind appeared, He saved us, not on the basis of deeds which we have done in righteousness, but according to His mercy, by the washing of regeneration and renewing by the Holy Spirit, whom He poured out upon us richly through Jesus Christ our Savior."

At this point Paul cannot contain his excitement and interjects, "By grace you have been saved, (Eph. 2:5b), a clause repeated in verse 8, with the added note that it is "by faith." Hoehner offers grammatical insight into this passage and shows that the passive voice is labeled by some grammarians and scholars as a divine passive where God is without doubt the subject. Sinners are being saved and brought to Christ by God's gracious act of redemption. The perfect tense expresses a completed and final action with continuing results that comes into the present time. The completed action occurred at the moment of their conversion. Here what is called in Greek the perfect periphrastic intensifies the present results of being saved. Hoehner comments:

> Although it could be translated "you have been saved" . . . the translation "you are saved" . . . better conveys the continuing results of being saved. In other words, God, by his grace, initially saves, but by that same grace he keeps believers safe or saved from God's wrath and from sin's grip of death from which they are delivered. On the other hand, one must not think that the perfect tense in itself guarantees future deliverance. It is the God behind the perfect tense that guarantees the future deliverance.[11]

Paul writes that God's great love caused him to make believers "alive together with Christ (by grace you have been saved), and raised us up with Him, and seated us with Him in the heavenly places in Christ Jesus" (Eph. 2:5–6). The Greek verbs translated as "raised us up," and "seated us," are both active, aorist verbs, which emphasize the absolute quality of these promises. It also emphasizes the "position" of each believer in Christ, right now, in the heavenlies. Although, experientially, believers are still working out their salvation here on earth, positionally the perfection of the believer has already taken place.

Just as important is living in the reality of that promise as a part of the heavenly community of God and Christ Jesus while yet here on earth in the midst of the sphere Satan rules. Our spiritual life with God is the conduit of all blessings received.[12] How would Christians be living without this saving work of God? What He has done not only gives an eternal blessing, an eternal salvation, but comes forth by the Holy Spirit in a new way to live. Yet Christians do not walk perfectly. Carnality (fleshliness) comes out and believers can often look like the lost in their walk (1 Cor. 3:1–3). This is why it is important for the child of God to grow up and mature so that sinful and harmful things may slough off in the Christian experience.

The future destiny of believers in God's presence in heaven is irrevocably certain because God sees them there now as a result of their faith in Christ. God's purpose in the salvation of lost men and women through faith in Christ is "in order that in the ages to come He might show the surpassing riches of His grace in kindness toward us in Christ Jesus." (Eph. 2:7). This verse is incomprehensible to the human mind. How can we process the thought of eternity? Yet God has created entire new persons for those now abiding in Christ. The old will pass away. This system is judged and will be destroyed. However, the believer will face an eternity walking with his Lord!

Christ explained it well to Martha at the occasion of the death of Lazarus. He told her "I am the resurrection and the life; he who believes in Me shall live even if he dies, and everyone who lives and believes in Me shall never die" (John 11:25–26). Two truths stand out in His words. Though a believer may physically die, that person still shall not die! Death is merely the entrance into the eternal state. The believer will receive a new resurrection body that is eternal, imperishable, and impervious to sin.

Summing up, in light of the human race's past condition and God gracious, loving redemption through Jesus Christ, Paul wrote that "by grace you have been saved through faith." (Eph. 2:8). He made it clear that salvation is "not of yourselves, it is the gift of God."

Some Christians consider the faith as God's gift, others the grace, implying that the person passively waits until God provides the faith and grace. In the Greek text, however, the word translated "that" (*touto*) is neuter, while the words translated "faith" and "grace" are both feminine. As a result, the "that" refers to the total work of salvation provided by God through Christ. This is not an unusual grammatical occurrence. There are numerous examples in Ephesians alone. "For example, in 1:15 *touto* refers back to the contents of 1:3–14, in 3:1 it refers back to 2:11–22, and in 3:14 it refers back to 3:1–13."[13] To emphasize the elimination of any kind of human effort, Brooke Foss Westcott writes that salvation "is not the result of a natural evolution of character, and yet more, it is not the result of self-originated and self-supported effort."[14]

Lenski comments on the grace and faith issue: "One often meets careless statements such as: 'Grace is God's part, faith ours.' Now the simple fact is that even in human relations faith and confidence are produced in us by others, by what they are and what they do; we never produce it ourselves. Even deceivers know that they must cunningly make their deceptions of such a nature that they may appear true and grand, and that they may thus produce faith in those whom they wish to deceive."[15]

Faith is never self-produced; faith is created in us. The faith that saves is created by the saving grace of God. Believers receive salvation "by means of faith." Faith is the trustful reception created in us by God, and this reception alone. It is distinguished from the subsequent activity of gratitude and works resulting from faith. Because of this, faith is essential. God brings about the faith, and the faith is an act of the will that lays claim to Christ's work on the cross for redemption. Those who trust Christ do so willingly; they are not simply robots with no consciousness as to the decision made. The work of the Holy Spirit in conversion, and faith, are but part of the processes that transpire in time (2 Thess. 2:13), though the person redeemed has been marked for salvation from eternity past (Eph. 1:4–5). From the human level, the person who does not believe is lost because he does not by faith receive the salvation he ought to receive.[16] And yet the divine work of redemption is absolutely essential in the cause of salvation.

Paul concludes by writing, "For we are His workmanship" (2:10)—what a wonderful summation of the believer's life! "For we are His [God's] workmanship," His *poiēma*. This Greek word means "a work, something made, the result of work"[17] (also the basis of our English word *poem*). And this was not work done to an object already alive spiritually, for we were dead in trespasses and sins. This work was done to a new creature, (2 Cor. 5:17), one who is "created in Christ Jesus for good works." The Greek word for "created" (*ktizō*) is also used in the LXX to speak of God's creation of the human race (Deut. 4:32). What Paul is describing is the re-creation of a human being in Christ Jesus, whereby that person becomes a believer. Grace is so awesome! It fashions a new life. It does not simply "reconstitute" or "remake" a new coat from old cloth. The child of God is now a completely new creature spiritually speaking, created for good works—"good works" from God's perspective, not from the world's viewpoint. Good works are not simply good acts. The good works Paul is describing have to do with what is done for God, for higher spiritual purposes.

---

### Salvation Is by Grace

*Believers have received grace (John 1:16).*

*Grace comes through the Lord Jesus Christ (John 1:17).*

*Believers are justified freely by grace (Rom. 3:24).*

*Believers are no longer under law, but under grace (Rom. 6:15).*

*Believers are called into the grace of Christ (Gal. 1:6).*

*Believers can come boldly unto the throne of grace (Heb. 4:16).*

*Hearts are established by grace (Heb. 13:9).*

*Believers are the heirs of the grace of life (Tit. 3:7).*

*God is the God of all grace (1 Pet. 5:10).*

---

And just as all believers were chosen by God in eternity past, so were these "works" prepared as well, emphasizing the totality of God's plan with those who are redeemed. He not only freely chose the elect, but also designed the good works they would then perform after being saved.

These verses make it clear that a plan is being carried out. Redemption of the lost brings about changed lives, and goodness begins to flow forth all planned and orchestrated by God! While there is evil in the world, there are no accidents or incidental happenings. God is in charge, and He knows where he is going with His divine plan.

This verse also answers another criticism. Stott explains: "Some critics have always . . . supposed that Paul's doctrine of salvation by grace alone actually encourages us to continue in sin. They are entirely mistaken. Good works are indispensable to salvation—not as its ground or means, however, but as its consequence and evidence."[18]

# United as God's People, Temple (2:11–22)

Within the context of the book of Ephesians as a whole, 2:11–22 stands as a kind of parallel to the preceding paragraph. In 2:1–10 the apostle Paul has reminded his gentile Christian readers of the awesome and dramatic change that the Lord had effected in raising them from death to new life in Christ. Now here in this latter passage the "once—now" expression appears again (vv. 11–13, 19). This time, however, providing a contrast in more specific terms: the readers' past is expressed in relation to Israel's previous privileged position in the saving plan of God, while the present is revealed in terms of their being brought near to God "through the blood of Christ" and to one another (gentile and Jewish believers) in Him.[19]

Verses 1–10 and 11–22 follow directly from 1:15–23, where Paul prays, hoping that those reading his letter might have a greater appreciation of God's power, which He had exercised on their behalf.[20]

At this point, with his "Therefore," Paul begins to summarize all the truth he has presented so far in chapter 2, in fact, in the entire letter. He reminds his primarily gentile "in the flesh" readers of the titles given them by Jews: frequently "gentile dogs" and always "uncircumcised" (v. 11). To be of the uncircumcised was a great blight on the gentile world. It not only conveyed a physical uncleanness but also a spiritual rejection by God. To be uncircumcised was the greatest description of ignominy the Jew could use to put forth a curse. Many Jews would ask, How could God love such people? By way of contrast and distinction, the Jews called themselves "the circumcision." Hoehner points out that "the Gentiles' lack of the external sign of circumcision also meant that they lacked five privileges that God had given the nation Israel,"[21] which are listed in verse 12.

Paul is not just speaking slightingly of circumcision, for he well knows that it was given by God to serve as the covenant sign from the days of Abraham onward (Rom. 4:11). Therefore it had to be clear that He was truly turning away His blessing and placing it upon the larger world of Gentiles.

Lenski points out that this function of circumcision, however, had ceased when the redemption was accomplished by Christ. Physical circumcision was not commanded by God for salvation. In fact, it never was. The Jews still sought to maintain it by their empty formalism and despised the "foreskin," which to a degree pointed to the Gentiles. "Paul thus speaks of foreskin and circumcision as being only a physical distinction, 'manmade' by the Jews, now artificial and thus valueless. Yet even then the distinction still indicated one thing, namely, that the 'foreskin,' the Gentiles, had never, like the Jews, been in contact with the saving institutions of God."[22]

This is the fact that Paul wants the gentile believers in Ephesus to remember because it is so meaningful to them personally when they consider what God has done for them. The Jewish believers in Ephesus will also hear Paul's message to their fellow gentile believers and praise God for the riches of His grace, which even reached out to the "foreskin." Paul is careful, however, to remove all occasion for pride among the Jewish believers, for their circumcision, as it is now only something handmade and of the flesh.[23]

Paul made it clear that this circumcision was "performed in the flesh by human hands" (v. 11), because elsewhere he emphasized the need for "circumcision . . . of the heart, by the Spirit" (Rom. 2:29; Phil. 3:3; Col. 2:11).

Here in Ephesians 2:11, Paul addresses the "former" position of the Gentiles who were now saved members of the Ephesian church. He calls for the Gentiles to remember again their old position before the revelation of salvation in Christ for both Jew and Gentile. Paul may have had in mind that the Gentiles would soon become arrogant about their position in Christ and look down at the Jews for their national rejection of the Lord. In other words, the Gentiles may have seen themselves on top and the Jews now on the bottom. The pagan Gentiles were once despised by the Jews, but the two now should be one in the spiritual body of Christ!

In time, history would be witness to a great tragedy in the church. Fewer and fewer Jews would come to Christ, and the Gentiles in the church would look down upon the Jews with great disdain and hatred. "Christendom" would become the instrument of violent persecution and use the excuse that the Jews were "Christ killers" in order to justify this hatred.

In verse 12 the apostle gives three specific details concerning the lost state of the Gentiles in the past. Their "lostness" was real. They were cut off from the revelations and the blessings of God. (1) They were separate from Christ. They were given no revelation of His coming to redeem humanity. However, the most recent revelation in God's plan for the human race had been the first advent of the Savior, the Christ. Still, He had come first to the Jew, then to the Gentile (Rom. 1:16). So, after Jesus had revealed God's plan for salvation, died, and risen again, the first who had heard were the Jews, who were also the first to believe and be saved. John the apostle made this clear when he wrote, "He came to His own, and those who were His own did not receive Him" (John 1:11). And there was a promise in Isaiah 9:2 that God would bring salvation to the Gentiles. The elder prophet Simeon, when he saw the baby Jesus, said "My eyes have seen Thy salvation, which Thou hast prepared in the presence of all peoples, 'A light of revelation to the Gentiles, and the glory of Thy people Israel'" (Luke 2:30–32).

Even before those events, however, the Gentiles had been separated from an acceptable relationship with God because they were (2) excluded from the commonwealth of Israel. During the dispensation of the Law, only the Jews were given the moral, civil, and ceremonial commandments to keep in order to be acceptable to God. These were not shared with the Gentiles. Only by becoming a proselyte, turning to the God of Israel, and being circumcised could a Gentile enter into an acceptable relationship with God during that period (Exod. 12:48).

Prior to the dispensation of the Law, reaching all the way back to the time of Abraham, Gentiles were excluded from having a proper relationship with God because (3) they were strangers to the covenants of promise. These covenants were first instituted by God with Abraham and included the promise of multitudes of descendants (Gen. 12:2; 13:16; 15:5), a land that his descendants would own forever (Gen. 13:14–15, 17; 15:7), and a legacy of blessing to all the families of the earth (Gen.12:3). Each of these provisions was expanded in future covenants made with Israel.

So, since the time of God's scattering of humanity at the Tower of Babel (Genesis 10), the time when God decided to stop treating all peoples as one homogeneous group, and called out a specific group—the descendants of Abraham through Isaac and Jacob—the remainder of humankind, the Gentiles, had "no hope" and had been "without God in the world." (Eph. 2:12). "Without God in the world" was a terrible indictment of Paul against the Gentiles. It conjures up hopelessness, helplessness, lostness, and rejection by God. Earlier theologians termed these descriptives "total depravity." God would by His sovereign grace re-reveal Himself through one people, the Jews. And it would be through them that He would at some time in history bring salvation to the gentile populations of the world.

With the coming of the gospel for all, there has been a change: "now in Christ Jesus you who formerly were far off have been brought near by the blood of Christ" (v. 13). A blessed program of redemption is now revealed to both the Jews and the Gentiles. There is no difference between these two classes during this new dispensation. The theocracy of Israel has been set aside, and God's grace is set forth for all humanity. The Gentiles were once far away from the Lord, but now the blood of Christ shed on the cross is the uniting factor. All who come to Him and believe that He died for their sins—both Jews and Gentiles—become children of God.

This was accomplished by the fact that Jesus Christ "is our peace" and has "made both groups into one" (Jewish believers and gentile believers) by destroying "the barrier of the dividing wall" (v. 14). A barrier stretched across the court in the temple in Jerusalem bearing an inscription prohibiting gentile worshippers from passing. One of the pillars of this "dividing wall" was excavated in 1871. It reads in Greek: "No man of another nation is to enter within this fence and enclosure round the temple. And whoever is caught will have himself to blame that his death ensues"[24] Paul used this architectural fact about the temple courtyard to reinforce the spiritual reality that Gentiles were truly cut off from God.

And because of their understanding of temple sacrifice and ceremony, the Jews certainly would have understood the expression in verse 13, "by the blood of Christ." They knew that redemption was accomplished only by the shed blood of a sacrificial animal. Christ become that sacrifice, and by its acceptance, both Jew and Gentile could be redeemed from sin and be graced with salvation.

Paul had been accused of violating the regulation of bringing Gentiles into the temple area with Trophimus (Acts 21:28b–29). Gentiles were permitted to convert to the Jewish faith but were considered inferior and not given equal rights and privileges. This was achieved "by abolishing in His flesh the enmity, which is the Law of commandments contained in ordinances" (Eph. 2:15). The ceremonial Mosaic Law denoted "the actual, existing enmity of Israel and non-Israel." John Eadie points out: "It was this hatred which rose like a party wall, and kept both races at a distance. Deep hostility lay in their bosoms; the Jew looked down with supercilious contempt upon the Gentile, and the Gentile reciprocated and scowled upon the Jews as a haughty and heartless bigot."[25]

In the Old Testament era the Jew fulfilled the law to the extent of his ability and secured temporary atonement for his sins from God and maintained fellowship with God by presenting the designated offerings in unconscious anticipation of Jesus Christ's final, perfect redemptive sacrifice for human sin (as a principle) and human sins (in particular). The purpose of Christ by His sacrificial death on the cross was "that in Himself He might make the two [Jew and Gentile], into one new man, thus establishing peace" (v. 15). Christ's objective was that He "might reconcile them both in one body to God through the cross" (v. 16).

Now that Christ has broken down the dividing wall of the Law and has joined together both Jew and Gentile, He can be about the work of reconciling them both to God. The "enmity" mentioned in verse 15 was between the Jews and the Gentiles. This "enmity" however, in verse 16, is that which stands between a holy God and sinful man. Neither case of enmity was one-sided. Just as both Jews and Gentiles hated each other, so too, man hated God and was rebellious, while God hated man's sin and held him under wrath and its condemnation. The elimination of both examples of enmity would require Christ's death on the cross to provide access to God for all humankind through His blood, thus making all people equal. His death would pay for the sins of everyone, regardless of being Jew or Gentile. By His death and expiation, accepted by God, the hostility between humanity and God comes to an end.

It is inconceivable that such a wonderful plan could be imagined by the human mind! The Bible, from Genesis to Revelation, gives us the unfolding revelation of a masterpiece of grace and mercy for the sinful human race. Salvation alone is a truth to bring praise to the Lord. There was no other way that redemption could be accomplished. Christ had to go to the cross for human salvation. Stott summarizes:

> This, then, was the achievement of Christ's cross. First, he abolished the law (its ceremonial regulations and moral condemnation) as a divisive instrument separating men from God and Jews from Gentiles. Secondly, he created a single new humanity out of its two former deep divisions, making peace between them. Thirdly, he reconciled this new united humanity to God, having killed through the cross all the hostility between us. Christ crucified has thus brought into being nothing less than a new, united human race, united in itself and united to its creator.[26]

This new "united human race" of which Stott speaks is, of course, not all of humanity. It is the church, the spiritual body of Christ. Jew and Gentile are now "reconciled" into this one body "to God through the cross" (Eph. 2:16).

With his coming he "preached peace to you who were far away and peace to those who were near" (v. 17; cf. Isa. 57:19). By way of prophetic support from the Old Testament for his thesis, Paul quotes the prophet Isaiah. In the quote, those who were "far away" were the Gentiles, and those who "were near" were the Jews. This passage comes from a section in Isaiah's prophecy (chaps. 54–57) where he speaks of God's Servant bringing salvation. The first section speaks of the salvation that will come to Israel; the second section, the salvation that will come to proselytes. Then, the section from which Paul quotes speaks of blessings that will be extended to Gentiles in the Millennium. When Christ returns to rule on earth, following Armageddon, when He has established peace throughout the world, the offer of peace with Christ will be extended to all the nations of the earth—those both *near* and *far*. While the Old Testament made it clear that the Gentiles would someday be offered salvation, no one could have conceived the way God would do this in the church. The ultimate redemption is still millennial. The church is but a parenthesis that shows that for now there is a postponement until God restores Israel back to the Promised Land.

However, through His divine insight, the Holy Spirit has shown Paul that this prophecy of redemption is also presently applicable in his explanation to the Ephesians regarding the joining of Jew and Gentile in one body, the church, though the church itself was never revealed in the Old Testament. That both Jew and Gentile would be so united in the same body would never have been understood. It must be remembered how far-off Gentiles were in morality and spirituality from the revelations the Jews enjoyed.

The present reality of the church is that in Christ "we both have our access in one Spirit to the Father" (Eph. 2:18). In Paul's reference to believers' "access . . . to the Father," A. R. Fausset and others noted that "there is allusion to the Introducer in Eastern courts: Jesus is our Bringer to God (1 Pet. 3:18)."[27] It depends on each individual to seize that access through faith in Christ's redemptive death on the cross, the efficacy of which was validated by God the Father by Christ's resurrection from the grave and his ascension to the Father's right hand in heaven. And that access is now open to both Jew and Gentile. Many believing Jews struggled with this wonderful revelation. This struggle was part of the context in the Jerusalem Council (Acts 15:1–18).

The doctrine of the Trinity is brought out in Ephesians 2:18. Hoehner, as many other commentators, called attention to the fact that "often in this book the work of the Trinity is seen. Here believers have access to God the Father through the Holy Spirit because of Christ's death on the cross"[28] The Son, the Holy Spirit, and God the Father are all mentioned in this verse. Each has a different function in the salvation process. The Trinity is defined as one God existing in three persons. This doctrine was opposed in the late second and early third century by a cult known as Monarchianism or Modalism. Modalism rejected the Trinity and simply said that the identity of persons is just a different way of describing God at any given moment. Or, God had different names—Father, Son, and Spirit—describing the different roles He played at different times. But the grammar of Scripture makes it clear that there are three distinct persons described as God—God the Father, God the Son, and God the Holy Spirit. The persons in the Godhead are complimentary and communicate with one another.

Paul goes on and describes the blessings and benefits now given to the Gentiles. The result when he wrote and now is that "you (gentile believers then and now) are no longer strangers and aliens, but you are fellow citizens with the saints (literally, "the holy ones," so designated as seen in Christ by God the Father) and are of God's household" (v. 19). Wood explains: "Two technical terms commonly denoting inferiority of status are contrasted with 'fellow citizens.' 'Foreigners' refers in particular to short-term transients; 'aliens' to those who had settled in a country of their choice. The latter were sojourners who received protection and legal status by paying a small tax, though they had no intrinsic rights."[29]

As such believers are "built upon the foundation of the apostles and prophets" (v. 20). Since prophets are listed following apostles, church age prophets are in view (cf. 3:5; 4:11; 1 Cor. 12:10, 28–29). For this building made up of believers in Christ, He is "the cornerstone." In the ancient building one properly squared stone was placed first at one corner, from which the entire foundation was laid out and the building constructed upon it. Fulfilling that graphic picture of the church, in Christ "the whole building being fitted together is growing into a holy temple in the Lord" (Eph. 2:21). This includes the Ephesian believers, who "also are being built together into a dwelling of God in the Spirit" (v. 22).

Some scholars try to argue that the church has been inserted into Israel. They somehow fold Israel and the church together, or argue that in some mysterious way the church is a new Israel. But this section (2:11–3:12) is not an argument for that position. The church is something brand-new, with both Jews and Gentiles as believers in Christ. Paul shows that "both groups are placed into one" with "the barrier of the dividing wall" broken down. There "two are made into one new man" and are placed "in one body," with "one access in one Spirit to the Father." There is now a new "household," a "whole building," being fitted together . . . growing into a holy temple in the Lord." Jew and Gentile now constitute a new building, a new structure. Hoehner concludes: "Paul has shown that though the Gentiles were formerly outside God's household, they are now one 'new man' with Jewish believers. This new entity is like a temple that is structured on the apostles and prophets, with Christ being the chief Cornerstone; it is indwelt by God through the agency of the Holy Spirit."[30]

Even today believers in Christ "as living stones, are being built up as a spiritual house" (1 Pet. 2:5).

## Study Questions

1. How does Paul describe the unregenerate condition of the Ephesians?

2. Who was the unknown motivator of their unregenerate manner of life?

3. What did God do for believers while they were still spiritually dead?

4. What is God's purpose in the salvation of human beings?

5. What does Paul call believers in relationship to God?

6. What were Gentiles called before they believed, and what was their position?

7. In his death on the cross, what did Christ do with regard to that separation between Jews and Gentiles?

# Section Two

# ALL ONE IN GOD'S PROVISION

## *EPHESIANS 3:1–4:16*

# CHAPTER 9

# The Stewardship Given to Paul
# Ephesians 3:1–21

## Preview:

*Now that Paul has explained how the Ephesian Gentiles have been saved through faith in Christ, he addresses the bigger picture of Gentile salvation in general. This dispensation is the age of grace, or the church age. Paul explains that it had been a mystery in times past, only now being revealed by God.*

## Paul's Reception of the Mystery (3:1–6)

After telling the gentile believers in the city of Ephesus to keep in mind what they once were and what God has now made of them by His grace, in particular that they together with all other believers (the Jews) are built together for a dwelling place of God, Paul continues by bringing to their minds his own great part in this work of God among the Gentiles (vv. 1–13). He reminds them of the intercession in prayer he continues to offer for them. He then reminds them of what he prays for and states its contents (vv. 14–21).

R. C. H. Lenski offers these thoughts regarding Paul's work: "Although he has been absent from Ephesus for about five years, Paul's inward connection with his readers is as close as it ever was when he worked in their midst. While he still addresses the gentile Christians (2:11), all that he says in both parts of this chapter has its great significance also for the Jewish Christians in Ephesus. In fact, in vv. 15 and 18 he also draws them in, for in his mind he ever sees the *Una Sancta* as a whole."[1]

Paul opened this sentence by tying it back with "For this reason" (v. 1) to what had been written in the preceding paragraph, if not in the letter, because he had in effect set forth the content of the mystery. He mentioned himself by name and described himself as "the prisoner of Christ Jesus for the sake of you Gentiles" (v. 1). Paul was a prisoner of Rome literally, but in the true sense he was imprisoned because of his ministry of the gospel to Gentiles. A. R. Fausset writes that Paul "marks Jesus' Messiahship as the origin of his being a 'prisoner,' owing to the jealousy of the Jews being roused at his preaching it to the Gentiles."[2]

Paul's entire ministry was a continual war between the Jewish and gentile factions. The gospel was always an object of contention and derision on both sides of the fence. But because he had seen the risen Christ on the road to Damascus, there was no turning back for the apostle. The reality of the Lord and His resurrection could not be disputed in his mind. He knew what he had experienced, and he was certain of the truth.

Charles Hodge points out that Paul's mission was to the Gentiles. It was with a special reference to them that he had received his calling and the gifts that went with that commission. When the Lord Jesus Christ appeared to him on his journey on the Damascus road, He said to him in so many words: "I have appeared to you for this purpose, to make you a minister and witness both of these things which you have seen and witnessed, and of those things by which I will appear unto you. I will deliver you from the people and from the Gentiles, to whom I am sending you, to open their eyes, and to turn them from darkness to light, and from the power of Satan unto God, that they may receive forgiveness of sins, and that they may have an inheritance among those who are sanctified by faith in Me" (Acts 26:16–18).[3]

Paul claims for himself "the stewardship [literally, *'economy* [house-rule]' or *dispensation*] of God's grace which was given to [him] for you [the Ephesians and other Gentiles, see Gal. 2:7–8]" (Eph. 3:2). This is called "the mystery of Christ" (Eph. 3:4), which is explained, "to be specific, that the Gentiles are fellow heirs and fellow members of the body, and fellow partakers of the promise in Christ Jesus through the gospel" (Eph. 3:6).

Paul here defines the gentile believers' participation, in this new dispensation, in three distinct areas, all of which were new to the Jewish believers. The Jews knew that the Gentiles would be blessed. This was foretold in the Abrahamic covenant (Gen. 12:3). However, here they learn that gentile believers are to be (1) "fellow heirs" (Eph. 3:6). This means an inheritance of some kind, but it is not to be mistaken for the land inheritance given to the Jews, which was also first promised in the Abrahamic covenant (Gen. 12:7). That was a promise made to Abraham and his descendants through Isaac, and through Jacob exclusively (those specific tribes that would make up the nation of Israel).

This inheritance is part of the overall participation plan, which includes the gentile believers being (2) "fellow members of the body," and (3) "fellow partakers of the promise of Christ Jesus through the gospel" (Eph. 3:6). Verse 5 clarifies the importance of this new revelation. Some argue that the church was actually revealed in the Old Testament but that knowledge was simply clouded and not fully understood. But this is not the case. Language could not be any more obvious that the revelation of the church was not made known until now: "revealed to His holy apostles and prophets in the Spirit." The *prophets* here would have to be the New Testament prophets and not of the Old. Something brand-new had begun. The messianic kingdom had been set aside but not obliterated in God's mind. God would restart the kingdom program with the Jews and someday bring them back to the land as promised. But for now the church age is what some call "the dispensation of grace."

All Jews and Gentiles who accept Christ as Savior become part of a new entity: the church, the living body of Christ. This inheritance is of those things now given to the church (v. 6). It covers all benefits that are in addition to salvation ("partakers of the promise of Christ through the gospel"), because in this new entity, Gentiles are *equal* with Jews in the sight of God ("fellow members of the body"). And it relates specifically to the promises mentioned by Paul earlier in 1:11, 14 and 18.

Moreover, since Jesus was a Jew and is the Jewish Messiah, the fulfillment of the Law, as well as the Christ of the Gentiles, this new entity, the church, gives Gentiles a new relationship with the Jews and Israel. Paul makes this very clear in Romans 11:17, speaking of the Gentiles being "wild olive" branches grafted in with the natural branches (the Jews). Gentiles in Christ must have a tender heart for God's chosen people (Deut. 14:2), those who are the "apple of His eye" (Zech. 2:8), for Israel's rejection is temporary. A remnant will be restored (Isa. 10:21–22; Rom. 9:27).

It is impossible to make these Old Testament verses and promises refer to anything else but to the Jewish people. For now the church is made up of Jews and Gentiles, but the day is coming when the Lord will restore the fortunes of Israel and bring about the promised messianic kingdom. This is what Peter had in mind when he spoke to his Jewish brothers following the miracle of Pentecost. Peter did not know God's timetable and thought that it was possible that if the Jews repented, the messianic kingdom could begin. "Repent . . . in order that times of refreshing may come from the presence of the Lord; and that He may send Jesus, the Christ appointed for you, whom heaven must receive until the period of restoration of all things about which God spoke by the mouth of His holy prophets from ancient times" (Acts 3:19–21). The Jews listening to him would have interpreted this as the promised messianic earthly reign of Christ, the son of David.

Meanwhile, for now, this truth about the present church age is called a mystery, not because it is hard to understand, but because it, as already shown, "in other generations was not made known to the sons of men, as it is has now been revealed to His holy apostles and prophets in the Spirit" (Eph. 3:5). Paul did not claim to be the exclusive recipient of the revelation of this mystery but its administrator to the Gentiles. Paul's statement "as I wrote before in brief" (v. 3) probably refers to his presenting the content of the truth earlier in this letter (2:11–22) without identifying it as "the mystery of Christ."

The dispensation of the church age began a new chapter in world history, not simply in sacred history. The world would never be the same. And very quickly the gospel would miraculously spread to the most important corners of civilization at that time. Some have speculated that it went all the way to the borders of Afghanistan, to Africa, and to the British Isles. This gospel included the salvation message for both Jews and Gentiles. No one could have imagined how far and wide the gospel of the grace of God could have spread in such a rapid manner.

### The "Mysteries" of the New Testament

Jesus revealed the mysteries of His kingdom to His followers (Matt. 13:11; Mark 4:11; Luke 8:10).

Salvation is from God's mysterious wisdom (1 Cor. 2:7).

The rapture of the church is called a mystery (1 Cor. 15:51).

The gospel is said to be a mystery (Eph. 6:19).

Sin and iniquity are called a mystery (2 Thess. 2:7).

Believers are urged to "hold fast" to the mystery of the faith (1 Tim. 3:9).

God's final work in history is called a mystery (Rev. 10:7).

Babylon the great harlot is described as a "mystery" (Rev. 17:5, 7).

## Paul's Ministry of the Mystery (3:7–14)

Paul wrote that he "was made a minister [*diakonos*, the basis for the English *deacon*] of the gospel" (v. 7). This was God's gift to him "according to the working of His power." Although on one hand Paul claimed for himself his full authority and prerogatives as a true apostle of Jesus Christ (cf. 1 Cor. 9:1–15a), at the same time he was deeply conscious of his past life as a persecutor of Christians and described himself here as "the very least of all saints" (cf. 15:9; 1 Tim. 1:13, 15b–16). To show how low the gospel could reach, however, Paul (then Saul) was saved. "The gift was bestowed," Marvin Vincent says, "in accordance with that efficiency which could transform Saul the persecutor into Paul the apostle to the Gentiles."[4]

Furthermore, as he writes here, "this grace was given, to preach to the Gentiles the unfathomable riches of Christ, and to bring to light [to everyone, Jew as well as Gentile] what is the administration ['dispensation, stewardship'] of the mystery which for ages [prior dispensations] has been hidden in God" (Eph. 3:8–9).

God is described as the one "who created all things," including the various dispensations, their content, and when that content should be revealed. His intent was that "the manifold wisdom of God might now be made known through the church [made up of Jewish and gentile believers on equal standing], to the rulers and the authorities in the heavenly places" (v. 10). These verses are explosive in their dramatic indication of how God had reconstructed history by the work of Christ on the cross. These are not *lightweight* matters but dramatic events that shook to the core the foundations of history. The full implications of what Paul is writing is too often ignored or passed over. Wood says: "What had been screened from the angelic hierarchy (cf. 1:21) is now to be declared through the body of Christ on earth (2:6–7). The ecclesiological implications of such verses as these are staggering indeed (cf. 1 Pet. 1:21). Through the mirror of the church, the angels of heaven see the glory of God."[5]

Paul reveals a fascinating fact. Throughout history, until the apostolic age (the dispensation of the church), God's angels did not understand His plan for humanity. This is what Paul is trying to communicate. What a breathtaking thought! Perhaps more remarkable was that the "manifold wisdom of God" concerning His plan, would be made know to these heavenly beings through the church. These "rulers and authorities" (Eph. 3:10) were spoken of earlier in 1:21 and are understood as being different orders of angelic beings in these verses.

These two Greek words referring to power (translated here as "rulers and authorities"), given in that order, actually occur ten times in the New Testament (Luke 12:11; 20:20; 1 Cor. 15:24; Eph. 1:21; 3:10; 6:12; Col. 1:16; 2:10, 15; Titus 3:1) and may refer to either men or angels in leadership positions.

Although these titles are used in 6:12 to refer to evil angels, there is not enough scriptural evidence given to ascribe them only to the fallen ones. This use in Ephesians 3:10 does not give a clear picture one way or the other; however, unlike 6:12, which speaks in context to the believers' battle against Satan, no such conflict is in view in chapter 3. Therefore, this may be referring to holy angels. Perhaps the best view is to consider both, especially since the "heavenly places" (v. 10) may refer to the realms in which both good and some evil angels reside. In fact, as Hoehner states: "God and Satan are seen conversing with one another in heaven (Job 1:6–12), and a struggle between good and evil angels is portrayed in heaven and on earth (Dan. 10:13, 20). Therefore it seems acceptable to suppose that both good and evil beings are being informed of the manifold wisdom of God."[6]

All this is "in accordance with the eternal purpose which He carried out in Christ Jesus our Lord" (Eph. 3:11). In chapter 1 the apostle spoke of God's eternal plan of salvation, though without a doubt, His plan includes more issues than simply redemption, as important as this is. He is in charge of His own universe, and He says of whatever He speaks, "Truly I will bring it to pass. I have planned it, surely I will do it" (Isa. 46:11b). The Lord adds: "I declared the former things long ago and they went forth from My mouth, and I proclaimed them. Suddenly I acted, and they came to pass" (48:3). The same divine plan is working in the church. And believers are objects of His grace and trophies of His redemptive goodness!

In these verses here in Ephesians 3 Paul once again returns to God's freedom as Creator and Sustainer. All that he has just revealed regarding the "mystery" and its unveiling: the joining of Jew and Gentile in a new entity, Paul's role as steward of this dispensation, the role of the church in making known the "manifold wisdom of God . . . to the "rulers and authorities" (v. 10). All of this was part of God's "eternal purpose" (v. 11). This may be better translated as "according to the purpose of the ages," speaking of the plan that God conceived and put into effect in eternity past. If what transpired in the past is part of God's eternal plan, how much more will take place in the future! God is not passive, and He is not impotent. While human beings are responsible, God is still sovereign. No person can reconcile these two truths. And the church is part of this magnificent plan. All who know Christ did not come to the revelation about Him by accident. God is the Author of His own history.

Paul started this line of thought back in the beginning of his letter to the Ephesians when he said, "just as He chose us in Him before the foundation of the world" (1:4); "He predestined us to adoption as sons" (1:5); and "We are . . . "created in Christ Jesus for good works, which God prepared beforehand" (2:10). Everything Paul has related to the Ephesians concerning the past, when the Jews and Gentiles were separated, to his present day, when a new entity, the church, was being born, to those events yet to happen, "the summing up of all things in Christ" (1:10) are part of one seamless, divine plan, conceived by God in eternity past in total personal freedom, without any requirements placed on Him or His decisions by anyone or anything. The purpose of this plan is simply to bring God glory.

Although the work of the church in carrying forth the gospel and building mature believers is extremely important, its ultimate purpose is to bring glory to God by manifesting His wisdom before the heavenly hosts, that they may bring greater praise to God.[7] John MacArthur says: "The church is not an end in itself but a means to an end, the end of glorifying God. The real drama of redemption can only be understood when we realize that the glory of God is the supreme goal of creation. . . . Even the fallen angels glorify God, though they do not intend to do so."[8]

As a result, in Christ "we have boldness and confident access [to God] through faith in Him" (v. 12). Paul closed this section by asking his readers "not to lose heart at my tribulations on your behalf, for they are your glory" (v. 13). It is by trusting the Lord that the believers can function and carry out their mission. Paul embedded the truth in his very soul so that he could be an example so the average Christian would see his determination in spreading the gospel. No one was more driven than the apostle. He was turned about dramatically on the road to Damascus. He had seen and heard the risen Christ. There was no doubt about the validity of the gospel message or about the facts of Christ presently residing in glory. And what was happening to Paul now, in his persecution and imprisonment, in a strange way benefited the believers and even brought glory to their stand for the truth.

This concept of tribulations ("afflictions," "suffering"), and glory working together, appears numerous times in Scripture. "Jesus said that he would enter his glory through suffering, and that his followers would have to tread the same path"[9] (see Luke 9:22; 24:26, 46). Here though, Paul is referring to *his* suffering bringing glory to the Ephesians. Undoubtedly, many of his followers suffered anguish over Paul's imprisonments, perhaps especially those in Ephesus who had sat under his teaching for three years.

However, Paul always offered a message of encouragement regarding suffering. He told the Romans, "I consider that the sufferings of this present time are not worthy to be compared with the glory that is to be revealed to us" (Rom. 8:18). He also gave concrete evidence to support his position, as when he told the Philippians, "I want you to know brethren, that my circumstances have turned out for the greater progress of the gospel . . . and that most of the brethren, trusting in the Lord because of my imprisonment, have far more courage to speak the word of God without fear" (Phil. 1:12, 14). There is no greater energizing of followers of a dynamic leader than to see that person being persecuted. It brought to the fore the priorities about the importance of the gospel, and how its message was so vital to the world—but also so despised! And what an example Paul exhibited by not shrinking back from the task assigned him by his risen Lord.

Paul is telling the Ephesians that he is suffering in prison because of the work he has done to further the cause of Christ. Part of that work was preaching the gospel in Ephesus and bringing believers together as a growing church. The Ephesian believers may now glory in their salvation because of Paul, and that is why he is being persecuted for his task of building the church of Jesus Christ, in which believers glory in their new state of being.

It was to be expected by Paul, and should be by all believers, that the more work done on behalf of Christ in this fallen world, the more persecution will quickly follow, but in the end, the more glory, and the more fruit that will be produced in the process. Many people came to Christ by witnessing the suffering of the saints. The Roman Empire was dramatically changed when the citizens saw the tenacity and the terrible martyrdom of those who were burned alive and torn apart by the lions in the arenas.

## Paul's Prayer for His Readers (3:14–21)

Paul now takes up the prayer he had intended to write in Ephesians 3:1, repeating the phrase "For this reason" (v. 14). Whether he actually knelt (literally, with the expression "bent the knees") as he wrote this letter or not, he certainly was in the attitude of supplication for his readers. His prayer was to "the Father" to emphasize the intimate relationship of the believer with God. He is the one "from whom every family in heaven and on earth derives its name." By stating this, Paul wants to remind his readers what their life now was all about. It had a higher purpose, and that purpose stretched all the way into heaven. But also, this verse shows the earnestness the apostle had for the care of those to whom he was writing. He truly kept them continually in his thoughts and prayers that they would be strengthened internally by the Lord.

Verse 15 sets forth an interesting statement and specific concept. Paul uses the Greek word *patria*, which means "family, clan, lineage,"[10] or it may mean something larger like "people" or "nation."[11] Some try to make the argument that this word should be given the definition of *patrotēs*, which means "fatherhood" as coming from the Father. *Patria*, however, is never found conveying this abstract concept.[12]

Paul seems to be saying that every family, whether in heaven (angelic) or on earth (human), is named by God the Father. Human beings have always been assigned descriptive names, and even some of the angels (including Satan) have names. Names identify and give meaning to the one mentioned. However, more may be meant in this verse. God did indeed start the process by naming Adam. In other cases, God had fathers name their own sons: Abraham named Ishmael and Isaac, Jacob named Benjamin, and David named Solomon.[13]

In other cases, God told the father what to name his child, as with Isaiah and Maher-shalal-hash-baz, Zacharias and his son, John (the Baptist), and Joseph and his son Jesus.[14] Hoehner says, "The present tense of the verb would seem to indicate that God is still naming every family because he is still creating them. Thus, every family, whether in heaven or on earth, has its origin in God as creator."[15] In biblical and in ancient cultures, names had greater significance and meaning. But the greater idea is that all are identified by God. He is the One who has given life to all. In that sense He owns all. Paul is not arguing for the "fatherhood of God" in the sense that now all have a "spiritual" relationship with Him. By the fall of Adam, all were cut off from such a relationship. He is "Father" only in the creative sense.

Paul's first request in this section is that God would grant believers "according to the riches of His glory, to be strengthened with power through His Spirit in the inner man" (v. 16). What does it mean to be strengthened "according to the riches of [God's] glory"? An example has been given concerning a millionaire. If he were to make a donation of a few hundred dollars, he would be giving *out of* his wealth. However, if he gave something on the order of $100,000, he would be giving *according to* his wealth. Simply stated, the more a person has, the greater the gift must be to qualify as being *according to* his wealth. Using this as an illustration, God is giving an infinite amount of strengthening from His storehouse of blessing. This idea is hard to grasp, because often the believer may not *experience* such generosity coming from a beneficent Master. The vicissitudes of life sometimes drag the believer down. Perspective is lost and depression may sour the Christian walk.

Knowing this fact is true, and knowing that God is the Creator, Sustainer and *Owner* of everything and the holder of *all* spiritual blessings, the mind is boggled at the amazing spiritual assets believers have when the Lord bestows such benefits on His children "according to the riches of His glory," "through His Spirit" (v. 16). Yet, this is exactly what Paul is requesting for the Ephesians.[16]

But what about the expression "inner man" (*esō*) versus the "outer man (*exō*)"? Paul first addresses this topic in Romans 7:21–23, where he speaks of the struggle between the evil that is present in him, that is, the "different law in the members of [his] body (vv. 21, 23). Paul in this Romans 7 passage is speaking of the outer man, because he contrasts these thoughts with the fact that he "joyfully concur[s] with the law of God in the inner man" (v. 22).

Paul's next mention is 2 Corinthians 4:16, where he speaks of the "outer man decaying," while the "inner man is being renewed day by day." Here he is contrasting the physical abuse he had been suffering as a witness for Christ with the spiritual gain received through spreading the gospel and seeing the work of God's grace. One should not be led to believe that there is a dichotomy going on and that the Christian is schizophrenic. The two descriptions, while different, still work together in the human being. One affects the other. It would be right to say, however, that the inner spiritual person controls what one is externally, in the body. To be inner controlled by God's Spirit is what believers need in the daily walk.

Now, in this prayer for the Ephesians, Paul is purely concerned with the "inner man" (Eph. 3:16) that it may be strengthened with power by the Father through the Holy Spirit. This formula for receiving divine power is first spoken of in reference to Jesus Christ (Acts 10:38). It is also in view when the apostles received power on Pentecost (1:8). Paul makes a similar request for the Romans in 15:13 and advises the Thessalonians that this was the method by which they received the gospel (1 Thess. 1:4–5). The Holy Spirit is the Father's agent in the world and the One who does His spiritual work within the believer. The Father and the Son still do specific work on their own in the life of the child of God, yet it is the Spirit who is the Helper and Enabler sent from the Father by the Son, who will do a marvelous work within (John 15:25–27; Acts 1:4–8). MacArthur comments: "Spiritual power is not the mark of a special class of Christian but is the mark of every Christian who submits to God's Word and Spirit. Like physical growth and strength, spiritual growth and strength do not come overnight. As we discipline our minds and spirits to study God's Word, understand it, and live by it, we are nourished and strengthened."[17]

The result of this strengthening is "that Christ may dwell [literally, 'be at home'] in your hearts through faith" (v. 17). This is more than trusting Christ by faith as Savior; it is permitting him to control and rule the life of the child of God.

Paul's next request builds on the first, which will result in the believer in whose heart Christ is at home "being rooted and grounded in love" (v. 17). This believer then, Paul says in so many words, "may be able to comprehend with all the saints what is the breadth and length and height and depth, and to know the love of Christ which surpasses knowledge" (vv. 18–19). Vincent, ignoring the frequent fanciful interpretations of these words, writes simply: "The general idea of vastness is expressed in these ordinary terms for dimension."[18] Then he adds: "Notice that the article (in the Greek text) is attached only to the first, *breadth*, all the rest being included under the one article; the intention being to exhibit the love of Christ in its entire dimension, and not to fix the mind on its constituent elements."[19]

Paul's prayer is that each believer "may be filled up to all the fulness of God " (v. 19). The idea of "filling" has to do with "control." God desires to control the heart, mind, and soul in order to carry out His will. How this works is difficult for Christians to comprehend, for one cannot "feel" something in the chest in a physical way. This benedictory sentence of the prayer has been used many times as a benediction to worship services. It acknowledges God's ability "to do exceeding abundantly beyond all that we ask or think, according to the power that works within us" and closes with "to Him [i.e., God the Father] be the glory in the church and in Christ Jesus to all generations, forever and ever [literally, 'unto the age of the ages'). Amen" (vv. 20–21). Again, these thoughts are so expansive they are hard to get ahold of. They seem to be but good theory as to how the Christian life works, but in reality they express the truth of what the Lord is doing in the lives of those who belong to Him.

Concerning Paul's benediction to this prayer (vv. 14–21) and to the closing of the first half of his letter to the Ephesians, Hoehner writes: "No human or angel (cf. 3:10) would ever think that Jews and Gentiles could function together in one body. But with God's power of love in each believer's life, Paul was confident that Jewish and gentile believers can function and love one another."[20]

This is an extraordinary thought, and it reflects something not fully known in the pagan world. The binding of Christian Jews and Gentiles together would never have been thought possible. Not only previously was there a great spiritual gulf dividing the two groups, but there was the whole cultural, social, and theological framework. The differences between Jews and Gentiles were considered insurmountable, but God was able to overcome them. This is why Paul ascribed "glory" to God, which is to be manifest "in the church," where this miracle of love will take place, "and in Christ Jesus," who made possible this union of Jewish and gentile believers.[21]

But what happens when believers fight and tear each other apart? Paul says the church can be carnal (*sarkikos*, "fleshly") with division and strife, with many in the congregation "walking like mere men" (1 Cor. 3:3b). The world sees the confusion and judges the believers as to their commitment to Christ and their fellowship with one another. The fellowship of the body of Christ is measured by the depth of love believers have for one another. If that care is not evident, the church will divide or take sides against one another with jealousy and strife (v. 3).

## Study Questions

1. Why does Paul call the truth he presented the "mystery of Christ"?

2. How does Paul define the "mystery of Christ"?

3. How does Paul describe himself?

4. What special ministry was given to Paul and not to the other apostles?

5. What purpose of God did the revelation of the mystery serve?

6. What does faith in Christ provide for the Christian?

7. How did Paul ask the Ephesian believers to react to his tribulations?

8. What was Paul's request to God the Father for the Ephesian believers?

# CHAPTER 10

# Unity and Diversity in the Spirit
# Ephesians 4:1–16

## Preview:
*Using the human body as his example, Paul explains how all believers are members of one body, the body of Christ, known as the church, which encompasses Jews and Gentiles. And just as the body is one with different parts that perform different functions, so is the body of Christ. We are all one in the Spirit, but we have been given different gifts with which to glorify God and edify the body.*

## Paul's Instructions to the Ephesians (4:1–16)

Charles Hodge explains how the apostle exhorts his readers to walk worthy of their vocation. Such a walk should be characterized by humility, meekness, long-suffering, and zeal to promote spiritual unity and peace (Eph. 4:1–3). The church is one because it is one body, has one Spirit, one hope, one Lord, one faith, one baptism, and one God and Father who is over, through, and in all its members (vv. 4–6).[1]

Consistent with this unity however, is the great diversity of gifts distributed by Christ according to His own will (v. 7). Psalm 68:18, which speaks of the Messiah giving gifts to men is offered as confirmation because it speaks of a divine person ascending to heaven, and this implies a preceding descent to the earth (Eph. 4:9–10). The apostle Paul applies this great psalm as an illustration of the work of Christ. The Lord will give gifts to those who are His own warriors. These gifts that Christ gives to His church are listed as various classes of ministries, apostles, prophets, evangelists, pastors, and teachers (v. 11). The Lord assigns these gifts for the edification of the church, that its members might be brought to a unity of faith and knowledge and to the full stature of Christ; that they should no longer be unstable as children, but be a firm, compact, and growing body in living union with Christ, its head (vv. 12–16).[2]

There is nothing like this spelled out in any other religion. Christianity gives responsibility to the members of the church. Of course there is leadership, but the building up of all the saints is the goal of the impartation of the gifts.

For the second time Paul reminds the Ephesian believers that he is "the prisoner of the Lord" (v. 1), which is part of the price he was paying to bring them and all the Gentiles the gospel. He wrote, in light of his sacrifice and God's infinite ability, "I, therefore . . . entreat you to walk in a manner [literally, 'keep on walking about'] worthy of the calling with which you have been called." This urging includes acting "with all humility and gentleness, with patience [literally, 'with patience or forbearance'), showing forbearance to one another in love." Richard Trench explains that Christian humbleness is "no mere modesty or absence of pretension, . . . nor yet a self-made grace," but "the esteeming of ourselves small, inasmuch as we are so; the thinking truly, and because truly, therefore lowly, of ourselves."[3]

With regard to Jesus' claim to be "gentle and humble in heart" (Matt. 11:29), Trench writes that this involved the recognition "of absolute dependence, of having nothing, but receiving all things from God. . . . In his human nature He must be the pattern of all humility, of all creaturely dependence."[4]

As a conclusion Paul urged them to be "diligent to preserve the unity of the Spirit in the bond of peace" (Eph. 4:3). Diligence means hard work, perseverance, and a zeal for a given pursuit. In verse 3 this diligence is to be applied to "preserving the unity of the Spirit in the bond of peace." Note the word, "preserving" or *tēreō* in Greek. This word means to "watch" or "guard."[5] Here the infinitive is being used. "The infinitive *tērein* from *tēreō* essentially means 'to keep, preserve' what is already in existence."[6] This is an important point to keep in mind.

Something new is not being created here. Something that has already been accomplished by the Holy Spirit is to be "maintained," "preserved." This would be the "unity of the Spirit." The Holy Spirit binds the believers together and works within each individually. Does the child of God "feel" something within the chest or heart that would indicate the Spirit's influence? No, but the question has to be asked again, "What would believers in Christ be like without the work of the Spirit of God within?"

But just what is this "unity" the apostle is speaking about? Since it is something that is already established by the Holy Spirit and then must be preserved by believers, it cannot be referring to the ecumenical movements today that try to unite all different denominations by only adhering to the lowest common denominators, such as some form of outward fellowship. It can only refer to the spiritual unity that exists among all true believers in Jesus Christ, not including those who simply make a profession but do not really believe. All of those who have trusted Christ make up the one true, "invisible" church. "Invisible" may not be the proper word to describe the fact that believers cut across the boundaries of the local church. All who have trusted in Him, no matter what nationality or language they speak, belong to this worldwide network of the saved. The members of the church are "sealed" by the Holy Spirit (1:13). The church, then, is a "universal" body made up of both Jews and Gentiles (2:15).

However, this begs the question, if this refers to the unity established by the Holy Spirit, and as will be shown in the following verses, is secured by God the Father, why should it need to be "preserved" by believers and even require a "diligent" effort to maintain that unity? (v. 3). This verse can only refer to preserving the "visible" exhibition of this "invisible" unity and fraternity. Without God and the work of His Spirit, there is no possibility of unity.

Because this is so important, what the lost world sees comes into play. Paul, after explaining in verses 1–2 how believers are to walk and act toward one another, gives the reason in verse 3. Through a walk showing love for God as well as love for one another, believers make visible the invisible unity that exists among Christians, extending their witness in the world past the proclamation of the gospel. This really impacts on the practical Christian walk through life. Unbelievers are faced every day with dysfunction, disunity, discord, and a general lack of love. What they see in the child of God becomes an occasion for witnessing of how the gospel truly changes the lives of those who claim the Lord Jesus as Savior. The position in Christ, and the Christian daily walk cannot be separated or disconnected! What believers believe must be practiced. What believers say must be lived out.

That which facilitates this walk, and this unity, is the "bond of peace" (v. 3), which binds all believers together. John MacArthur comments, "It is the bond that Paul described in Philippians as 'being of the same mind, maintaining the same love, united in spirit, intent on one purpose' (2:2). Behind this bond of peace is love, which Colossians 3:14 calls 'the perfect bond of unity.'"[7]

Paul then returns to his theme of the mystery of the unity of gentile and Jewish believers on equal standing in Christ—"one body and one Spirit," and reminds them that they were "called in one hope of your calling" (Eph. 4:4).

He continues listing the unities in Christ—"one Lord, one faith, one baptism" (v. 5). The last item mentioned is not ritual baptism, important as that is as a witness to one's faith in Christ, but the spiritual truth that "by one Spirit we were all baptized into one body, whether Jews or Greeks, whether slaves or free, and we were all made to drink of one Spirit" (1 Cor. 12:13). Ephesians 4:4–6 stands out as an anthem of Christian theology or small doctrinal nugget. These verses have often been incorporated into church creeds throughout church history. They explain in a nutshell the essentials of what Christianity is all about. Concerning verse 5, Marvin Vincent writes: "The connection with the preceding verses is as follows: I exhort you to *unity*, for you stand related to *the Church*, which is *one* body in Christ; to the *one Spirit* who informs it; to the *one hope* which your calling inspires; to the *one Lord*, Christ, in whom you believe with *one common faith*, and receive *one common sign* of that faith baptism. Above all, to the *one God and Father*."[8]

The final and preeminent unity Paul lists is "one God and Father of all, who is over all and through all and in all" (v. 6). In some ways this verse is difficult to explain or grasp. It is all inclusive, expansive, and wraps up all of creation, all of history, and all things under the authority, power, and control of God the Almighty! The verse proclaims Him as the Sovereign God but also the originator of everything, in the sense of Father! However, some have taken the verse in another way. Paul is making God the Father of "all" believers only. In this way, He owns all in the church, is over all with His authority, and working in all of the saints to carry out His intents and purposes.

How does God carry out this authority and providence within His church? At this point Paul introduces and presents his argument of how Christ has assigned spiritual gifts. He develops this also in some detail elsewhere (Rom. 12:4–8; 1 Cor. 12:1, 4–11, 27–31). He calls the spiritual gift "grace," which it certainly is—an unmerited favor and bestowal from God only. He is not writing about innate human talent but about specific spiritual gifts to carry out His purposes with His church. He also says that "to each one of us" a spiritual gift "was given" (Eph. 4:7), a point also made in his other discussion of spiritual gifts (1 Cor. 12:7, 11). As an encouragement to many Christians, James Robinson Boise notes from the Greek text that "in the general distribution of gifts, not one individual, however obscure, is overlooked."[9] The implication also is made that a Christian may be given more than one spiritual gift. The assignment of spiritual gifts by Christ took place upon his ascension to God the Father's right hand in heaven, the support of which truth is presented in the slightly altered quotation of Psalm 68:18. Vincent writes: "The Psalm is Messianic, a hymn of victory in which God is praised for victory and deliverance. It is freely adapted by Paul, who regards its substance rather than its letter, and uses it as an expression of the divine triumph as fulfilled in Christ's victory over death and sin."[10]

Paul's quotation of the phrase "He ascended" (Eph. 4:8) leads to a digression to point out that the ascension of Jesus Christ to heaven required first of all his descension as the Son of God from heaven in incarnation "to the lower parts of the earth" (v. 9). A. T. Robertson comments: "If the *anabas* is the Ascension of Christ, then the *katabas* would be the Descent (Incarnation) to earth and *tēs gēs* ("of the earth") would be the genitive of apposition. What follows in verse 10 argues for this view."[11]

Paul is emphasizing that Jesus is not merely a mortal man but the eternal Son of God incarnate, who, after fulfilling his ministry on earth of living and being sacrificed for people's sins, "ascended far above all the heavens, that He might fill all things" (v. 10). He is the one in whom "all things hold together" (Col. 1:17). Some critics have wrongly argued that the doctrine of the Trinity and the deity of Christ are barely, if at all, mentioned in the Bible. But this is certainly not so. The apostle Paul is arguing in the strongest manner for the deity, sovereignty, and preeminence of Christ as God the Son. No one can look carefully at these verses and deny this fact.

Here in Ephesians 4:11 Paul writes that Christ "gave some as apostles, and some as prophets, and some as evangelists, and some as pastors and teachers." Harold Hoehner notes, "Evangelists were those engaged in spreading the gospel, similar to present-day missionaries."[12] It has been well noted that this verse lists four groups of gifted men, not five. The pastors (literally, shepherds), responsible for guiding and comforting the people under their care, are also to be teachers, instructing them in the truth and will of God (1 Tim. 3:2; Titus 1:9). Vincent points out: "The omission of the article from *teachers* seems to indicate that pastors and teachers are included under one class. The two belong together. No man is fit to be a pastor who cannot also teach, and the teacher needs the knowledge which pastoral experience gives."[13]

However, this knowledge should also include not only practical knowledge but biblical and doctrinal knowledge. This is why pastors should be well trained in a full understanding of the Bible. Some pastors step into the pulpit simply motivated by enthusiasm and zeal. Though this is important, it is not enough. If one is called to the *position* of pastor, that person must also be called to the *process* of proper biblical education and training.

The apostles (*apostolos*, literally, "sent ones, messengers") identified in the formal sense the original eleven, plus Saul (Paul), appointed by the risen Christ. The term *apostle* was also used of James (Gal. 1:19), Barnabas (Acts 14:14), Silas and Timothy (1 Thess. 2:6 with 1:1), and Andronicus and Junius

(Rom. 16:7). The apostle Paul was on the same level as "a true apostle," the twelve, because he performed "signs and wonders and miracles" as they did (2 Cor. 12:11–13). The others were not on the same level though they were extremely important to the development of the early church. Today it can be said that all believers are *apostles* of the Lord, using a little *a*. The average Christian does not have apostolic authority as was ascribed to only a few in the beginning of the New Testament period.

Paul next mentions prophets in Ephesians 4:11. He is not referring here to the twelve apostles or to himself, but to a host of gifted men who had great teaching skills. It must be remembered that the full canon of Scripture had not been given—the New Testament was not finished. Therefore there were those who had certain revelatory skills to "teach" truth that had not as yet been recorded in letters. Only a few of these prophets foretold future events (Acts 21:10–11). But instead they spoke "to men for edification and exhortation and consolation" (1 Cor. 14:3). Evangelists were those who proclaimed the gospel, such as Philip (Acts 21:8; cf. 8:5–6, 12, 40).

Paul personified all four groups of gifted men. Our Lord's purpose in providing all four types was "for the equipping of the saints for the work of service" for "the building up of the body of Christ" (Eph. 4:12). The Greek word used here for "equipping" is *katartismos*. It has in view "preparation," "restoration," and even, in medical circles, the "setting of a bone."[14] Paul uses it to tell the Corinthians to be "made complete" (2 Cor. 13:11). The saints of God require all of this preparation, restoration, mending, and much more to become mature disciples equipped to do the work of "service," which is *diakonias* in Greek (from which we get *deacon*), which seems to come from a root word meaning "to labor" or "to run through the dust."[15] This gives a graphic picture of the "work of service, to the building up of the body of Christ" (Eph. 4:12). Many pastors believe they are in the "work of service" as full-time ministers. But by looking at the verse carefully, one may note that Paul is actually saying that the saints, the church members themselves, are in the work of service, or in the ministry. The pastors are to see themselves first and foremost as teachers who then equip the church members to have their own work of service by exercising the gift granted them.

In many churches and denominations today, this essential focus of ministry has been twisted or laid aside. Many Christians today believe that their "service" is to bring unsaved people to a church service to hear the gospel and hopefully be saved. Many pastors propagate this error through ignorance, and the result is a body of believers who are immature and ill-equipped, because every church service is an evangelistic meeting and not an equipping session to bring the flock to maturity in the Word.

Believers today need to learn that the role of pastor-teachers is different from that of evangelists and that pastor-teachers are to spend their time "equipping" the saints so that they may do the "work of service to the building up of the body of Christ" (v. 12). And there is much work in any church that needs to be done. This includes not only the physical labor but the caring and encouragement of each other as believers so that the body of Christ will be "built up." This certainly includes, as well, going forth into the world to proclaim the gospel to the unsaved and "always *being* ready to make a defense to everyone who asks you to give an account for the hope that is in you, yet with gentleness and reverence" (1 Pet. 3:15). This work is for the congregation to do. All Christian ministry and service are not to be laid at the door of the pastor-teacher.

This issue is probably one of the most misunderstood issues in most church congregations. Most believers in the assembly leave much of the ministry in the hands of the "paid pros," the full-time professional pastors. This fosters a weak and impotent body of believers who should have their own ministry, exercising their own gifts. It takes away their privilege and calling to serve Christ in a very personal way. As MacArthur explains, "From the saints who are equipped God raises up elders, deacons, teachers, and every other kind of worker needed for the church to be faithful and productive. Spiritual service is the work of *every* Christian, *every* saint of God. Attendance is a poor substitute for participation in ministry."[16]

The goal is that "we all attain to the unity of the faith and of the knowledge of the Son of God to a mature man, to the measure of the stature which belongs to the fulness of Christ" (v. 13). This is an ideal set forth by the apostle Paul. The body of Christ should be functioning in a whole and complete way, but often there is impotence and disunity. The church is then weakened and has but limited witness in the world. Hoehner comments: "As each believer functions in accord with the gift(s) Christ has given him (v. 7), the body as a whole enjoys unity (cf. vv. 3–6) and becomes more spiritually mature (v. 15), more like Jesus Christ in all His fullness (cf. 1:23; 3:19)."[17]

The Lord is continually striving with His church, working toward this goal of maturity, and will continue to do so until Christ returns to claim His spiritual body and bride. Certain forces are always opposing congregations: carnality, squabbles, divisions, doctrinal impurity, immorality, and more.

When the goal of completing the church is reached, Paul writes, "We are no longer to be children, tossed here and there by waves, and carried about by every wind of doctrine, by the trickery (literally, "dice-throwing"),of men, by craftiness in deceitful scheming" (v. 14). To the contrary, Paul desires that "speaking the truth in love, we are to grow up in all aspects into Him who is the head, even Christ" (v. 15). He is the one from whom "the whole body, being fitted and held together by that which every joint supplies, according to the proper working of each individual part, causes the growth of the body for the building up of itself in love" (v. 16). "The leading thought of the paragraph, unity in diversity, and the dependence of the whole for its growth on each individual part, is most impressive."[18] Boise concludes, "The value and importance of each individual member of the Christian church, however humble the station, is here strikingly presented"[19] Hodge adds: "As then the human body, bound together by the vital influence derived from the head through appropriate channels and distributed to every member and organ according to its function, constantly advances to maturity; so the church, united as one body by the divine influence flowing from Christ its head through appropriate channels, and distributed to every member according to his peculiar capacity and function, continually advances towards perfection."[20]

In the same way as in the human body no one part, whether hand or foot, can live and grow unless it is in union with the body, so union with Christ's mystical body is the one indispensable condition of growth for every individual believer.[21] The church must be established in love. This love is the separator of a church that is just a businesslike association that is without heart and a church in which the love "from" God makes the differences in what is happening in that assembly.

John the apostle drives home this point in his last epistles. Those who are born of God love Him as Father, but they also love the other believers who are born of God. Loving other Christians means that we love God (1 John 5:1–3). The new commandment is to "love one another" (2 John 1:5). John said of those he was writing to that others could bear witness of their love "before the church" (3 John 1:6). The ones he was writing to were both walking in the truth and walking in love (v. 1–7).

## Study Questions

1. How does Paul ask the Ephesian believers to live their lives?

2. What unities do believers have in Christ?

3. When were the grace gifts given to believers by Christ according to Paul?

4. Can a believer have more than one gift?

5. What was the purpose of Christ's giving gifted people to the church?

6. Does the phrase "pastors and teachers" refer to two different kinds of gifted people?

7. How is the relationship between Christ and the church described in human figures?

## Section Three

# ALL ONE IN GOD'S PURPOSE

## EPHESIANS 4:17 – 6:24

# CHAPTER 11

# The Believer's Walk in Christ
# Ephesians 4:17–32

## Preview:

*As is Paul's usual pattern, presenting first doctrinal truth for the believer's heart and mind, he now gives practical examples to the Ephesians, that they may walk in their faith before a fallen world.*

## One in Godly Living (4:17–32)

The apostle, having in the preceding section taught that the Lord Jesus had destined his church to perfect conformity to Himself and made provision for that end, as a natural consequence, solemnly and openly calls on those who profess to be believers in Christ to live in accordance with this high calling. In so many words, Paul was saying, "This *therefore* I say and testify in the Lord, that the child of God from now on goes about not as the other Gentiles and pagans walk, in the vanity of their minds." *To testify*, in this case, means to solemnly commit just as one does who calls upon God to bear witness to the truth and importance of what he says.[1]

When Paul emphatically told the Ephesian believers "walk no longer just as the Gentiles also walk" (v. 17), he was pointing out the need for godly living as a witness to the transforming power of Christ (cf. Rom. 12:2). Some may have been convicted to simply go on and live as before, wallowing in the sins of the immoral gentile world. But they had to break away because they now represent the Lord who saved them by His death on the cross. While breaking away may not have been easy, they had the enabling power of the Holy Spirit and the Word of God as the guide as to how to live.

The early church was a miracle in that many new converts were able to walk away from their past life and journey in the sunshine of spiritual and moral integrity. However, many struggled to make the break from the past life. For some victory comes quickly; for others it can be a painful new beginning.

Ephesians 4:17–19 are akin to Paul's message to the Romans. "They became futile in their speculations, and their foolish heart was darkened" (Rom. 1:21). Paul goes on: "Professing to be wise, they became fools" (v. 22). And "God gave them over in the lusts of their hearts to impurity" (v. 24). These verses in Romans 1 and Ephesians 4 contribute to what is called in theology "*total depravity.*" The weight of the degradation and sin of humanity is heavy. Paul is reminding the believers that this was their past; this is how they used to walk. This lifestyle has to be abandoned and forsaken.

This appears to be the pattern the unsaved follow in moral descent. First, the thinking process of humanity becomes "futile." This Greek word is defined as "pertaining to being useless on the basis of being futile and lacking in content—'useless, futile, empty, futility.'"[2] This is the definition Paul gives to the mind-set of the unsaved Gentile. An unsaved person's mind-set is useless, empty, and futile because it can in no way bring glory to God. Every thought begins with the individual and ends with him or her. Anything accomplished for the greater good is done with reference to the "good" as determined by that person and not by God. Therefore it has no real meaning except in the realm of selfishness and greediness.

This is what is meant by "being darkened in their understanding" (Eph. 4:18). Apart from a true, communicative relationship with God (available only through Jesus Christ), man's mind is unable to see truth and discern good from bad. It is like moving through total darkness, unable to see properly. It is difficult sometimes to imagine how blind the human race is to spiritual and moral matters. And there is certainly no way for humanity, apart from the work of the Holy Spirit, to know of God and His love for His creatures!

Part of the reason for their depraved spiritual state is the "hardness of their heart" (v. 18). The unsaved do not seek God (Rom. 3:11), and even more, they are enemies of God (5:10). The unsaved are dead in their sins and unable, in any way, to move toward God (John 6:44). While it would be easy for believers to throw stones at the lost, it must be remembered that all Christians were at one time in the same state of condemnation and depravity (Eph. 2:2–3). If it were not for God's mercy and grace (vv. 4–5), where would the believer be today? There is no salvation apart from this active grace that draws the lost to come into the light of the gospel. One of the most telling faults of the Pharisees and leaders of Israel was their heavy judgments against sinners. Jesus countered this hypocrisy in the story about the woman taken in adultery (John 8:1–11). Whatever He wrote on the ground caused all of the accusers to slip away (vv. 6, 8–9). His told the woman not to sin again: "Go your way. From now on sin no more" (v. 11).

The heaviness of this separation from God, this darkness holding sway over the thought process, and this hatred for God due to sin, results in "the hardness of heart," or "callousness" (Eph. 4:18–19). This Greek word, *apalgeō* is "from *apo*. . . denoting privation, and *algeō* . . . to feel pain. To grow or become insensible, void of or past feeling."[3] Eventually, the unsaved person's hatred for God leads that one to lose all feeling for anything except that which pleases oneself. All peoples of all cultures and nations are existing in a state of lostness. The more depraved the culture, the more selfishness rules the society. All caring and feeling can break down without a proper relationship to God.

History is filled with such examples of nations that were wallowing in sin and injustice. Russia in the nineteenth is a fitting example. The nation was tearing itself apart with assassinations of the leadership, corruption in high places, slavery, and cruelty in all strata of the society. The Russian orthodox church was impotent spiritually and could offer no spiritual solace to the darkness and turmoil.

When goodness and spirituality are lost, in this callous state it is easy for the unsaved to give themselves "over to sensuality, for the practice of every kind of impurity with greediness" (v. 19). Only those things that delight the senses, with a mind exclusively directed toward one's self-interest, can, at this point, offer any pleasure to those without God in the world.

Paul is working hard, trying to clarify to the gentile Ephesians that this was how they walked prior to salvation and why they were no longer to consider this a viable way to live. Ephesus was a major city in the Roman Empire and had every kind of delight to offer, including pagan religions, foremost of which was the worship of Diana (or Artemis) at her great temple, which was considered one of the seven wonders of the world. The worship of Diana involved much sexual activity of every kind. John MacArthur says that "male and female roles were interchanged, and orgiastic sex, homosexuality, and every other sexual perversion were common."[4]

This was the world in which the Ephesians had formerly participated and in which they were still surrounded as they attempted to live the Christian life.

Only their personal relationship with Christ, and leading by the Holy Spirit, could keep them pure and separate as believers.

In writing that the Ephesian believers "did not learn Christ in this way" (v. 20), the way of overt sin, the apostle was alluding to the fact that he was not the person who founded the church in Ephesus. He did stop there when returning to Judea from his second missionary journey and "entered the synagogue and reasoned with the Jews" without staying (Acts 18:19b–20), but he left Aquila and Priscilla there (v. 19a). They, together with Apollos (18:24–26), undoubtedly were the ones who founded the church (v. 27).

The Ephesian believers were taught the "truth is in Jesus" (Eph. 4:21). A. R. Fausset points out, "There is no article" before the word translated "truth" in the Greek text . . . 'Truth' is truth in its essence and perfection in Jesus."[5] This meant "in reference to your former manner of life, you lay aside the old self."

Although the Christian does have a continuing battle with sin, this passage (v. 21) is referring to an event that occurred at the time of salvation. "Lay aside," is a Greek aorist, infinitive verb that speaks of something done once, for all time. It would be better translated "You laid aside." It is not an imperative or command. For those in Ephesus who had, "heard Him," and had "been taught in Him" (v. 21), salvation had brought a new beginning. They laid aside the "old self" (otherwise known as the "old man," Rom. 6:6; Col. 3:9), the depraved sin nature that totally ruled their lives before being saved. Believers have to learn to walk away from, abandon the old practices that were a part of the past life. Some sins seem to fall off more quickly while others linger and bring destruction in the life of the child of God. Each believer struggles with different sins. Some evils are more tenacious than others.

The Greek word translated "lay aside" speaks in terms of tossing aside clothing or laying down military arms. Why must this "old self" be cast aside? Because it is "being corrupted," which is a present Greek participle denoting an ongoing process. This Greek participle may be regarded as either a middle or passive form, so it could mean that one "is corrupting himself" or "is being corrupted" (by an outside source). Since the old self is totally depraved from inception, perhaps the present middle participle is to be preferred. As R. C. H. Lenski says, it is "in harmony with . . . the lusts in which the old man indulges [and by this] he plunges himself down progressively into everlasting ruin or destruction."[6] What Lenski is saying is that some sins are difficult to get past and can bring permanent ruin.

This continual corruption occurs "in accordance with the lusts of deceit" (v. 22)—in other words, "working with" or "in harmony with" the lusts of deceit. The "lusts of deceit" reach all the way back to the Garden of Eden, for that is where wickedness and deception entered into the realm of humanity. When Satan told Eve, "You surely shall not die!" (Gen. 3:4), deceit was born. Then, when the deceit and rebellion were accepted and sin was born, the floodgates of lust were opened to the family of the human race. Ever since, when the lost heed the voice of deceit to feed lust, wicked and evil mushrooms and society becomes more and more corrupt. Only through salvation in Christ can a believer "lay aside," or "put off" the old self, which is continually corrupted by lust.

The Ephesians were then commanded to keep on being "renewed in the spirit of your mind" (Eph. 4:23), which is a continuing process. This involves a once-for-all reckoning and a continued awareness of putting "on the new self, which in the likeness of God has been created in righteousness and holiness of the truth" (v. 24). Becoming a Christian means on one hand, on the positional level, becoming a new person—putting off the old self and putting on the new self. This is all tied to the decision to trust Jesus Christ and his finished work of salvation. But on the other hand, it implies the continuing work of being "renewed in the spirit of your mind" (v. 23). A. Skevington Wood writes: "Christian converts are to undergo a radical reorientation of their mental outlook. This can only take place under the influence of the Holy Spirit, acting on the human spirit as it affects the realm of thought."[7]

At this point Paul becomes very specific. Looking ahead and summarizing what follows in the remainder of this chapter, Harold Hoehner writes: "Each of the following five exhortations about a believer's conduct has three parts: (1) a negative command, (2) a positive command, and (3) the reason for the positive command."[8]

Verse 25 begins with "therefore." In other words, on the basis of what has just been said ["be renewed in the spirit of your mind" (v. 23); "put on the new self" (v. 24)], do the following as the apostle lays out in the verses that follow. Paul then goes on to reiterate one of the Ten Commandments, which commands, "Laying aside falsehood, speak truth." Here Paul uses the same Greek root verb *apotithēmi* to speak of "laying aside falsehood" that he uses in verse 22 in reference to the "laying aside" of the old self, which occurred at salvation. Here the verb is also in the aorist tense, speaking of something that is to be done once for all time. When a person becomes a born-again believer in Jesus Christ, some changes are to be made immediately, one of which is to stop lying to people, period.

The verses in this entire section may be telling as to what the Ephesians were wrestling with in their carnal nature. It was probably reported to Paul that these believers had great difficulty in their relationships. Their sins came to the surface, and they were continually hurting each other in their practical walk. It was as if the life patterns were set even though they had trusted Christ as Savior. But the apostle Paul would not let them have any excuses. They had to change how they lived and related to others.

Paul could have just given the command to stop lying and moved on, but to make sure there is no misunderstanding, he then gives the positive response, "Speak truth, each one of you, with his neighbor" (v. 25). Paul brought his positive response statement forward from the Old Testament prophet Zechariah (8:16), combining the Hebrew version with the Septuagint rendering. God, through Zechariah, in this verse, was advising the remnant of Israel who had returned from Babylonian captivity on how to relate to one another, based on the fact that He had decided to "do good to Jerusalem and to the house of Judah" (v. 15), and that they should not fear.

Paul takes this Old Testament directive and brings it to the Ephesians, adding "for we are members of one another" (Eph. 4:25). This relates back to the previous chapters where Paul describes believers as being parts of the "body," which, along with Christ the head, make up the church (2:21–22; 3:6; 4:4, 12, 15, 16). On 4:25 MacArthur adds, "The word *neighbor* is defined by the phrase *members of one another* and means fellow Christians. We are to *speak truth* to everyone and in every situation, but we have a special motive to be truthful with other believers, because we are fellow members of Christ's Body, the church, and therefore *members of one another*."[9] Lying was a characteristic way of life in the ancient Middle Eastern world. It was not, however, to mark the life of the Christian.

Quoting Psalm 4:4, Paul then commands, "Be angry, and yet do not sin" (v. 26). Notice that he does not write, "Do not be angry," because there is a proper place and time for righteous anger, or righteous indignation, as seen in Jesus Himself when He was questioned for healing on the Sabbath (Mark 3:1–5) and when he drove the moneychangers and sellers of sacrificial animals out of the temple in Jerusalem (John 2:13–16).

Furthermore, when angry, believers are not to sin in deed (in action), thought, or word. One way to avoid this is to "not let the sun go down on your anger" (Eph. 4:26). To carry anger into the night and over into the next day is to allow it to fester in one's own mind and to devise further actions against those with which there is a conflict. Righteous indignation is to express anger against some blatant injustice in which someone is maligned or hurt. Leftover anger gives "the devil an opportunity" (v. 27) to come in and foster more destructive words. The thoughts of the mind fester and grow into a sense of having to retaliate and say more hurtful words. Wood expresses the position of most Bible commentators about a Christian's righteous anger when he writes: "A Christian's exasperation or provocation, however justifiable, must not be allowed to simmer overnight. If this advice is followed, the devil will be afforded no leeway. He will have no place to move. Instead, we must leave a place for the wrath of God, because vindication is his prerogative (Ro 12:19)."[10]

> ## The Devil's War against Believers
>
> Satan desired to "sift" Peter (Luke 22:31).
>
> As an adversary, he desires to devour believers "as a roaring lion" (1 Pet. 5:8).
>
> Believers are to stand against the schemes of the devil (Eph. 6:11).
>
> New converts to Christ can be "condemned" by the devil (1 Tim. 3:6).
>
> Satan can tempt believers (1 Cor. 7:5).
>
> Satan can gain an advantage of believers (2 Cor. 2:11).
>
> Satan may hinder the work of believers (1 Thess. 2:18).
>
> An overseer of the church can be caught in the snare of the devil (1 Tim. 3:7).
>
> Believers must resist the devil (James 4:7).
>
> At the church of Smyrna, the devil desired to cast believers into prison and test them (Rev. 2:10).

Stealing was another practice of the ancient Middle Eastern world, so Paul commands, "Let him who steals steal no longer" (Eph. 4:28). Instead, Paul writes to the one tempted to steal that he must "labor, performing with his own hands what is good." As a result, he "may have something to share with him who has need." Hoehner concludes, "Work has many benefits: it provides for a person's material needs, it gives him something useful to do (something that is beneficial to himself and others), and it enables him to help others materially."[11] As he wrote just before this, "This is true Christian charity"[12]

Christians are to "let no unwholesome (literally, "rotten" as a rotten fish) word proceed from your mouth" (v. 29). This would include profanity and inappropriate language of any kind. To the contrary the speech of Christians should be "only such a word as is good for deification according to the need of the moment." The desire is "that it may give grace to those who hear."

Paul commands his readers, "Do not grieve [literally, 'Do not make a habit of grieving,' or 'stop grieving'] the Holy Spirit of God, by whom you were sealed for the day of redemption" (v. 30). Here, in the midst of Paul's practical behavioral instructions to the Ephesians, he gives a command concerning the treatment of the Holy Spirit. Although no clue is given for Paul's digression, much may be learned by this statement. The Greek word translated "grieve" means "to afflict with sorrow . . . to be sad or sorrowful . . . to cause grief or offend."[13] It is a present tense verb meaning that the action is done continually, or in this case, is not to be done continually ("do not continually sadden or offend the Holy Spirit of God"). When most believers sin, they forget the consequence that harms the relationship with the Spirit of God. He is a person and not simply a "force." He can be grieved and feel the pain of the disobedience of the child of God. He is always indwelling the Christian. This command coming from the apostle confirms this truth about the "personhood" of the Holy Spirit. Cults frequently try to identify the Holy Spirit and argue that He is but an "energy," or "force," robbing Him of His personhood. An "energy" or "force" however, cannot be saddened, made sorrowful, or offended.

The time period for this behavior is also given: "by whom you were sealed for the day of redemption" (v. 30). Christians are "sealed" by the Holy Spirit at the moment they believe in Jesus Christ as their personal Savior. The "day of redemption" is the day when a believer goes on to glory either by death or rapture. This sets the time period for not grieving the Holy Spirit as the time of the believer's walk on earth. The day of redemption is about the period of final and complete sanctification. For now, the Holy Spirit is working in believers' lives to conform them to the image of Christ.[14] Previously Paul had discussed this sealing work of the Spirit and of the final redemption that will result in the final, complete, and triumphant "praise of His glory" (1:13–14).

Knowing this, how does one then "grieve" the Holy Spirit? In this immediate context of 4:30–31, bringing slander and evil words against another believer is the cause of this grief. But there is certainly more. The most important consideration must be that the Holy Spirit of God is "holy"; therefore any activity or thought of the believer that is unholy would offend Him.[15] This naturally would include any effort of a believer to harm others or to live in a worldly fashion, such as not heeding Paul's instructions in the previous verses. A good example of this would be Ananias and his wife, Sapphira, in Acts 5:1–10.

The Spirit of God is also referred to as the "one Spirit" (Eph. 2:18; 4:4), which speaks of the fact that He is one person, and that there is only one Holy Spirit! This means that anything that disrupts His work with the church harms the unity or purity of the body of believers. This definitely grieves the Spirit.[16]

John Stott observes: "One might add that because he is also the 'Spirit of truth', through whom God has spoken, he is upset by all our misuse of speech, which has been Paul's topic in the preceding verse."[17]

Paul continues by ordering his readers to "Let all bitterness and wrath and anger and clamor and slander be put away from you along with all malice" (v. 31). These are obviously negative attributes so characteristic of non-Christians. Speaking of wrath in this verse, Vincent explains, "What is commanded in verse 26 is here forbidden, because [it is] viewed simply on the side of human passion."[18] Vincent continues and supports his position by pointing out that "clamor" is the "outward manifestation of anger in vociferation or brawling."[19]

In opposition to living this way, the apostle commands believers to "be kind [literally, 'keep on being kind'] to one another, tender-hearted, forgiving [literally, 'showing grace to']) each other, just as God in Christ also has forgiven [once for all] you" (v. 32). The standard for how the child of God is to treat the fellow believer is found in how God provided grace for us in salvation. This then is an extremely high standard and to a degree cannot be met. What believer can show the same depth of grace and mercy that God has shown in Christ? But this is the standard and this is the goal that is set before the Christian. Henry Alford writes that this verse describes Christians as "Doing as a body for yourselves that which God did once for you all."[20] God's grace in Christ is the ultimate standard of forgiveness (Isa. 38:17; 43:25; Mic. 7:19) to which in the final analysis no one can attain.

## Study Questions

1. How is the lifestyle of unregenerate Gentiles described spiritually?

2. Who most likely founded the church at Ephesus?

3. Discuss the relationship between Ephesians 4:23–24 and Romans 12:1–2.

4. How did Paul describe the change of lifestyle of the Christian in human terms?

5. Why should the Christian not let any anger pass from day to day?

6. How does un-Christian behavior affect the Holy Spirit?

7. Who should be the example and pattern of our forgiveness as Christians?

# CHAPTER 12

# To Walk in Faith Is to Imitate God
# Ephesians 5:1–33

### Preview:

*Paul continues giving practical examples of Christian behavior for the Ephesians to follow and expands his view from the individual's general walk to a specific relationship: that of husband and wife, both in private and in public.*

## Walking as Imitators of God (5:1–21)

In effect Paul summed up all of his commands and recommendations to this point by writing, "Be [literally, 'keep on becoming') imitators [the Greek word from which our English word 'mimic' is derived] of God . . . as beloved children [literally, 'born ones, infants']" (v. 1). All of us know how children, especially little ones, imitate their parents, both consciously and unconsciously. Paul commanded true children of God to do the same. Paul also commanded his readers to "walk [literally, 'keep on walking about']) in love" (v. 2). Once again Christ is the example—"just as Christ also loved you and gave Himself up for us, an offering and a sacrifice to God" (v. 2). *Love* should be permeating the life of the believer. It is difficult for mortals to fully understand how this love should be doing this in the life. Believers can become angry and get distracted with the daily grind of existence, especially in a hostile and imperfect world. And children of God struggle with his their own sins. But Christ is the example. He gave Himself up to the cross for our sins. If He did this out of love, that kind of love becomes the pattern for the believer. A. R. Fausset comments that the word *offering* "expresses *generally* His presenting Himself to the Father, as Representative, undertaking the cause of our lost race (Ps. xi. 6–8), including His *life* of obedience, though not excluding of His body for us (Heb. x. 10). Usually an *unbloody offering*, in the limited sense. 'Sacrifice' refers to His *death* for us exclusively."[1]

> ## How the Child of God Is to Walk
>
> *Believers are to be careful how they walk (Eph. 5:15).*
>
> *Believers are to walk as wise (Eph. 5:15).*
>
> *Believers are to walk in "newness of life" (Rom. 6:4).*
>
> *Believers are not to walk after the flesh (Rom. 8:4).*
>
> *Believers are to walk honestly (Rom. 13:13, "behave properly").*
>
> *Believers can walk sinfully as the lost (1 Cor. 3:3).*
>
> *Believers are to walk by faith (2 Cor. 5:7).*
>
> *Believers are to walk in the Spirit (Gal. 5:16).*
>
> *Believers are to walk worthy of the Lord (Col. 1:10).*
>
> *Believers are to walk "in Him" (Col. 2:6).*
>
> *Believers are to walk in wisdom (Col. 4:5).*
>
> *Believers are to walk worthy of God (1 Thess. 2:12).*
>
> *Believers are to walk in the light (1 John 1:7).*
>
> *Believers are to walk in truth (3 John 4).*

Describing the sacrificial offering of Christ as a "fragrant aroma" (v. 2) is illustrated by the atonement offering set forth in Leviticus 4:31. It is important to notice that Christ's sacrifice is "to God," not to Satan as some theologians teach. God is the One accepting this offering. It is not an appeasement to God or to Satan! God is the One offended by the sins of humanity. But again, it is not simply an appeasement offering. It is only right that sin must be punished. Yet how can God punish sin without rejecting forever the sinner? By substituting for sinners on the cross, the sinner is no longer a sinner. However, sinners must acknowledge and accept the sacrifice made by Christ for themselves. They must consciously cling to Him as the Lamb who took their place as offenders.

After the positive summary instructions, Paul returned to the negative ones about specific sins. My translation of this passage reads, "But fornication and every impurity and covetousness should not be mentioned [literally, 'named'] among you as fitting for holy ones" (v. 3). Those who have been redeemed are now declared holy because they are seen by the Lord as relating to His Son. Believers are placed into the spiritual body of Christ (1 Cor. 12:12–13). This is a miracle work of God. It is His new reckoning of the believing individual, making that one a child of God.

Getting back to the issue of the Christian walk, we find Paul continuing to reject "obscenity [literally, that which is "shameful"] and foolish talk or coarse joking, which are out of place for the child of God. But now Paul wants something else coming forth from the believer, and that is thanksgiving (Eph. 5:4). Harold Hoehner describes thanksgiving as "appreciation for others" that brings about helpfulness for someone else.[2] He says that "Paul was not intimating that humor itself is sin, but that it is wrong when it is used to destroy or tear down others."[3] He could then be describing cynicism and the making of jokes that are destructive to one's personality. Nothing is more harmful than a personal "put down," whereby one is demeaned, though it is couched with some form of humor. People can destroy with their actions but also with their words!

This contrast of views is a definite wake-up call to the Ephesians, because the sinful environment was still wreaking havoc in how the new believers were behaving. They were living life as they had done before. There was little control over the mouth, the attitudes, and the way of life. The Ephesians were living in a pagan culture that was not sensitive to coarseness and kindness toward others. But even more, the people of this culture mixed sexual activity with religious worship. Before receiving Christ, they had been participants in this lifestyle.

The first contrast noted is one of being self-centered versus being God-centered. The "filthiness" (or obscenity), "silly talk," and "coarse jesting" were all self-centered pursuits, whereas "giving thanks" involves taking the mind off of oneself and focusing on the God of Scripture.[4] These statements might be considered Paul's instructions to the Ephesians on how to clean up the remaining immoral residue of their previous lives. This is a struggle for all believers who have had a substantial unsaved period of life before coming to the Lord. The habits of a lifetime do not easily pass away just because one becomes a Christian. It takes a decided effort of praying, giving thanks, and spending time in God's Word. As Paul told the Romans, "do not be conformed to this world, but be transformed by the renewing of your mind, that you may prove what the will of God is, that which is good and acceptable and perfect" (Rom. 12:2).

The second contrast involves focusing on the sexual context of Paul's statements in relation to the previous lifestyle of the Ephesians. The loose sexual attitude of the Ephesians, prompted by their prostitute-laden pagan religion, led to a cheapening of this great gift from God. This resulted in self-centered vulgar thoughts that were expressed in "silly talk," and "coarse jesting" (Eph. 5:4). Now that these Ephesians were believers, they needed to have a proper, God-oriented view of sexual relations and be thankful to God for them. Sex is a gift from God, but because of sin, it can be distorted, abused, made light of, and even destroyed. Almost all societies that have failed first degenerated into obscenity by open, immoral sexual behavior. The world often accuses believers in Christ of being anti-sex and overly prudent, even to the point of saying that Christianity is against the sex act. But this is a complete misrepresentation of the truth. John Stott concludes:

> The reason why Christians should dislike and avoid vulgarity is not because we have a warped view of sex, and are either ashamed or afraid of it, but because we have a high and holy view of it as being in its right place God's good gift, which we do not want to see cheapened. All God's gifts, including sex, are subjects for thanksgiving rather than for joking. To joke about them is bound to degrade them; to thank God for them is the way to preserve their worth as the blessings of a loving Creator.[5]

The unusual construction translated "For this you know with certainty" (v. 5) is used, A. T. Robertson suggests, because the knowledge came from their own experience.[6] He says that no "immoral [Gk. *pornos*, from which the English word *pornography* is derived], or impure person or covetous man who is an idolater [desiring and seeking to possess more—Paul properly called such a person 'an idolater,' his possessions being his god], has an inheritance in the kingdom of Christ and God [literally reading, 'of the Christ and God']." This condemnation describes persons whose lives are characterized by these ungodly qualities, not persons who at one time or another might slip and sin. Believers can fail and practice wickedness. This is not how the child of God is characterized in Christ, but carnality and walking in the flesh can suddenly overtake that person and bring about sin.

The apostle James warns of this happening: "Each one is tempted when he is carried away and enticed by his own lust. Then when lust has conceived, it gives birth to sin; and when sin is accomplished, it brings forth death" (James 1:14–15). James may certainly be referring to physical death but not the loss of salvation. He also may be describing the terrible consequences of evil in the life of the child of God. It is deathlike and sometimes brings a permanent scarring in the Christian walk.

Paul warned the Ephesians against being deceived by "empty words" (Eph. 5:6), possibly referring to the false belief that the Christian can "continue in sin that grace might increase" (Rom. 6:1-2, 15-16), or the Gnostic heresy that sin affects only the body, which will die and be destroyed, while salvation affects the eternal soul (Col. 2:4-8). This last view reflects the growing cultish idea that there is a dichotomy in the spiritual realm. One can live one way though hold to beliefs that reflect something different. While Christians have a body, soul, and spirit, these human attributes are related and mysteriously connected. Believers are but *one* in essence and are not divided up into separate and disconnected parts. This growing incipient Gnosticism would deeply damage Christian thinking in the decades following the early church period. The Gnostic heresy would inflict damage in every area of New Testament doctrine.

Although speaking to a predominantly gentile audience, Paul, as a Jew, had a great knowledge of their false religions and knew that they had lying prophets, i.e. those who would "deceive you with empty words" (Eph. 5:6). Not only had he been confronting false teachers, who were either Judaizers or representatives of pagan beliefs and philosophies (such as the Areopagus [Acts 17:22]), he knew, from the Old Testament writings, how often the Jews had been misled, listening to these false messengers as if they represented God (e.g., 1 Kings 18:21-22; Jer. 5:31; 6:13; 14:14; 23:32).

Likewise, Paul knew of the suffering of the Jewish nation under the wrath of God, foremost being the Assyrian captivity of Israel and the Babylonian captivity of Judah and the attendant violence, torture, and death that even the righteous suffered because of the "sons of disobedience" (Eph. 5:6). The apostle knew that this degree of disobedience, especially in moral issues, was not limited to Israel. God's wrath would fall on unfaithful Israel but also on the wickedness of the sinful nations of the world. The Lord's judgment can fall on both Jew and Gentile, but His grace can also be dispensed to both (Rom. 11:21-24). In God's sight right is right and sin is sin. All human beings may receive either His grace or His judgment. The personal issue comes down to trust and belief or unbelief (v. 23).

James Robinson Boise writes: "The question is raised by the expositors whether the anger of God in this life, or in the future life is here referred to. . . . Clearly the statement is a general truth with no specified limitations. Wherever the sons of disobedience are, there the anger of God comes upon them."[7]

The apostle Paul further writes, "Therefore, do not be partakers with them" (Eph. 5:7). This can mean "Do not become" or "Stop being" partakers with them! Paul acknowledges the fact that the Ephesian believers "were formerly darkness" (v. 8)—not just *in* darkness, but *characterized by* darkness. As a result of trusting the Lord Jesus Christ, however, "now you are light in the Lord" (v. 8). The Ephesian believers have a responsibility, therefore, to "walk [literally, 'keep on walking about'] as children [literally, 'born ones'] of light." Paul urged them and us to "learn [by testing and proving] what is pleasing to the Lord" (v. 10). The parenthetic statement in verse 9 describes "the fruit of the light" as "all goodness and righteousness and truth," qualities of the triune Godhead. The joining of fruit and light is interesting, first, because the Lord Jesus described both Himself and His disciples as "the light of the world" (John 8:12; 9:5; Matt. 5:14), and second, because fruit is related to the ministry and control of the Holy Spirit in a believer's life (Gal. 5:22–23, 25; cf. John 15:4–5, 8).

Since the Ephesian believers are now "light in the Lord" (Eph. 5:8), Paul commands them, "Do not participate [literally, 'have no fellowship or part- nership'] in the unfruitful deeds of darkness, but instead even expose them" (v. 11; see John 3:19–21). A. R. Fausset writes: "Sins, being terminated in themselves, are called 'works' ('deeds' in the NIV), not 'fruits' (Gal. 5:19, 22). Their only fruit, if the term is to be used (Deut. xxxii. 32), is 'death.'"[8] The Word of God places great emphasis on what comes out of the life of a person. Thoughts and actions are seen as working together. This is what makes the Bible so different from other so-called religious revelations. The Scriptures will not let one believe one thing and then act differently. Human responsi- bility for decisions and actions is seen throughout the Word of God. Paul will not allow these new Ephesian Christians to simply claim a *belief* in Christ without a *life* in Christ!

The reason is that "it is disgraceful even to speak of the things which are done by them in secret" (Eph. 5:12). Christians are transparent in the eyes of the Lord and therefore should be equally transparent in the eyes of others. It is humanly impossible to live a perfect life, but that is the goal, the standard, for the spiritual life! It may be put this way: the work of physical light and of Christians as spiritual light is to expose and dispel darkness (see Matt. 5:15–16). Paul continues, "But all things become visible when they are exposed by the light," because "everything that becomes visible is light" (Eph. 5:13).

Robertson writes, "Turn on the light . . . Often the preacher is the only man brave enough to turn the light on the private sins of men and women or even those of a community."[9] The poetic verse that follows is believed by some apparently to be addressed to the unbeliever: "Awake, sleeper, and arise from the dead [the spiritually dead], and Christ will shine on you" (v. 14). However, it still could be applied to believers and be meant to sober them up as to how they were living. This is not "a direct quotation of Old Testament

Scripture (though they contain echoes of Isa. 60:1 and possibly Isa. 9:2; 26:19; 51:17; 52:1). Most likely this section is an early baptismal hymn based on Isa 60:1. Paul is soon to mention hymns in the context of worship (v. 19), so that this may well have been a liturgical chant addressed to those about to be baptized (cf. I Tim. 3:16)."[10] This may or may not be true, though it is certain that the early church worshiped by singing and reading of the Psalms to uplift those attending the congregational meetings.

Once again Paul concludes his counsel with "Therefore be careful how you walk [literally, "walk about"], not as unwise men, but as wise" (Eph. 5:15). The Greek actually reads, "Therefore you all continually see carefully how you walk." The Greek word *blepō* [to see] not only refers to ordinary vision, but "can also be used for conceptual perception, 'to perceive,' even abs[olutely] in the sense, 'to have insight.'"[11] It is also being used here as a command from Paul. He served at their church for three years; he knew the culture they came from and that still existed all around them. He cannot stress strongly enough the need for these believers to continually be observant as to where they will go and what they will do.

They are to walk as "wise [Gk., *sophos*]" men. This Greek word dates back to the sixth century BC and "in general . . . denotes a materially complete and hence unusual knowledge and ability."[12] For these Christians this "unusual knowledge and ability" was to come from Paul's teachings and other Scripture, as well as the leading of the Holy Spirit. Only in this way could these believers avoid the temptations and pitfalls of the pagan culture in which they lived.

Paul goes on: "making the most of your time [literally, 'buying up the time'], because the days are evil" (v. 16). Christianity is not a spectator sport. Believers are to "buy up" or "redeem" their time because they exist in a sinful, dying world. Because the world offers such distractions in entertainment and materialism, it is difficult to really believe it is such an evil environment for human existence. The average person may wrongly think this is a "good place" and that it has only a few sinful inclinations. It is only through divine revelation, the Word of God, that the true condition of the world is revealed. John the apostle wrote in his first epistle that we know "the whole world lies in the power of the evil one" (1 John 5:19). "The power of" is in italics. Many commentators believe this should be left out and that John is implying that the world is actually lying in bed in fornication with the devil! This would certainly be a more graphic interpretation. As Stott observes: "All of us have the same amount of time at our disposal, with sixty minutes in every hour and twenty-four hours in every day. None of us can stretch time. But wise people use it to the fullest possible advantage. They know that time is passing, and also that *the days are evil.* So they seize each fleeting opportunity while it is there. For once it has passed, even the wisest people cannot recover it."[13]

"The days are evil [Gk., *ponēros*] (Eph. 5:16), which may also mean, "painful," "grievous," "full of sorrow and affliction."[14] What better description exists for the world, not only in Paul's time but also today? The Bible is the only true record of God's revelation to humankind, so those who know this fact are required to share it with those who don't. Only in obedience to God's will do believers "redeem" their time: studying God's Word, sitting under solid biblical teaching, fellowshipping with other believers, spreading the gospel message, and generally living their faith before a world in decay. All of this comes down to what really counts. It has to do with priorities that are spiritual and not simply temporal. While believers can enjoy all that God has bestowed in His world, still spiritual issues should occupy the basic thrust of existence. And there is a place for giving proper attention to the temporal: shelter, work, food, and rest. Children of God also can have fun, be friendly, and interact with others on a very human level. It is not necessary for Christians to wear a sober and serious face all the time!

Paul writes, "So then do not be [literally, 'stop becoming'] foolish, but understand what the will of the Lord is" (v. 17). Often "foolishness" is equated with laughter and lightness, but Paul is not calling believers to be super-serious, not exhibiting any enjoyment whatsoever. To Paul foolishness has to do with making decisions and acting in a contrary manor that is self-destructive.

Paul reiterates the need to be wise by stating the opposite and coupling it to a duty. In verse 16 he tells readers to be wise and redeem their time. Here he says, "Do not be foolish, but understand what the will of the Lord is." Knowing God's will and acting upon it (redeeming your time) is being a wise Christian, one who realizes that this pattern was modeled by our Lord Jesus Christ for our benefit. "Jesus said to them, 'My food is to do the will of Him who sent Me, and to accomplish His work'" (John 4:34).

This is the effective life of the Christian: knowing then doing. One cannot "do" properly without first "knowing," and knowledge comes from the study of God's Word. Then again, one may "know" much but not share that knowledge through edification of the body or sharing God's truth with the unsaved. Pursuing an incomplete existence is foolish.

The apostle also writes, "Understand what the will of the Lord is" (v. 17), which involves the realization that God's will for every believer is both "general" and "specific." The "general" will could imply that believers are to be "conformed to the likeness of Christ." The "general" will of God, is found in the Bible. These issues are clear, and what the Lord wants for the child of God is spelled out in so many verses here in Ephesians. However, God's "specific" will for a Christian's life will be realized in certain things that each individual Christian must do that may be different and distinct from what is necessary for another.

John MacArthur puts it this way: "Although his plans and directions for each believer are not found in Scripture, the general principles for understanding them are there."[15] And Stott adds, "To be sure, we shall find general principles in Scripture to guide us, but detailed decisions have to be made after careful thought and prayer and the seeking of advice from mature and experienced believers."[16]

Paul now takes the opportunity to spell out some important general principles: For health reasons wine mixed with water was frequently recommended in ancient times. And this could easily lead to excess (see 1 Tim. 5:23). Paul commands, "Do not get drunk [or 'stop getting drunk'] with wine, for that is dissipation [or 'profligacy']" (Eph. 5:18). This was an appropriate warning. As in modern cultures, drunkenness or alcoholic dependency was a major problem. These new believers had to consider long and hard their testimony as they struggled with drinking too much wine. Hoehner explains that this passage contains "the idea of profligate or licentious living that is wasteful. . . . In this verse the literal sense of incorrigibility seems best, for a drunken man acts abnormally. Rather than controlling himself, the wine controls him."[17]

"But," the apostle continues, "be filled [literally, 'keep on being filled, controlled'] with the Spirit" (v. 18). Hoehner points out that "each Christian has all the Spirit, but the command here is that the Spirit have all of him. The wise walk, then, is one that is characterized by the Holy Spirit's control."[18]

This "control" is illustrated in verse 19. In the Greek text, instead of "speak" being a verb, it is a participle, "speaking," describing the result of being filled or controlled with the Spirit. The Holy Spirit should be in charge of the believer's life. Paul first uses the imperative ("keep on being controlled") and then shows what will come out of the one being controlled. The believer's words will reflect the inner attitudes that are generated by the work of the Spirit of God. Christians have to learn to "let go and let God"! Our speaking "to one another" should be "in psalms, and hymns and spiritual songs." Once again the Greek text continues with a participle, "singing and making melody with your heart to the Lord."

Verse 19 is referring to fellowship between believers when they meet to study God's Word. This is the time when believers speak "to one another" in this manner. The children of the Lord who are filled by the Holy Spirit want to offer praise whether they are alone or together with other believers, so they "speak to one another," or seek fellowship through "psalms and hymns and spiritual songs." The whole purpose is to make "melody with your heart to the Lord." If one has difficulties in life, this is impossible to do from the natural inclination. Thus it must be prompted by the inner work of God's Spirit. He must take charge in the soul and in the heart. To have joy and peace in the midst of chaos has to come from Him.

Church history is full of the stories of the martyrs who went to their deaths with total acceptance and peace.

Only the heart of a believer can take a psalm, hymn, and/or spiritual song and use it to make a "melody" to the Lord. This has nothing to do with singing ability; this is the true vocal praise and worship of a believer to God. The greatest unsaved vocalist on earth is totally incapable of making a pleasing melody to God from the inner recesses of the soul. One has to be in close fellowship with the Lord and be controlled by the Holy Spirit for this to happen. Yet the Spirit-filled (controlled) believer can scarcely be restrained from such activity, whether a good vocalist or not. The "heart" is what speaks to the Lord.

The sentence continues with another present participle: "always giving thanks for all things in the name of our Lord Jesus Christ to God, even the Father" (v. 20). Paul wants to make sure that his readers understand the new and close relationship they now have with God. He is the heavenly Father in contrast to what they knew before of the Greek and Roman gods. They were but stone deities with which no one could relate. These gods had to be placated. Their anger often had to be abated because of their emotional capriciousness. It is said that to still the gods the Greeks would often stand on the seashore and toss chunks of meat into the sky to calm the deities. This is a far cry from the God of the Jewish people. While He is a God of justice, He is also full of mercy—and His children can call Him Father!

In reference to what the believer should give thanks for, Charles Hodge remarks:

> We are to give thanks *for all things;* afflictions as well as for our joys, say the ancient commentators. This is not in the text, though Paul, as we learn from other passages, gloried in his afflictions. Here the words are limited by the context, *for all our mercies. In the name of the Lord Jesus.* The apostles preached in the name of the Lord Jesus; they wrought miracles in his name; believers are commanded to pray in his name; to give thanks in his name, and to do all things in his name.[19]

Finally, instead of using a simple verb, the closing statement is again a participle: "and be subject [submitting] to one another in the fear of Christ"

(v. 21). All of these participles used in this long paragraph are present tenses, meaning continuing and linear action.

Back in verse 15, Paul told the Ephesian believers that they should "not walk as unwise men but as wise." In verse 18 he added, "Be filled with the Spirit." Subjecting oneself to another is truly an example of both of these commands, because a natural person will not do it. The Greek word translated as "subject" is an old military term meaning "to line up under."[20] Generally unsaved people will not willingly place themselves under someone else unless compensated or coerced in some way. Hoehner adds, "Unbelievers tend to take great pride in individualism and independence, which leads to selfishness."[21]

The rebellious human heart wants freedom from the control of another—and this also applies to the servitude even to God. But Christians are to act differently and are to acquiesce to the other person. This does not mean a loss of identity which most people fear. But it has in view a companionship and relationship whereby the two or more are sharing the joy of the Christian experience.

Believers, however, exhibit wisdom and the filling of the Spirit by doing this very thing. For while, within the Trinity, all members of the Godhead are equal, when it comes to the function of the Trinity, it becomes evident that the Son has willingly subjected Himself to the Father, and the Holy Spirit has willingly subjected Himself to the Son; therefore believers are to "be subject one to another in the fear of Christ." The present generation, especially in America, dislikes the idea of submission to someone else. But if that submission is to God, the person has peace, protection, and safety. He will do His children no harm; nor will He unduly oppress them. But the human spirit prefers freedom over servitude, even if it is just.

Believers are to be subject to one another "in the fear [or reverence] of Christ" (v. 21). He can be trusted. After all, He went to the cross to be our personal Redeemer. The apostle Paul was so moved by this sacrificial gesture that he willingly became a servant of Christ. He refers to this voluntary servitude at the beginning of three of his letters (Rom. 1:1; Phil. 1:1; Titus 1:1). This is the key for believers, for these instructions Paul has just given and the ones to come. Believers should not fear serving one another, though this does not mean that one should become a "doormat" to an abusive and carnal fellow Christian. As Stott says, "Those who are truly subject to Jesus Christ do not find it difficult to submit to each other as well."[22] And Klyne Snodgrass concludes, "Mutual submission is love in action. It brings equal valuing and is the power by which a *Christian* community establishes itself."[23] A heart does not fear binding itself to another heart when each person is in submission to God and does not have any personal axes to grind or selfish agendas to fulfill.

The final participle ("submitting," "subjecting") (Eph. 5:21) also properly serves as the introductory statement for all the interpersonal commandments that follow in the next section of the letter. Wood comments that "the basic principle of Christian submissiveness (v. 21) that governs the community life of the church applies also to social relationships. Paul selects the most conspicuous of these and shows how they are transformed by a prior obedience to Christ. . . . The gospel places such relationships as these on a revolutionary new footing, since all are subjected to the lordship of Christ."[24]

## One in Personal Relationships (5:22–5:33)

In the Greek text the verb "be subject" (v. 22) does not occur, but the idea is carried over from verse 21. The apostle has created a long, running sentence that begins with the idea of being filled (controlled) by the Holy Spirit (v. 18). This is one of the most powerful concepts in all of Paul's theology about the Christian life. This filling may be compared to the skill it takes to ride a bicycle. It would be difficult to figure out what is happening in the brain that finally results in the process of balancing oneself. The rider is not fully conscious of what is happening! So it is with the filling of the Spirit of God. How is this done? The only thing the believer is somewhat aware of has to do with *submission*. And even that process is difficult to explain!

In the Greek text of verse 22 the nouns translated "wives" and "husbands" are literally "women" and "men," but the marital relationship obviously is meant, for the apostle Paul adds "your own [literally, 'one's own']." The reason for this submission in the marital relationship is that "the husband is the head of the wife as Christ also is the head of the church. Paul makes a special point of emphasis when he adds, "He Himself" (v. 23; see 1 Cor. 11:3; 12:12–13, 27). The relationship of husband and wife, therefore, is a sacred one because it illustrates and witnesses to Christ's relationship to "the church," over which it is said: "He Himself being the Savior of the body" (Eph. 5:23). Therefore, "as the church is subject to Christ, so also the wives ought to be to their husbands in everything." Comparing the submission of the wife to her husband to that of the church to Christ, Boise writes: "There can be nothing debasing, nothing except what is dignified and noble in the subjection of the church to Christ. While it is complete, it is also a loving, confiding, ennobling subjection. To this, and this only, wives are exhorted."[25]

The modern women's liberation movement, including some women within the church, consider these directions demeaning in spite of their spiritual significance. When fulfilled in light of the commands to husbands that follow, however, they become appropriate and necessary for the calm operation of a biblical home honoring to God. It is also important to note that Paul is arguing his points here on the basis of what is *doctrinally* correct and not what is simply a *cultural* issue.

It is important that the Bible not be interpreted simply in the light of what is happening presently in the culture. False interpretations can come about because of social pressures to make the Scriptures say what we want them to say. Interpretation must be based on what was going on at the time of the writing. One cannot impose thoughts and ideas upon the text that are not there. The Word of God cannot be bent to say just what we want it to say.

The counterpart to what the apostle has said to wives is the command to husbands to "love your wives," with the standard being, "just as Christ also loved the church" (v. 25). A seminarian once went to his professor and said, "Sir, I have a problem. I think I love my wife too much." Thinking for a moment, the teacher asked, "Do you love her as much as Christ loves the church?" The student answered, "Of course not!" The professor came back with, "Then you had better get with it!" The point became obvious. The standard for the love husbands should have for their wives is the pattern set by Christ in His love for His own, the church. And no human being can love that much. Wood explains: "Greco-Roman society held that wives had obligations to their husbands, but not vice versa. Christianity introduced a revolutionary approach to marriage that equalized the rights of wives and husbands and established the institution on a much firmer foundation than ever before. . . . Paul chooses a verb that insists that the love of a Christian man for his wife must be a response to and an expression of the love of God in Christ extended to the church."[26]

This love (Gk., *agapē*) is not just the emotional love of friendship (Gk. *philia*; the difference between the two is seen in John 21:15–17), or the love of sexual partners (Gk. *eros*; the word is not used in the Bible), although both of those kinds of love also should exist between husbands and wives. It is the self-giving, sacrificial love God displayed in providing salvation for sinful humankind (John 3:16) and exhibited by Christ, who "loved the church and gave Himself up for her" (Eph. 5:25). Christ's goal in doing this was "to sanctify her, having cleansed her by the washing of water with the word."

With this thought Paul is saying that the way a husband loves his wife results in the strengthening of her spiritual life. She becomes more secure spiritually in her walk with the Lord. The husband does for her something like what Christ does as we are related to Him.

The washing that the apostle is describing is not about water baptism, though many in "high" churches hold this position. Ceremonial water baptism is not in view but a genuine cleansing of the heart and soul. Nevertheless, many commentators come close to endorsing the view of some kind of baptismal regeneration or baptismal effectiveness brought about by the ritual of water. Hoehner says emphatically, "This is not baptismal regeneration, for that would be contrary to Paul's teaching in this book as well as all his other writings and the entire New Testament."[27] The objective in making the church holy was to "present to Himself the church in all her glory [as his bride], having no spot or wrinkle or any such thing, but that she should be holy and blameless" (v. 27).

Turning to another illustration of the self-sacrificing love husbands should have for their wives, Paul wrote that "husbands ought to love their own wives as their own bodies" (v. 28a). It is with this thought that the comparison of Christ and the husband comes into play. The husband can bring about a certain blessing on the human level to his spouse. He is good to her just as Christ is to His church. The reality is that the man "who loves his own wife loves himself" and shows that he understands that he will receive a benefit (v. 28b). While love may be a one-way expression of giving, more than likely there is a residual effect.

Paul goes on and points out that "no one ever hated his own flesh, but nourishes and cherishes it" (v. 29). The great example again is Christ, who similarly treats with love "the church, because we are members of His body" (v. 30). The Lord Jesus voluntarily went to the cross for those He loved. So, in like manner, the husband is to sacrifice himself because of his love for his wife. Quoting Genesis 2:24, Paul writes, "For this cause [literally, 'therefore'] a man shall leave his father and mother and shall cleave to his wife; and the two shall become one flesh" (Eph. 5:31).

Paul's quoting of Genesis 2:24, after stating that believers are members of Christ's body, leads Henry Alford to draw this analogy: "Adam's deep sleep, wherein Eve was formed out of his opened side, is emblematic of Christ's death, which was the birth of the Spouse, the Church."[28] The Christian marriage that grows, matures, and flourishes shows in some small way the depth of commitment that Christ has for His own. But even that near *perfect* marriage cannot plumb the depths and reach the heights of how much Christ loves the church. A mature Christian marriage is but a shadow of how much the Lord cares for the believers.

Paul then says about the church and Christ's relationship to it: "This mystery is great" (Eph. 5:32). This is true both in the biblical sense, of a great truth now revealed, but also in the fact that it was hidden in the past. But, as already mentioned, and in the normal sense, it is simply a spiritual fact that is too difficult to understand. Paul explains that this is "with reference to Christ and the church."

The apostle then sums up his discussion of marital relations by saying, "Let each individual among you also love his own wife even as himself; and let the wife see to it that she respect [literally, 'treat reverentially'] her husband" (v. 33). With this verse he describes the Christian marriage as a distinct mutual relationship that cuts two ways. There is to be in the Christian marriage a giving and a receiving—reciprocal responses as to how each is to treat the other. Such a passage removes the charge that for the woman there is "slavery" in marriage. It must be remembered, however, that in a marriage between unbelievers, the couple may live in a most unholy way, bringing about abuse and mistreatment, but this is not the way of Christian marriage. Believers have to learn how to relate in the marriage, and Christ's love for the church is the clear example. Both the Old and New Testaments honor marriage, which is set forth as an institution of sanity and protection. The Bible never condones abuse against the wife. And in return the wife is to respect her husband. Paul sets this argument forth in the form of commands. Christian spouses do not have options in these matters.

In summary: wives then should be subject to their husbands as the church is to Christ. But it is to be a two-way street. The husband is responsible for the love in the marriage. The motive to this subject is a regard to the Lord (v. 22). The ground of this relationship is that the husband is the head of the wife as Christ is the head of the church (v. 23). This subjection is not confined to any one sphere in the marriage, but to every aspect, yet it does not imply slavery. Both the husband and the wife are individuals yet still form a bond, a oneness that cannot be fully explained (v. 24). The best way Satan can destroy individuals is to bring division in the marriage. When there is discord in the home, the ones often most harmed are the children. This is the way the devil is able to destroy lives and place a blight on the Christian witness. Hodges comments:

> Husbands should love their wives. 1. The measure of this love is Christ's love for the church for whose redemption he died, vs. 25–27. 2. The ground of love is in both cases the same—the wife is flesh of her husband's flesh, and bone of his bone. So the church is flesh of Christ's flesh and bone of his bone. Husband and wife are one flesh; so are Christ and the church. What is true of the one is true of the other, vs, 29–31. 3. The

union between Christ and his church is indeed of a higher order than that between husband and wife—nevertheless the analogy between the two cases is such as to render it obligatory on the husband to love his wife as being himself, and for the wife to reverence her husband, vv. 32–33.[29]

## Study Questions

1. How should Christians live their lives as children of God?

2. What types of daily action does Paul reject for Christians?

3. In what terms did Paul vividly describe the change in a person when regenerated?

4. Why should the Christian expose the unfruitful works of darkness?

5. How is the overflowing fullness of the Holy Spirit manifested in one's daily life?

6. Why should Christian wives be subject to their husbands?

7. What two reasons are given for Christian husbands to love their wives?

8. What is the result when a man and a woman become husband and wife?

# CHAPTER 13

# Standing Strong in the Lord
# Ephesians 6:1-24

### Preview:

*In his concluding chapter to the Ephesians, Paul finishes his discussion of the believer's outward walk expanding beyond the relationship between husband and wife to include the whole family (children and parents) and other close relationships (slaves and masters). Paul then explains the tools for standing strong in the Lord by using armor and sword as examples of the believers' defensive and offensive weapons in defending their faith.*

## Family and Other Relationships (6:1-9)

From marital relationships, Paul turns to family relationships. First he addresses children, commanding them, "Obey your parents in the Lord, for this is right" (v. 1). The question may be asked, are these children born again, or have they not as yet accepted Christ as their Savior? More than likely they are somewhat mature in age since they can "reason" with what Paul is writing to them. And he commands them to act in a spiritual way and obey the Word of God. John Stott has another view, adding: "Child obedience belongs to that realm which came in medieval theology to be called 'natural justice.' It does not depend on special revelation; it is part of the natural law which God has written on all human hearts."[1] But this may not be the case, since the apostle quotes Scripture and tells how children are to relate to parents.

If Stott is correct, it means that the obedience of children is not exclusive to the Christian ethic. It was taught by both Greek and Roman moralists, as well as by Stoic philosophers. They saw the obedience of a son as being self-evident.[2]

Stott continues: "Much earlier, and in oriental culture, one of the greatest emphases of Confucius was on filial respect, so that still today, though centuries later, Chinese, Korean and Japanese customs continue to reflect his influence. Indeed, virtually all civilizations have regarded the recognition of parental authority as indispensable to a stable society."[3]

Paul, to support his directions, quotes from the Ten Commandments—"Honor your father and mother" (Exod. 20:12; Deut. 5:16)—and points out that this "is the first commandment with a promise" (Eph. 6:2). The apparent discrepancy here, since the second commandment also has a promise (Exod. 20:6; Deut. 5:10), is thus explained by A. Skevington Wood: "It seems most likely that 'first' here means first in importance. The rabbis regarded this commandment as the weightiest of all"[4]

Such commandments to children imply that the parents are teaching their flock at home, not only in word, but also in example. If this is not done, children will absorb the practices and attitudes of the culture. They will then go to war with the parents, not understanding that they are not simply obeying them but the Lord who sets forth the need for their obedience to those who are raising them up. Basically, the delinquency of children is disobedience to what God says and not simply what the parents say.

To support the point he is making, Paul continues the quote: "That it may be well with you, and that you may live long on the earth" (Eph. 6:3), here adapting for gentile believers the Jewish aspect of the promise, "in the land the Lord your God is giving you." Paul then addresses parents, particularly fathers, writing, "Do not provoke your children to anger" (v. 4). James Robinson Boise writes: "The address is to fathers as the heads of families; possibly, also, because they might be more liable than mothers to severity, or even harshness. Such is the usual explanation; yet the question arises, may not *hoi pateres* be understood here in the sense of *parents*, as in Heb. 11.23?"[5]

In the Greek text in Ephesians 6:1 the word translated "parents" is *geneousin*, meaning "the ones who generated (gave life to)" you. In verse 4 the Greek *hoi pateres* is clearly a reference to fathers. Our present culture, because of broken families, has become more and more matriarchal rather than patriarchal. Young boys especially need the strong discipline and leadership of a dad. To fathers Paul says, "Bring them up in the discipline and instruction [literally, 'admonition'] of the Lord." The ultimate source of this instruction is not from the parents but from God. The child is not obeying the parents "only," but the Lord. It is significant that the Bible places the primary responsibility for this raising of children on fathers, while today it falls on mothers.

This is certainly not meant to diminish the very important role of mothers in child development. Both parents bring to the family their own special influences that fit exactly their gender. The ideal home has both loving and Spirit-led parents meant by the Lord to impart proper spiritual, moral, social, and intellectual maturity in the growth of the youngsters.

Paul discusses last the household relations between slaves and masters (v. 5). Slavery was a common social arrangement in ancient history, even as it remains today in some parts of the world. There was generally speaking two levels of slavery: (1) slaves purchased from a slave pool or those made slaves who had been captured in war; and (2) those who became indentured slaves—that is, they voluntarily submitted themselves to a master for life. Whichever, kind treatment of the slave is what Paul is most concerned for. It must be remembered that many slaves could not have survived in that culture unless they lived under this arrangement. Most of their needs were taken care of, and they did not lack for shelter and food. In what he writes here, Paul does not make a distinction as to the class of slavery he has in view.

"In this appeal Paul was addressing a numerous class," says Marvin Vincent. "In many cities of Asia Minor, slaves outnumbered freemen"[6] As mentioned, a large number of the people captured in war from conquered cities and lands frequently were taken as slaves (Exod. 1:8–11; Lev. 25:44). Then as now a slave trade existed (Gen. 7:27–28). How then should slaves act toward their masters, especially after they became believers?

Paul writes, "Slaves, be obedient to those who are your masters [literally, 'lords'], according to the flesh with fear and trembling, in the sincerity of your heart, as to Christ" (Eph. 6:5). "As to Christ" implies that they are actually serving Him. They are accepting their position in life while bringing honor to His name. They should do this as a witness even though the master may not be a believer. This seems to be Paul's point as he continues on with his thought: "not through eye service as men-pleasers, but as slaves of Christ, doing the will of God from the heart. With good will render service, as to the Lord, and not to men, knowing that whatever good thing each one does, this he will receive back from the Lord, whether slave or free" (vv. 6–8). The apostle reinforces his point by writing again, "With good will render service, as to the Lord, and not to men." It would take strong spiritual insight for the Christian slave to realize that his position of servitude, at that time in his life, was as if he were serving Christ. Most slaves would naturally be resentful and bitter because of their loss of freedom and because of their bondage. Charles Hodge adds:

> Servants should be obedient to their masters. This obedience should be rendered—1. With solicitude. 2. With singleness of mind. 3. As part of

their obedience to Christ, v. 5. Therefore, not only when observed by men or from the desire to please men, but as serving Christ and desiring to please him; rendering their services with readiness as to the Lord and not to men; because they know that at his bar all men, whether bond or free, shall be treated according to their works, vs. 6–8.[7]

---

### The Christian Walking in Obedience

Salvation is "the obedience of faith" (Rom. 1:5).

Believers are to obey the gospel resulting in righteousness (Rom. 6:16).

Believers are to conform their thoughts to the obedience of Christ (2 Cor. 10:5).

Believers are to be as obedient children (1 Pet. 1:14).

Believers are to purify the soul in obeying the truth (1 Pet. 2:11).

---

Whether one is in slavery or walks about in freedom, the issue of responsibility becomes paramount. One must be continually doing what is right, what is good, because God will judge and give back a reward for so doing what honors Him. All believers are leveled before the scrutiny and judgment of God. He sees the actions and He knows the heart. He does not give slack as to one's social position. He judges on the basis of what one does in the place one finds himself or herself.

Masters do not get off easily either. They are to live a life of responsibility as to how they treat their slaves. Paul concludes this section and writes to "masters [literally, 'lords']," obviously Christian masters, whom he commanded to "do the same things to them" (v. 9), that is with respect and sincerity of heart as to the Lord. He directed them to "give up threatening" because the masters know that "both their [the slaves'] Master [literally, 'Lord'] and yours is in heaven, and there is no partiality [literally, 'respect of person'] with Him" (v. 9). In these times there was no such thing as democracy as we now understand it, yet the seeds of equal treatment are given in these verses. All stand equal before God; and all must be treated in an equal manner in His sight. These seeds of equal treatment would grow in democratic societies centuries later. But such fair treatment has a theological mandate in the words of the apostle Paul. A. R. Fausset writes: "Christ will not regard such present distinctions in His future judgments. The slave that has acted faithfully for the Lord's sake, though the master may not repay his faithfulness, shall have the Lord for his Paymaster. The freeman (in the sense of master) who has done good for the Lord's sake, though man may not reward him, has the Lord for his debtor (Prov. xix. 17)."[8]

## One in Resisting Satan's Forces (6:10–20)

The apostle now shifts gears and goes to another subject that was heavy on his mind and heart. He was concerned that here in Ephesus the believers should be aware of the satanic struggle that waged war against their witness. He had already written about how the devil exercised control over the unbelievers in the world (Eph. 2:1–3). Now he writes about how Satan has made the world his slave, and how the minds of the lost were blinded by his insidious evil activities. But his work of rebellion even spills over to the walk of the child of God. Whether the believer realizes it or not, a war is taking place.

For the Christian this conflict is not only real, it is difficult and dangerous. The believer can be wounded and sidetracked in the spiritual walk. This conflict can be one in which true believers are often morally and spiritually damaged. Many Christians of good faith may succumb to Satan's assaults. Great mistakes are often committed and serious loss incurred from ignorance of the nature of this struggle and of the appropriate means for defending against Satan's strategies.

Satan is clever in how he makes his attacks against the church. He is aware of personal weaknesses, moral slips, and often the lack of trust in the Lord. He plots his warfare to fit the times, the culture, and the seasons of temptations. He knows what works best to trip up the saints in carrying out their Christian witness. He knows what makes them discouraged and how best to assault their citadels of faith.

Regarding spiritual warfare, Hodges notes: "Men are apt to regard it as a mere moral conflict between reason and conscience on the one side, and evil passions on the other. They therefore rely on their own strength, and upon the resources of nature for success. Against these mistakes the apostle warns his readers. He teaches that every thing pertaining to it is supernatural."[9]

The source of strength for such warfare is not found in nature. Neither is the conflict between the good and bad principles of human nature. Paul shows that believers belong to both a spiritual and a natural world, and are engaged in combat in which the higher powers of the universe are involved. Satan knows how to outsmart the child of God. His intellect is far superior over that of mortals. And while he is not omnipresent, not everywhere at one time, his intelligence and comprehension is far beyond what we can imagine.

This spiritual conflict is real and not simply imaginary. There are evil forces that swirl about energized by the demon world over which the devil has charge. The demons are his servants and lackeys who do his bidding. This conflict is serious and is not to be carried on with straws picked up by the wayside as armament. Believers contend with superhuman enemies and thus need, not only superhuman strength, but also divine armor and weapons.[10]

Having reached his last instructions, Paul writes, "Finally [cf. Gal. 6:17], be strong [literally, 'keep on being strengthened'] in the Lord, and in the strength of His might" (Eph. 6:10). The basis for accomplishing this order is to "put on [cf. 4:24] the full armor [the Greek word *panoplia* comes into English as *panoply*] of God, that you may be able to stand firm against the schemes of the devil [the Greek word *methodia* comes into English as *methodology*]" (v. 11). The point is that Satan has a strategy, a plan, a program, for destroying the believer and his spiritual witness, his influence and character. It is hard for human beings to fully conceive of the *near* spiritual world of demonic activity. And it is equally difficult to understand how Satan and his troops of fallen angels can reach into the realm of the physical and affect the world of the living.

### How Paul Wants the Believer to be Dressed

Put on the armor of light (Rom. 13:12).

Put on the Lord Jesus Christ (Rom. 13:14).

Be clothed with Christ (Gal. 3:27).

Put on the full armor of God (Eph. 6:11).

Take up the full armor of God (Eph. 6:13).

Gird your loins with truth (Eph. 6:14).

Put on the breastplate of righteousness (Eph. 6:14, cf. 1 Thess. 5:8).

Wear the shoes of the preparation of the gospel of peace (Eph. 6:15).

We desire to be clothed with our dwelling from heaven (2 Cor. 5:2).

Put on the breastplate of faith and love (1 Thess. 5:8, cf. Eph. 6:14).

Put on the helmet of the hope of salvation (1 Thess. 5:8, cf. Eph. 6:17).

Peter adds, clothe yourself with humility (1 Pet. 5:5)

It is important also to know that the believer cannot do anything without the strength that actually comes from the Lord Himself. We do not have the innate personal power to overcome the devil's powerful and evil influence. The Christian must "let go and let God," as the old saying is. He cannot be personally victorious. The victory belongs to the Lord. The forces of evil pull and push on the child of God, in what way, we cannot fully grasp. But the Word of God tells us this is so.

Harold Hoehner points out, "The form of the Greek imperative 'put on' . . . indicates that believers are responsible for putting on God's (not their) 'full armor . . . with all urgency'"[11] We need God's panoply because "our struggle is not against flesh and blood, but against the rulers, . . . powers, . . . world forces of this darkness (personal translation), . . . spiritual forces of wickedness in the heavenly places" (v. 12). There is no way that mere mortals can overcome such awesome power originating from the world of evil. Believers must appropriate and wear divine protection; otherwise they will be defeated.

For emphasis Paul repeats the command he gives in verse 11 to "take up the full armor of God" with the desired result that "you may be able to withstand in the day of evil, and everything having been done, to stand" (v. 13, my paraphrase). Is the average Christian always able to see the sudden attack coming, the thrust and jab that will knock him off his feet? Every child of God has to answer *no*. Believers are not more intelligent than Satan. It is easy to fall asleep and be unaware of the coming personal assault!

It is also important to note that for a complete defense against the satanic strategy, the believer must be fully armed, completely clothed with all the defensive weaponry that God affords. It is further important to realize that believers are not to go on the attack against Satan. We cannot win in ourselves against his power. To be able to stand firm and resist is the most we can accomplish.

After commanding, "Stand firm, therefore" (v. 14), Paul proceeds to list the weapons of spiritual warfare in God's panoply, all of which are defensive and protective except one—"the sword [literally, 'short sword or dagger'] of the Spirit, which is the word of God" (v. 17), which is able to supply both defense and protection. The Greek word translated "word" is *rhēma*, which means a spoken word or saying, not *logos*, which means a written word. An excellent example of this use of the Word (*rhēma*) of God is Jesus' responses to the devil's temptations in the desert after his fasting for forty days and forty nights (Matt. 4:1–11; Luke 4:1–13). William Hendriksen adds:

> In all the preceding sections Paul has described salvation as being, on the one hand, the product of God's sovereign grace, on the other hand the promised reward of human effort, the latter being made possible from

start to finish by the former. These two elements—divine grace and human responsibility—are again most beautifully combined in this closing section. Man must equip himself with a full suit of arms, that is, it is he who must put it on. It is also he, he alone, who must use this entire panoply. Nevertheless, the weapons are called "the full armor of *God*." It is *God* who has forged them. It is *God* who gives them. Not for one single moment is man able to employ them effectively except by *the power of God*.[12]

---

### Believers Are Strengthened in the Lord

The gospel is the power of God unto salvation (Rom. 1:16).

Abraham grew strong in the Lord (Rom. 4:20).

The word of the cross to the saved is the power of God (1 Cor. 1:18).

Christ is the power of God and the wisdom of God (1 Cor. 1:24).

Believers need to know the power of Christ's resurrection (Phil. 3:10).

Christ gave power to Paul (Phil. 4:13; 1 Tim. 1:12).

God gives to believers power, love, and a sound mind (2 Tim. 1:7).

Timothy is urged by Paul to be strong in the Lord's grace (2 Tim. 2:1).

The Lord empowered Paul in the proclamation of the gospel (2 Tim. 4:17).

Believers are protected by the power of God through faith (1 Pet. 1:5).

Paul wants believers to be strengthened with all of the power of God (Col. 1:11).

---

Wood observes, "The several items of the soldier's armor appear in the order in which they would be put on."[13] First is "having girded yourself around the loins with truth" (v. 14, my paraphrase), being put in place last of the clothing and first of the equipment for work or warfare to hold the loose garments tight and to provide a place to hang the short sword or dagger. The "girding" is accomplished by the use of long strips of leather or cloth. It tightens up the stomach area, which is most vulnerable for being sliced open with a forceful jab of the sword or spear. It is *truth* that gives the most protection. Fausset says: "As the girdle . . . kept all together, so that an ungirded soldier would be a contradiction in terms,—just so Truth is the band and expediter of the Christian's work in the conflict, without which all his armour would be but encumbrance."[14] It is possible that Paul is referring to the truth of Scripture and not simply truth in general, though the old saying "All truth is God's truth" may be applicable. Since Scripture records that, when the Lord comes to judge the earth, "righteousness will be the belt about His loins, and faithfulness the belt about His waist" (Isa. 11:5), it seems best to conclude that it refers to the truthfulness of the warrior.

The intended thought of the next clause is, "having put on the breastplate of righteousness" (Eph. 6:14). Hoehner states that this "refers not to justification, obtained at conversion (Rom. 3:24; 4:5), but to the sanctifying righteousness of Christ (1 Cor. 1:30) practiced in a believer's life. As a soldier's breastplate protects his chest from an enemy's attacks, so sanctifying , righteous living (Rom. 6:13; 14:17) guards a believer's heart against the assaults of the devil (cf. Isa. 59:17; Jas. 4:7)."[15] The believer also needs to have shod his feet "with the preparation of the gospel of peace" (v. 15). In other words, as he moves about in life, it is the gospel of personal salvation that gives him mobility and becomes a large part of how he is identified. The gospel of Christ's death and resurrection for sinners is always a part of the Christian witness.

It is important to understand that in ancient days, top quality sandals were required to solidly secure the warrior's feet. This was needed preparation for long marches and battles in rough terrain. Wood writes: "The military successes both of Alexander the Great and of Julius Caesar . . . were due in large measure to their armies being well shod and thus able to undertake long marches at incredible speed over rough terrain."[16] Thus the believer will face the attacks of Satan's minions and will need the assurance that comes from the good news that permanent peace with God has been secured through saving faith in the Lord Jesus Christ. This does not mean that all will go automatically for the believer. There is satanic hatred for the truth of the gospel of Christ. The cross is an ignominious symbol to the world. It reminds human beings that they are sinners in need of a divine Savior. This is offensive to the lost.

Continuing on with a single simple sentence, Paul directs the believers to take up "the shield of faith" (Eph. 6:16). In the writings of the Greek philosopher Homer, the word *thureos,* translated "shield," describes a large shield in the shape of a door. But it is made of wood covered with tough animal skin to protect most of the warrior's body from the arrows and darts of the enemy attackers. With this shield of faith, the apostle has in mind trusting God in daily living. By this defense the believer will be able to "extinguish all the flaming missiles of the evil one [the devil, Satan]." The missiles were flaming arrows that often would come as darts reigning down from the sky on the unprepared troops below. A. T. Robertson comments: "These darts were sometimes ablaze in order to set fire to the enemies' clothing or camp or homes."[17]

Roman soldiers often created a mass, or phalanx, with the shields linked and locked together over their heads. This would shield the troops from raining fiery arrows or flying stones. Only by trusting God and Christ can the believer be spared from the blazing arrows launched by Satan!

To complete the armor of the believer, he is now commanded to "Take [an imperative parallel to 'stand,' v. 14] the helmet of salvation" (v. 17). Because this headpiece was uncomfortable, it was usually put on last and handed to the warrior by an assistant. This protected the vulnerable part of the body left unprotected by other armor. It is usually identified by commentators as the assurance of salvation and an ultimate place in the presence of God. The head and the skull protect the brain, the seat of the thinking processes, so this piece of armor is essential for cognizance and awareness. The believer needs to have his thoughts protected!

"The sword of the Spirit," as already shown, and mentioned here in verse 17, although usually identified as the sole offensive weapon in the armor, is included in a list of protective armor and under the basic command, "Stand firm." This too is a defensive posture against the attacks of Satan and his minions. Believers are not told to "attack" or "charge" Satan. The sword then is to be used as a defensive weapon when under attack. Vincent explains: "The word of God serves both for attack and to parry the thrusts of the enemy. Thus Christ used it in His temptation. . . . It is the sword *of the Spirit,* because the Spirit of God gives it and inspires it. The Spirit's aid is needed for its interpretation."[18]

Paul also requests that believers "pray at all times in the Spirit, and with this in view, be on the alert with all perseverance and petition for all the saints" (v. 18). Why should prayer be offered at all times for the other Christians? It is because all those in Christ are faced with the same opposition. Satan is alive and well on planet Earth! He has the lost in his hands, and when possible, he will attack the child of God with equal fury. Prayer should be used not only for our own desires and needs, but for others as well. The familiar rhyme says: "Satan trembles when he sees/ the weakest saint upon his knees."

Paul closes his discussion about prayer by requesting the Ephesian believers to "pray on my behalf, that utterance may be given to me [literally, 'the word, message'] in the opening of my mouth, to make known with boldness the mystery of the gospel, for which I am an ambassador in chains" (vv. 19–20a). This is Paul's second reference to his being in prison (3:1). Because of his close walk with the Lord and his faithful ministry of the gospel, the apostle is seldom thought of as being in need of prayer, but his leadership made him the special target of Satan's attacks. That need for intercessory prayer is true of our pastors and Christian leaders today as well. Paul continues: "that in proclaiming it I may speak boldly, as I ought to speak" (v. 20b). Hoehner comments: "Here Paul probably did not refer to witnessing or preaching the gospel of Christ. Instead, he may have referred to his need to be bold (twice he said "fearlessly") and clear regarding the 'mystery of the gospel' when he would be on trial before Caesar in Rome (when and if the Jewish accusers would make charges against him). The Romans looked on the Christians as a sect of the Jews, and the Jews considered them as a heretical group."[19]

If and when a trial took place, Paul needed to make clear that Christianity was neither a sect of Judaism or a heretical group, but indeed, a brand new entity, the church: Christ's body, made up of Jewish and gentile believers.

This brings to mind Paul's lengthy discussion of this "mystery of the gospel" in 2:11–3:11. For this reason Paul was "an ambassador in chains."[20] He never mentions this confinement to get sympathy but simply to let his readers know of the reality of what he was going through for the sake of Christ. An ambassador (*presbeuō*) was generally an older man, an elder, who represented the king or a governing official. What Paul is writing is a twist of meaning. An ambassador would not be put in chains but would be free to deliver a message and return to his master. But this was not true of the apostle. For representing the Lord Jesus Christ, he was incarcerated and confined, and ultimately killed for his service.

## Conclusion (6:21–24)

"Tychicus," from the province of Asia (Acts 20:4), was the companion of Paul who carried this letter to the Ephesians and other churches in the province of Asia (cf. Col. 4:7). Wood called attention to the fact that verses 21 and 22 are "almost a word-for-word parallel with Col. 4:7–8. Nowhere is the connection between these two captivity letters closer than here."[21] He also writes nearly the same thing in 2 Timothy 4:12 and Titus 3:12. Here in Ephesians he is called "the beloved brother and faithful minister [the Greek word *diakonos* comes into English as *deacon*] in the Lord" (Eph. 6:21). Paul was sending Tychicus for the "very purpose" that the Ephesians "may know about us, and that he may comfort your hearts" (v. 22).

Paul's closing benediction is "Peace be to the brethren, and love with faith, from God the Father and the Lord Jesus Christ. Grace be with all those who love our Lord Jesus Christ with a love incorruptible [literally, 'with incorruptibility, immortality']" (vv. 23–24). This is longer than most of Paul's closing benedictions, but not nearly as long as the one ending Romans (16:25–27). The many similarities in subject and wording between this letter and the one to the Colossians are due to the fact that both were written at the same time and delivered by the same messenger. Colossians was addressed to a specific church and has many personal references and greetings (Col. 4:7–15), while Ephesians is more general and designed to be a circular letter to be read by all the churches in the province of Asia. It may have been delivered first to the church in Laodicea (v. 17b) and become identified with the church in Ephesus because it ended up there. Paul's letter to the Ephesians had special significance for the first-century church because of its emphasis on the unity of the church in Christ. It had that same significance for the church through the centuries and for the church today. Hoehner writes about the close of the Ephesian letter:

> The conclusion of this letter (6:21–24) illustrates to believers the kind of love and oneness that Paul had been demonstrating throughout the book. Although imprisoned in Rome, his thoughts were for the welfare of the Ephesian believers. In light of this he sent Tychicus to them to report on his situation. His purpose was to comfort them. In addition, he sent a letter (now known as the Book of Ephesians) to instruct them in doctrine and their daily walk. His greetings to them were more impersonal than the greetings in some of his other letters. This may have been due to great changes in the congregation over the two years since he had seen them or it could have been because the letter was encyclical.[22]

Hodge concludes:

> Want of love for Christ must deserve final perdition, and love to him must include preparation for heaven. This of necessity supposes Christ to be God. Want of love to him must imply enmity to God. It is all a delusion for anyone to think he can love the Infinite Spirit as manifested in nature, or in the Scriptures, if he does not recognize and love that same God in the clearest revelation of his character, in his most definite personal manifestation, and in his most intimate relation to us, as partaking of our nature, loving us, and giving himself for us.[23]

Loving Christ must include adoring admiration of His person, a great desire for His presence, a zealousness for His glory, and devotion to His service. These characteristics do not need to be ecstatic, but they must be controlling.[24]

## Study Questions

1. What reasons does Paul give for children to obey their parents?

2. How should fathers deal with their children?

3. Why are slaves directed to be obedient to their masters?

4. Why should masters treat their slaves properly and without threatening?

5. Why should the believer put on the full spiritual armor of God?

6. What are the elements of the Christian's armor of God, and what is their purpose?

7. What Christian ministry should accompany our standing against Satan and his hosts while we are dressed in the armor of God?

8. Why did Paul ask the Ephesians to pray for him?

# Bibliography

Best, Earnest. *Ephesians*. International Critical Commentary. Edited by J. A. Emerton and C. E. B. Cranfield. Edinburgh: T. & T. Clark, 1998.

Bruce, F. F. *Commentary on Galatians*. Grand Rapids: Eerdmans, 1992.

Dunn, James D. *The Epistle to the Galatians*. London: A. & C. Black, 1993.

Eadie, John. *Commentary on the Epistle to the Ephesians*. Grand Rapids: n.p., 1883.

Hendriksen, William. *Galatians and Ephesians*. Grand Rapids: Baker, 1982.

Hodge, Charles. *Commentary to the Epistle to the Ephesians*. Grand Rapids: Eerdmans, n.d.

Hoehner, Harold W. *Ephesians: An Exegetical Commentary*. Grand Rapids: Baker, 2002.

Lenski, R. C. H. *The Interpretation of St. Paul's Epistles to the Galatians, Ephesians, and Philippians*. Minneapolis: Augsburg, 1937.

Lightfoot, J. B. *J. B. Lightfoot's Commentary on the Epistles of St. Paul*. 4 vols. Peabody, MA: Hendrickson, 1993.

Luther, Martin. *Galatians*. Wheaton: Crossway, 1998.

MacArthur, John. *Ephesians*. The MacArthur New Testament Commentary. Chicago: Moody, 1986.

———. *Galatians*. The MacArthur New Testament Commentary. Chicago: Moody, 1987.

O'Brien, Peter T. *The Letter to the Ephesians*. Grand Rapids: Eerdmans, 1999.

Stedman, Ray C. *Expository Studies in Ephesians 1–3*. Waco: Word, 1976.

Stott, John R. W. *The Message of Ephesians*. Downers Grove, IL: InterVarsity, 1979.

Westcott, Brooke Foss. *Saint Paul's Epistle to the Ephesians*. New York: Macmillan, 1906.

# Notes

## GALATIANS—Introduction

1.   T. Wilson and K. Stapley, eds., *What the Bible Teaches: Galatians, Ephesians* (Kilmarnock, Scotland: John Ritchie, 1983), 3.

2.   Ibid.

3.   Ibid.

4.   Donald K. Campbell, in John F. Walvoord and Roy B. Zuck, eds., *The Bible Knowledge Commentary*, New Testament (Wheaton: Victor, 1983), 588.

5.   Wilson and Stapley, *What the Bible Teaches*, 4–8.

6.   F. F. Bruce, *Commentary on Galatians* (Grand Rapids: Eerdmans, 1992), 3–5.

## Chapter 1—A True Apostle Defends the True Gospel

1.   Ronald Y. K. Fung, *The Epistle to the Galatians*, The New International Commentary on the New Testament (Grand Rapids: Eerdmans, 1988), 36.

2.   James D. Dunn, *The Epistle to the Galatians* (London: A. & C. Black, 1993), 26.

3.   R. C. H. Lenski, *The Interpretation of St. Paul's Epistles to the Galatians, Ephesians, and Philippians* (Minneapolis: Augsburg, 1961), 27.

4.   Donald K. Campbell, in John F. Walvoord and Roy B. Zuck, eds., *The Bible Knowledge Commentary*, New Testament (Wheaton: Victor, 1983), 290.

5.   Frederic Rendall, in W. Robertson Nicoll, ed., *The Expositor's Greek Testament* (reprint; Grand Rapids: Eerdmans, 1990), 150–51.

6. John MacArthur, *Galatians,* The MacArthur New Testament Commentary (Chicago: Moody, 1987), 13.

7. Henry Alford, *Alford's Greek Testament,* 4 vols. (Grand Rapids: Guardian, 1976), 2:4.

8. Fung, *Galatians,* 3.

9. Ibid., 3–4.

10. Ibid., 4.

11. Ibid.

12. Ibid., 5.

13. Ibid.

14. Ibid., 7, 8.

15. MacArthur, *Galatians,* 20.

16. Ibid., 20–21.

17. Dunn, *Galatians,* 51.

18. MacArthur, *Galatians,* 22.

19. Ibid., 55.

20. Lenski, *Galatians, Ephesians, and Philippians,* 52.

21. Nicoll, *Expositor's Greek Testament,* 154.

22. MacArthur, *Galatians,* 26.

23. Ibid., 27.

24. Ibid.

25. Fung, *Galatians,* 63–64.

26. Lenski, *Galatians, Ephesians, and Philippians,* 58.

27. Ibid., 58.

28. Ibid., 59.

29. Dunn, *Galatians,* 71.

30. A. R. Fausset, *A Commentary on the Old and New Testaments,* 6 vols. (Grand Rapids: Eerdmans, 1945), 6:375–76.

31. Nicoll, *Expositor's Greek Testament,* 156.

## Chapter 2—Paul Defends the Gospel in Jerusalem and Antioch

1. R. C. H. Lenski, *St. Paul's Epistles to the Galatians, Ephesians, and Philippians* (Minneapolis: Augsburg, 1961), 66.

2. Donald K. Campbell, in John F. Walvoord and Roy B. Zuck, eds., *The Bible Knowledge Commentary*, New Testament (Wheaton: Victor, 1983), 593.

3. James D. Dunn, *The Epistle to the Galatians* (London: A & C Black, 1993), 86.

4. James Boice, *Zondervan NIV Bible Commentary* (Grand Rapids: Zondervan, 1999), 2:713–14.

5. Lenski, *Galatians, Ephesians, and Philippians*, 71.

6. W. Robertson Nicoll, *The Expositor's Greek Testament*, 5 vols. (Grand Rapids: Eerdmans, 1990), 3:160.

7. John MacArthur, *Galatians*, The MacArthur New Testament Commentary (Chicago: Moody, 1987), 42.

8. Ibid., 42–43.

9. Boice, *Zondervan NIV Bible Commentary*, 2:715–16.

10. Dunn, *Galatians*, 115–16.

11. A. R. Fausset, *A Commentary on the Old and New Testaments*, 6 vols. (Grand Rapids: Eerdmans, 1945), 6:378.

12. Ronald Y. K. Fung, *The Epistle to the Galatians*, The New International Commentary on the New Testament (Grand Rapids: Eerdmans, 1988), 107.

13. MacArthur, *Galatians*, 51–52.

14. Lenski, *Galatians, Ephesians, and Philippians*, 90–91.

15. Campbell, in Walvoord and Zuck, *Bible Knowledge Commentary*, 378.

16. Fung, *Galatians*, 113.

17. Ibid., 114.

18. Martin Luther, *Galatians* (Wheaton: Crossway, 1998), 87–88.

19. MacArthur, *Galatians*, 58.

20. Lenski, *Galatians, Ephesians, and Philippians*, 112–13.

21. Ibid., 119.

## Chapter 3—Paul Defends the Gospel through Explanation

1. Marvin Vincent, *Vincent's Word Studies in the New Testament* (New York: Scribner, 1918), 4:110.

2. James Boice, *Zondervan NIV Bible Commentary* (Grand Rapids: Zondervan, 1999), 2:720.

3. Ronald Y. K. Fung, *The Epistle to the Galatians*, The New International Commentary on the New Testament (Grand Rapids: Eerdmans, 1988), 129.

4.   Martin Luther, *Galatians* (Wheaton: Crossway, 1998), 127.

5.   Ibid.

6.   James D. Dunn, *The Epistle to the Galatians* (London: A. & C. Black, 1993), 159.

7.   Boice, *Zondervan NIV Bible Commentary*, 2:721.

8.   Donald K. Campbell, in John F. Walvoord and Roy B. Zuck, eds., *The Bible Knowledge Commentary, New Testament* (Wheaton: Victor, 1983), 597.

9.   William Hendriksen, *Galatians and Ephesians* (Grand Rapids: Baker, 1982), 124.

10.  Dunn, *Galatians*, 169.

11.  Ibid.

12.  Luther, *Galatians*, 151.

13.  Campbell, in Walvoord and Zuck, *Bible Knowledge Commentary*, 598.

14.  R. C. H. Lenski, *St. Paul's Epistles to the Galatians, Ephesians, and Philippians* (Minneapolis: Augsburg, 1961), 169.

15.  Luther, *Galatians*, 168.

16.  Ibid., 147.

17.  A. T. Robertson, *Word Pictures in the New Testament* (New York: Harper & Brothers, 1931), 4:297–98.

18.  Lenski, *Galatians, Ephesians, and Philippians*, 185.

19.  Boice, *Zondervan NIV Bible Commentary*, 2:727.

20.  A. R. Fausset, *A Commentary on the Old and New Testaments*, 6 vols. (Grand Rapids: Eerdmans, 1945), 6:386.

21.  Campbell, in Walvoord and Zuck, *Bible Knowledge Commentary*, 601.

## Chapter 4—Do Not Turn Back to Enslavement

1.   R. C. H. Lenski, *St. Paul's Epistles to the Galatians, Ephesians, and Philippians* (Minneapolis: Augsburg, 1961), 210.

2.   William Hendriksen, *Galatians and Ephesians* (Grand Rapids: Baker, 1982), 165.

3.   Ibid.

4.   Ibid.

5.   James D. Dunn, *The Epistle to the Galatians* (London: A. & C. Black, 1993), 223.

6.   James Boice, *Zondervan NIV Bible Commentary* (Grand Rapids: Zondervan, 1999), 2:731.

7. Ibid.

8. Martin Luther, *Galatians* (Wheaton: Crossway, 1998), 222.

9. Ibid., 225.

10. Dunn, *Galatians,* 243.

11. Ibid.

12. J. B. Lightfoot, *J. B. Lightfoot's Commentary on the Epistles of St. Paul,* 4 vols. (Peabody, MA: Hendrickson, 1993), 1:179.

13. Donald K. Campbell, in John F. Walvoord and Roy B. Zuck, eds., *The Bible Knowledge Commentary, New Testament* (Wheaton: Victor, 1983), 603–4.

14. Luther, *Galatians,* 228.

## Chapter 5—Be Free in Christ and Walk by the Spirit

1. James Boice, *Zondervan NIV Bible Commentary* (Grand Rapids: Zondervan, 1999), 2:735.

2. Martin Luther, *Galatians* (Wheaton: Crossway, 1998), 245.

3. Donald K. Campbell, in John F. Walvoord and Roy B. Zuck, eds., *The Bible Knowledge Commentary, New Testament* (Wheaton: Victor, 1983), 605.

4. William Hendriksen, *Galatians and Ephesians* (Grand Rapids: Baker, 1982), 198.

5. Ibid.

6. Boice, *Zondervan NIV Bible Commentary,* 2:736–37.

7. Campbell, in Walvoord and Zuck, *Bible Knowledge Commentary,* 606.

8. J. B. Lightfoot, *J. B. Lightfoot's Commentary on the Epistles of St. Paul,* 4 vols. (Peabody, MA: Hendrickson, 1993), 1:207.

9. A. R. Fausset, *A Commentary, Critical and Explanatory, on the Old and New Testaments,* 2 vols. (Hartford: S. S. Scranton, 1872), 2:337.

10. Boice, *Zondervan NIV Bible Commentary,* 2:738.

11. Lightfoot, *Epistles of St. Paul,* 1:210.

12. Boice, *Zondervan NIV Bible Commentary,* 2:739.

13. Luther, *Galatians,* 275.

14. A. T. Robertson, *Word Pictures in the New Testament* (New York: Harper & Brothers, 1931), 4:312.

15. Ibid., 275.

16. Fausset, *A Commentary,* 2:337.

17. Ibid.

18. Campbell, in Walvoord and Zuck, *Bible, Knowledge Commentary*, 608.

19. Lightfoot, *Epistles of St. Paul*, 1:212.

20. Ibid.

21. Ibid., 1:213.

22. Campbell, in Walvoord and Zuck, *Bible Knowledge Commentary*, 609.

## Chapter 6–Responsibilities of Christian Fellowship

1.   Martin Luther, *Galatians* (Wheaton: Crossway, 1998), 289.

2.   James Boice, *Zondervan NIV Bible Commentary* (Grand Rapids: Zondervan, 1999), 2:744.

3.   Donald K. Campbell, in John F. Walvoord and Roy B. Zuck, eds., *The Bible Knowledge Commentary, New Testament* (Wheaton: Victor, 1983), 610.

4.   Henry Alford, *Alford's Greek Testament*, 4 vols. (Grand Rapids: Guardian, 1976), 3:63.

5.   Boice, *Zondervan NIV Bible Commentary*, 2:745.

6.   Campbell, in Walvoord and Zuck, *Bible Knowledge Commentary*, 610.

7.   A. T. Robertson, *Word Pictures in the New Testament* (New York: Harper & Brothers, 1931), 4:317.

8.   Luther, *Galatians*, 297.

## EPHESIANS–Introduction

1.   Peter T. O'Brien, *The Letter to the Ephesians* (Grand Rapids: Eerdmans, 1999), 2.

2.   Ibid.

3.   Ibid.

4.   Ibid., 3.

5.   Harold W. Hoehner, *Ephesians: An Exegetical Commentary* (Grand Rapids: Baker, 2002), 80.

6.   Ibid., 83.

7.   Ibid., 84.

8.   Ibid., 86.

9.   E. J. Banks, *International Standard Bible Encyclopedia* (Grand Rapids: Eerdmans, 1939), 2:961.

10. *Zondervan Pictorial Encyclopedia of the Bible, ed.* E. M. Blaiklock (Grand Rapids: Zondervan, 1975), 2:324–32.

11. Hoehner, *Ephesians*, 87.

12. Ibid.

13. Ibid.

14. Ibid., 87–88.

15. Ibid., 88.

16. O'Brien, *Ephesians,* 4.

17. Henry Alford, *Alford's Greek Testament,* 4 vols. (Grand Rapids: Guardian, 1976), 3:8.

18. O'Brien, *Ephesians,* 4.

19. Ibid.

20. Hoehner, *Ephesians,* 23.

21. Ibid.

22. J. Llewelyn Davies, *The Epistles of St Paul to the Ephesians, the Colossians, and Philemon* (London: Macmillan, 1884), 9–10.

23. Earnest Best, *Ephesians,* ed. J. A. Emerton and C. E. B. Cranfield (Edinburgh: T. & T. Clark, 1998), 33–34.

24. Ibid.

25. Ibid., 64.

26. Ibid.

27. Hoehner, *Ephesians,* 104.

28. Ibid., 105.

29. O'Brien, *Ephesians,* 35.

30. Ibid.

## Chapter 7—Blessings Obtained through Redemption

1. Walter Bauer, Wilbur F. Gingrich, and Frederick W. Danker, *A Greek-English Lexicon of the New Testament and Other Early Christian Literature* (Chicago: University of Chicago Press 1979), Logos Software ed., n.p.

2. John Eadie, *Commentary on the Epistle to the Ephesians* (Grand Rapids: np, 1883), 2.

3. Harold W. Hoehner, *Ephesians: An Exegetical Commentary* (Grand Rapids: Baker, 2002), 140.

4. A. R. Fausset, *A Commentary on the Old and New Testaments,* 6 vols. (Grand Rapids: Eerdmans, 1945), 6:398.

5. Bauer, Gingrich, Danker, *Greek-English Lexicon,* n.p.

6. Hoehner, *Ephesians,* 140.

7.   Brooke Foss Westcott, *Saint Paul's Epistle to the Ephesians* (New York: Macmillan, 1906), 5–6.

8.   Hoehner, *Ephesians,* 140.

9.   T. K. Abbott, *The Epistles to the Ephesians and the Colossians* (Edinburgh: T. & T. Clark, 1974), 4.

10. Charles Hodge, *Commentary to the Epistle to the Ephesians* (Grand Rapids: Eerdmans, n.d.), 27.

11. Hoehner, *Ephesians,* 175.

12. Ibid.

13. Ibid.

14. Ibid., 175–76.

15. Ibid., 176.

16. Ibid.

17. Klyne Snodgrass, *Ephesians,* The NIV Application Commentary (Grand Rapids: Zondervan, 1996), 49.

18. Hoehner, *Ephesians,* 177.

19. Bauer, Gingrich, Danker, *Greek-English Lexicon,* n.p.

20. John R. W. Stott, *The Message of Ephesians* (Downers Grove, IL: InterVarsity, 1979), 38.

21. Ibid.

22. Hoehner, *Ephesians,* 202.

23. Ibid.

24. Spiros Zodhiates, *The Complete Word Study Dictionary: New Testament* (Chattanooga: AMG, 1992), 1471.

25. Markus Barth, *Ephesians 1–3,* The Anchor Bible (New York: Doubleday, 1974), 82–83.

26. Harold W. Hoehner, in John F. Walvoord and Roy B. Zuck, eds., *The Bible Knowledge Commentary, New Testament* (Wheaton: Victor, 1983), 618.

27. Henry Alford, *Alford's Greek Testament,* 4 vols. (Grand Rapids: Guardian, 1976), 3:75.

28. *"Dispensation,"* in *A Theological Wordbook* (Nashville: Word, 2000), 99.

29. Bauer, Gingrich, Danker, *Greek-English Lexicon,* n.p.

30. Hoehner, *Ephesians,* 226–27.

31. Ibid.

32. Hodge, *Ephesians,* 57.

33. D. Miall Edwards, *"Seal,"* in *The International Standard Bible Encyclopedia* (Grand Rapids: Eerdmans, 1939), 4:2709.

34. Hoehner, *Ephesians,* 238–39.

35. Hoehner, in Walvoord and Zuck, *Bible Knowledge Commentary,* 616.

36. Ibid.

37. Peter T. O'Brien, *The Letter to the Ephesians* (Grand Rapids: Eerdmans, 1999), 127.

38. Eadie, *Ephesians,* 76.

39. O'Brien, *Ephesians,* 130.

40. Ibid.

41. Ibid.

42. Hoehner, in Walvoord and Zuck, *Bible Knowledge Commentary,* 620.

43. Hoehner, *Ephesians,* 259.

44. J. Armitage Robinson, *St. Paul's Epistle to the Ephesians: An Exposition* (London: MacMillan, 1915), 40.

45. R. C. H. Lenski, *St. Paul's Epistles to the Galatians, Ephesians, and Philippians* (Minneapolis: Augsburg, 1961), 397.

46. Ibid.

47. Ibid.

48. Hoehner, *Ephesians,* 272.

49. Ray C. Stedman, *Expository Studies in Ephesians 1–3* (Waco: Word, 1976), 90.

50. Hoehner, *Ephesians,* 275.

51. Ibid., 277.

52. Ibid.

53. Ibid, 278.

54. Bauer, Gingrich, Danker, *Greek-English Lexicon,* n.p.

55. Hoehner, *Ephesians,* 278.

56. Ibid., 279.

57. Ibid., 280.

58. Ibid.

59. O'Brien, *Ephesians,* 152.

60. Ibid.

## Chapter 8—From Death to Life in Christ

1.   Harold W. Hoehner, in John F. Walvoord and Roy B. Zuck, eds., *The Bible Knowledge Commentary, New Testament* (Wheaton: Victor, 1983), 622.

2.   John R. W. Stott, *The Message of Ephesians* (Downers Grove, IL: InterVarsity, 1979), 73.

3.   Ibid.

4.   Peter T. O'Brien, *The Letter to the Ephesians* (Grand Rapids: Eerdmans, 1999), 160.

5.   Ibid.

6.   A. Skevington Wood, *Zondervan NIV Bible Commentary* (Grand Rapids: Zondervan, 1994), 2:757.

7.   Harold W. Hoehner, *Ephesians: An Exegetical Commentary* (Grand Rapids: Baker, 2002), 317–18.

8.   Ibid., 321–22.

9.   Ibid., 324.

10.   T. K. Abbott, *The Epistles to the Ephesians and the Colossians* (Edinburgh: T. & T. Clark, 1974), 48.

11.   Hoehner, *Ephesians,* 333.

12.   John MacArthur, *Ephesians,* The MacArthur New Testament Commentary (Chicago: Moody, 1986), 60.

13.   Hoehner, *Ephesians,* 343.

14.   Brooke Foss Westcott, *Saint Paul's Epistle to the Ephesians* (New York: Macmillan, 1906), 32.

15.   R. C. H. Lenski, *St. Paul's Epistles to the Galatians, Ephesians, and Philippians* (Minneapolis: Augsburg, 1961), 422–23.

16.   Ibid.

17.   Spiros Zodhiates, *The Complete Word Study Dictionary: New Testament* (Chattanooga: AMG, 1992), 1190.

18.   Stott, *Message of Ephesians,* 84–85.

19.   O'Brien, *Ephesians,* 183.

20.   Ibid.

21.   Hoehner, in Walvoord and Zuck, *Bible Knowledge Commentary,* 625.

22.   Lenski, *Epistles to the Galatians, Ephesians, and Philippians,* 431.

23.   Ibid.

24.   J. Armitage Robinson, *St. Paul's Epistle to the Ephesians: An Exposition* (London: MacMillan, 1915),, 59–60.

25. John Eadie, *Commentary on the Epistle to the Ephesians* (Grand Rapids: np, 1883), 174.

26. Stott, *Message of Ephesians,* 102.

27. A. R. Fausset, *A Commentary on the Old and New Testaments,* 6 vols. (Grand Rapids: Eerdmans, 1945), 6:405.

28. Hoehner, in Walvoord and Zuck, *Bible Knowledge Commentary,* 626.

29. Wood, *Zondervan NIV Bible Commentary,* 2:761.

30. Hoehner, in Walvoord and Zuck, *Bible Knowledge Commentary,* 628.

# Chapter 9—The Stewardship Given to Paul

1. R. C. H. Lenski, *St. Paul's Epistles to the Galatians, Ephesians, and Philippians* (Minneapolis: Augsburg, 1961), 461.

2. A. R. Fausset, *A Commentary on the Old and New Testaments,* 6 vols. (Grand Rapids: Eerdmans, 1945), 6:406.

3. Charles Hodge, *Commentary to the Epistle to the Ephesians* (Grand Rapids: Eerdmans, n.d.), 160.

4. Marvin Vincent, *Vincent's Word Studies in the New Testament* (New York: Scribner, 1918), 3:381.

5. A. Skevington Wood, *Zondervan NIV Bible Commentary* (Grand Rapids: Zondervan, 1994), 2:764.

6. Harold W. Hoehner, *Ephesians: An Exegetical Commentary* (Grand Rapids: Baker, 2002), 460.

7. John MacArthur, *Ephesians,* The MacArthur New Testament Commentary (Chicago: Moody, 1986), 96.

8. Ibid.

9. John R. W. Stott, *The Message of Ephesians* (Downers Grove, IL: InterVarsity, 1979), 128.

10. Walter Bauer, Wilbur F. Gingrich, and Frederick W. Danker, *A Greek-English Lexicon of the New Testament and Other Early Christian Literature* (Chicago: University of Chicago Press 1979), Logos Software ed., n.p.

11. Ibid.

12. Hoehner, *Ephesians,* 474.

13. Ibid., 475.

14. Ibid.

15. Ibid.

16. MacArthur, *Ephesians,* 102.

17. Ibid., 105–6.

18. Vincent, *Word Studies,* 3:385.

19. Ibid., 385.

20. Harold W. Hoehner, in John F. Walvoord and Roy B. Zuck, eds., *The Bible Knowledge Commentary, New Testament* (Wheaton: Victor, 1983), 632.

21. Ibid.

## Chapter 10—Unity and Diversity in the Spirit

1.   Charles Hodge, *Commentary to the Epistle to the Ephesians* (Grand Rapids: Eerdmans, n.d.), 197–98.

2.   Ibid.

3.   Richard Chenevix Trench, *Synonyms of the New Testament* (Grand Rapids: Eerdmans, 1948), 150.

4.   Ibid.

5.   Spiros Zodhiates, *The Complete Word Study Dictionary: New Testament* (Chattanooga: AMG, 1992), 1380.

6.   Harold W. Hoehner, *Ephesians: An Exegetical Commentary* (Grand Rapids: Baker, 2002), 510.

7.   John MacArthur, *Ephesians,* The MacArthur New Testament Commentary (Chicago: Moody, 1986), 128.

8.   Marvin Vincent, *Vincent's Word Studies in the New Testament* (New York: Scribner, 1918), 3:386–87.

9.   James Robinson Boise, in Nathan E. Wood, ed., *Notes, Greek Text of Paul's Epistles* (Boston: Silver, Burdett and Co., 1896), 378.

10. Vincent, *Word Studies,* 3:388.

11. A. T. Robertson, *Word Pictures in the New Testament* (New York: Harper & Brothers, 1931), 4:536.

12. Harold W. Hoehner, in John F. Walvoord and Roy B. Zuck, eds., *The Bible Knowledge Commentary, New Testament* (Wheaton: Victor, 1983), 635.

13. Vincent, *Word Studies,* 3:390.

14. Walter Bauer, Wilbur F. Gingrich, and Frederick W. Danker, *A Greek-English Lexicon of the New Testament and Other Early Christian Literature* (Chicago: University of Chicago Press 1979), Logos Software ed., n.p.

15. Zodhiates, *Complete Word Study Dictionary,* 430.

16. MacArthur, *Ephesians,* 155.

17. Hoehner, in Walvoord and Zuck, *Bible Knowledge Commentary,* 635.

18. James Robinson Boise, in Nathan E. Wood, ed., *Notes, Greek Text of Paul's Epistles* (Boston: Silver, Burdett and Co., 1896), 382.

19. Ibid., 382.

20. Hodge, *Ephesians,* 244.

21. Ibid.

## Chapter 11–The Believer's Walk in Christ

1. Charles Hodge, *Commentary to the Epistle to the Ephesians* (Grand Rapids: Eerdmans, n.d.), 248.

2. J. P. Louw and E. A. Nida, *Greek-English Lexicon of the New Testament: Based on Semantic Domains,* electronic ed. of 2nd ed. (New York: United Bible Societies, 1996).

3. Spiros Zodhiates, *The Complete Word Study Dictionary: New Testament* (Chattanooga: AMG, 1992), 202.

4. John MacArthur, *Ephesians,* MacArthur New Testament Commentary (Chicago: Moody, 1986), 166.

5. A. R. Fausset, *A Commentary on the Old and New Testaments* (Grand Rapids: Eerdmans, 1945), 6:412.

6. R. C. H. Lenski, *St. Paul's Epistles to the Galatians, Ephesians, and Philippians* (Minneapolis: Augsburg, 1961), 565.

7. A. Skevington Wood, *Zondervan NIV Bible Commentary* (Grand Rapids: Zondervan, 1994), 2:772.

8. Harold W. Hoehner, in John F. Walvoord and Roy B. Zuck, eds., *The Bible Knowledge Commentary, New Testament* (Wheaton: Victor, 1983), 637.

9. MacArthur, *Ephesians,* 184.

10. Wood, *Zondervan NIV Bible Commentary,* 2:773.

11. Hoehner, in Walvoord and Zuck, *Bible Knowledge Commentary,* 637.

12. Ibid.

13. Zodhiates, *Complete Word Study Dictionary,* 929.

14. John R. W. Stott, *The Message of Ephesians* (Downers Grove, IL: InterVarsity, 1979), 189.

15. Ibid.

16. Ibid.

17. Ibid.

18. Marvin Vincent, *Vincent's Word Studies in the New Testament* (New York: Scribner, 1918), 3:397.

19. Ibid.

20. Henry Alford, *Alford's Greek Testament,* 4 vols. (Grand Rapids: Guardian, 1976), 3:127.

## Chapter 12—To Walk in Faith Is to Imitate God

1.   A. R. Fausset, *A Commentary on the Old and New Testaments*, 6 vols. (Grand Rapids: Eerdmans, 1945), 6:415.

2.   Harold W. Hoehner, in John F. Walvoord and Roy B. Zuck, eds., *The Bible Knowledge Commentary, New Testament Edition* (Wheaton: Victor, 1983), 638.

3.   Ibid.

4.   John R. W. Stott, *The Message of Ephesians* (Downers Grove, IL.: InterVarsity, 1979), 192.

5.   Ibid., 193.

6.   A. T. Robertson, *Word Pictures in the New Testament* (New York: Harper & Brothers, 1931), 4:542.

7.   James Robinson Boise, in Nathan E. Wood, ed., *Notes, Greek Text of Paul's Epistles* (Boston: Silver, Burdett and Co., 1896), 389.

8.   Fausset, *Commentary on the Old and New Testaments*, 6:416.

9.   Robertson, *Word Pictures*, 543.

10. A. Skevington Wood, *Zondervan NIV Bible Commentary* (Grand Rapids: Zondervan, 1994), 2:776.

11. G. Kittel, G. W. Bromiley, and G. Friedrich, eds., *Theological Dictionary of the New Testament*, vols. 5–9, ed. Gerhard Friedrich; vol. 10, comp. Ronald Pitkin (Grand Rapids: Eerdmans, 1964–c. 1976), Logos Software ed., n.p.

12. Ibid.

13. Stott, *Message of Ephesians*, 202.

14. Spiros Zodhiates, *The Complete Word Study Dictionary: New Testament* (Chattanooga: AMG, 1992), 1198.

15. John MacArthur, *Ephesians*, The MacArthur New Testament Commentary (Chicago: Moody, 1986), 226.

16. Stott, *Message of Ephesians*, 203.

17. Hoehner, in Walvoord and Zuck, *Bible Knowledge Commentary*, 640.

18. Ibid.

19. Charles Hodge, *Commentary to the Epistle to the Ephesians* (Grand Rapids: Eerdmans, n.d.), 306.

20. A. T. Robertson, *Word Pictures in the New Testament* (New York: Harper & Brothers, 1931), 4:544.

21. Harold W. Hoehner, *Ephesians: An Exegetical Commentary* (Grand Rapids: Baker, 2002), 717.

22. Stott, *Message of Ephesians,* 208.

23. Klyne Snodgrass, *Ephesians,* The NIV Application Commentary (Grand Rapids: Zondervan, 1996), 311.

24. Wood, *Zondervan NIV Bible Commentary,* 2:777.

25. Boise, *Notes, Greek Text of Paul's Epistles,* 393.

26. Wood, *Zondervan NIV Bible Commentary,* 2:778.

27. Hoehner, in Walvoord and Zuck, *Bible Knowledge Commentary,* 641.

28. Henry Alford, *Alford's Greek Testament,* 4 vols. (Grand Rapids: Guardian, 1976), 6:418.

29. Hodge, *Ephesians,* 308–9.

## Chapter 13—Standing Strong in the Lord

1. John R. W. Stott, *The Message of Ephesians* (Downers Grove, IL: InterVarsity, 1979), 238–39.

2. Ibid., 239.

3. Ibid.

4. A. Skevington Wood, *Zondervan NIV Bible Commentary* (Grand Rapids: Zondervan, 1994), 2:780.

5. James Robinson Boise, in Nathan E. Wood, ed., *Notes, Greek Text of Paul's Epistles* (Boston: Silver, Burdett and Co., 1896), 396.

6. Marvin Vincent, *Vincent's Word Studies in the New Testament* (New York: Scribner, 1918), 3:404.

7. Charles Hodge, *Commentary to the Epistle to the Ephesians* (Grand Rapids: Eerdmans, n.d.), 356.

8. A. R. Fausset, *A Commentary on the Old and New Testaments* (Grand Rapids: Eerdmans, 1945), 6:420.

9. Hodge, *Ephesians,* 373.

10. Ibid.

11. Harold W. Hoehner, in John F. Walvoord and Roy B. Zuck, eds., *The Bible Knowledge Commentary, New Testament* (Wheaton: Victor, 1983), 643.

12. William Hendriksen, *Galatians and Ephesians* (Grand Rapids: Baker, 1982), 270.

13. Wood, *Zondervan NIV Bible Commentary,* 2:783.

14. Fausset, *Commentary on the Old and New Testaments,* 3:420.

15. Hoehner, in Walvoord and Zuck, *Bible Knowledge Commentary,* 643.

16. Wood, *Zondervan NIV Bible Commentary,* 2:784.

17. A. T. Robertson, *Word Pictures in the New Testament* (New York: Harper & Brothers, 1931), 4:551.

18. Vincent, *Word Studies*, 3:410–11.

19. Hoehner, in Walvoord and Zuck, *Bible Knowledge Commentary*, 644.

20. Ibid.

21. Wood, *Zondervan NIV Bible Commentary*, 2:785.

22. Harold W. Hoehner, *Ephesians: An Exegetical Commentary* (Grand Rapids: Baker, 1982), 878.

23. Hodge, *Ephesians*, 398.

24. Ibid.

# About the Authors

John Witmer was a professor of systematic theology at Dallas, Head Librarian for an extended period, and in his later years held the position of Library Archivist. He was also appointed as Assistant Professor Systematic Theology Emeritus. Dr. Witmer was a regular contributor to numerous Christian periodicals and one of the major contributors to the theological volume The Theological Wordbook and authored Immanuel. Dr. Witmer passed away in January 2007. Mal Couch completed Dr. Witmer's initial work on this commentary.

Mal Couch is founder and former president of Tyndale Theological Seminary and Biblical Institute in Fort Worth, Texas. He previously taught at Philadelphia College of the Bible, Moody Bible Institute, and Dallas Theological Seminary. His other publications include *The Hope of Christ's Return: A Premillennial Commentary on 1 and 2 Thessalonians, A Bible Handbook to Revelation, and Dictionary of Premillennial Theology.*

# About the General Editor

Edward Hindson is professor of religion, dean of the Institute of Biblical Studies, and assistant to the chancellor at Liberty University in Lynchburg, Virginia. He has authored more than twenty books, served as coeditor of several Bible projects, and was one of the translators for the New King James Version of the Bible. Dr. Hindson has served as a visiting lecturer at Oxford University and Harvard Divinity School as well as numerous evangelical seminaries. He has taught more than fifty thousand students in the past twenty-five years.